Foundations for
Educational
Ministry

FOUNDATIONS FOR EDUCATIONAL MINISTRY

C. RICHARD EVENSON
Editor

YEARBOOKS IN CHRISTIAN EDUCATION
VOLUME III   FORTRESS PRESS

YEARBOOKS IN CHRISTIAN EDUCATION, Volume III

This yearbook is the third in a series of annual volumes
to be produced jointly by the Boards of Parish Education of
The American Lutheran Church and the Lutheran Church in America.

Printed in U.S.A.

2875D71   1-1044

Foreword

"What are you folks thinking about these days?"

That's a reasonable question for any community to ask of its educational leaders. It is especially appropriate to ask when a new educational effort is being shaped and planned. Such an effort is underway in The American Lutheran Church and the Lutheran Church in America. The chapters of this yearbook are addressed to foundational concepts expressed in a *Central Objective for Educational Ministry in the Parish: ALC/LCA,* first in a series of working documents prepared by joint staff task forces in looking toward the later seventies.

But as soon as any answer is given to the question, that answer is at least partially out of date, because the process of staff thinking and planning is constantly being shaped and modified by successive stages of staff work, and by reviews from board members and consultants. As the joint work has proceeded, *Age-Level Objectives for Educational Ministry in the Parish: ALC and LCA* and *Age-Level Proposals for Educational Ministry in the Parish* have been stated. Each has contributed to further shaping of emphases growing out from the *Central Objective.* Even proposals of a *Strategy for Developing Educational Ministry in the Parish* mold the basic ideas yet further as they seek to provide functional forms by which the objectives might be undertaken and achieved.

Yet the direction of thought made visible in the *Central Objective* is evident throughout, and it is appropriate to examine, to extend, and to test that direction rigorously.

This yearbook offers a more extended statement of direction from the perspective of staff members, together with an examination of that direction from the perspective of educators outside the staff. There are two exceptions. The chapter on God's activity was written by a member of the Board of Parish Education, LCA, who participated intensively with staff as a consultant. The anticipated response to Pichaske's chapter on the Concept of the Church was not completed.

During the next several years, many factors will shape whatever educational ministry the church can offer in the late seventies. But the conceptual foundations underlying the functional programs will give that ministry the bases for whatever clarity or uncertainty it will offer to the church.

C. Richard Evenson

Contributors

REV. ARVID E. ANDERSON, Educational Research Specialist, Board of Parish Education, Lutheran Church in America, Philadelphia, Pennsylvania.

DR. VERNON E. ANDERSON, Graduate School of Education, University of Maryland, College Park, Maryland.

DR. WALLACE J. ASPER, Professor of Religion, California Lutheran College, Thousand Oaks, California.

MR. HENRY BERTNESS, Board Member, Division of Parish Education, The American Lutheran Church, Minneapolis, Minnesota.

REV. HERBERT BROKERING, Special Assistant to the Executive Director, Division of Parish Education, The American Lutheran Church, Minneapolis, Minnesota.

DR. CHARLES R. BRUNING, Director of Clinical Experiences, College of Education, University of Minnesota, Minneapolis, Minnesota.

DR. C. RICHARD EVENSON, Executive Director, Division of Parish Education, The American Lutheran Church, Minneapolis, Minnesota.

DR. W. KENT GILBERT, Executive Secretary, Board of Parish Education, Lutheran Church in America, Philadelphia, Pennsylvania.

DR. LOREN E. HALVORSON, Associate Professor of Church and Society, Luther Theological Seminary, St. Paul, Minnesota.

7

Mr. Wendell Johnston, Secretary for Administrators, Leadership Development Department, Division of Parish Education, The American Lutheran Church, Minneapolis, Minnesota.

Dr. Luther E. Lindberg, Chairman, Department of Leadership Development, Board of Parish Education, Lutheran Church in America, Philadelphia, Pennsylvania.

Rev. Donald R. Pichaske, Director of Editorial Work, Board of Parish Education, Lutheran Church in America, Philadelphia, Pennsylvania.

Dr. John H. Reumann, Professor of New Testament, Lutheran Theological Seminary, Philadelphia, Pennsylvania.

Dr. J. Harlan Shores, Professor of Education, University of Illinois, Urbana, Illinois.

Dr. William D. Streng, Professor of Christian Education, Dean of Faculty, Wartburg Theological Seminary, Dubuque, Iowa.

Rev. Edward W. Uthe, Director of Long-Range Planning, Board of Parish Education, Lutheran Church in America, Philadelphia, Pennsylvania.

Contents

Chapter I

Historical Foundations

C. RICHARD EVENSON

Educational ministry among Christian believers at the present time exists as the current manifestation of a long history. Plans and projections for future possibilities will have to grow out of that history and this present situation.

A BELIEVING COMMUNITY

An Identity to Build

Consciousness of selfhood is a mark of what it means to be human. Consciousness of others perceived to be like oneself is the beginning of human community. Response to others in that community is the basis for communication and for the interaction that can maintain or destroy the community. Participation in the interests and activities of the community develops the interdependence that gives rise to a sense of belonging, sharing, and purposing together. These basic experiences are essential to the formation and continuance of any human community including the community of belief.

They are so essential that every community of belief must give particular attention to ways they can be encouraged and guided so that the identity of the community is maintained. To fail in building the identity of the community is to allow it to become a community of *different* belief, or to dissolve its very existence.

Events to Remember

The Christian community of the past two thousand years, and the children of Israel in the twenty centuries before that, have always placed much emphasis on great events to be remembered. The reality and the mystery of God's call to Abraham, the redemption from bondage in Egypt, the prophets' view of their nation, the life and death and resurrection of Jesus, the experiences and reflections of the church —all these are events to be remembered. The reason for remembering certain great events is that the believing community saw God moving in their midst in those moments. Indeed, it is that very interpretation that establishes the identity of the believing community, and gives it a model for interpreting its present situation and finding meaning in it. Without their memory there is no Christian community.

Perspective to Develop

The present involvements of life are sufficiently different from those faced by believers in the past that interpreting what current situations might mean must ever be undertaken anew—and now. These new situations call for new interpretations—but specific guides can seldom be found in the remembered events and interpretations from the past. For this work the believing community must develop in its members a perspective by which they can perceive, respond to, and participate in all the events and involvements of their lives. One need not be a theologian to think theologically if one can perceive God at work and making himself known in our present time.

Stance to Take

Because persons are different and life is so complex, the members of any believing community are bound to find that their perspectives and interpretations of what things mean, while similar in many ways, will differ—sometimes sharply. Then it becomes necessary for the believing community to adopt a stance which can be accepted as normative by all its members. Such a stance is a shared confession of belief, framed in a given time and situation. But soon it too becomes an interpretation remembered and, after a time, a later agreement in the community of belief may modify or supercede it.

Faith to Share

Throughout all the experiences and tasks of a believing community it is essential that its life and conversation have the quality of a faith that is shared. When the sense of personal conviction becomes eroded the community of belief is weakened. When faith is being shared the believing community is strengthened.

SUCCESSIVE WAYS OF TRANSMITTING BELIEFS, EVOKING FAITH

The History of Israel and the Church

The history of the Christian Church, and of the congregation of Israel before it, is the history of a believing community that has clearly shown each of the characteristics stated above. Further, it is a history that has shown remarkable variety of ways in which a believing community can induce qualities of life together in its members.

When Israel lived in tents, the patriarch told and retold to his tribal "household" the great events of their past and his belief in God, who has done wonders among them. When Israel became a nation the people "came up" to Shiloh and to Jerusalem for a great national expression of faith in their festival gathering and at their temple. The rhythm of the seasons and the pattern of their lives were interpreted as in the sight of God. When Israel was captive in Babylon the people of God invented the synagogue, a local house of meeting together, for instruction and worship. After the sermon the rabbi stayed in the pulpit for questions from the congregation—a marvelous educational forum.

When the people of God were first called Christians and sought to convey their faith, they had to do it secretly and in small, intimate groups. For more than two-hundred years they lived under persecution. In small fellowship groups they recounted what Jesus had said and done; they discussed earnestly what their views should be on ethical questions arising out of the situation in which they found themselves.

13

When the emperor Constantine became a Christian, it became popular for everyone to follow suit. Pagan temples were made into churches and crowds came. Basic information from the Hebrew scriptures and from Christian tradition and writings had to be conveyed to people who knew nothing of them. The priest became a teacher. The fourth-century pulpit became a chair of instruction, built up high to provide a primitive public address system.

When learning and literacy were low, drama taught every man the stories to know and the viewpoints to hold.

When the state began providing education it taught its own religion in its own schools. With the spread of schools children were separated from the rest of the community, and the idea of Christian education became related to child education in the rudiments.

When colonists brought the church to America they had no state to supply leadership or education in religion. They had to provide their own schools—church schools.

Now, mass communication has lessened the enthusiasm for the school as a place to go and sit at the feet of a learned man. The idea of a learning community may offer a possible new direction, one where interest and concern would be of greater significance than age-level or organizational structure.

LUTHERAN LEARNING PATTERNS AND TEACHING EFFORTS IN NORTH AMERICA

Catechism, Bible, Hymnbook

All Lutherans in America have a colonial or immigrant heritage, and their sense of the essential in Christian education still reflects the bare minimum of what could be packed and taken along to the new world: catechism, Bible, and hymnbook. This is not bad in itself —Christians should always be ready to travel light—but it has sometimes caused them to apply the limitation and approach to everyone, regardless of age, interests, or situation.

Culture and Religion

In their efforts at Christian education, Lutherans have experienced much the same sequence of relationships between culture and religion as other American religious groups. First the newcomers clung desperately to the old world culture and regarded it practically at one with their religion. (Many early Lutheran education efforts were called simply "German school", or "Norwegian school".) Next, as people sought to divest themselves of the old world culture, those who desired to retain their religion found themselves striving hard to separate religion from their culture—both the old and the new. Sunday school became known for its Bible-only content. Joking references to any religious viewpoint notoriously unrealistic and unrelated to the stuff of life as "Sunday school religion" became commonplace. Now Lutherans, along with other Christians struggling to relate their religion to the culture, find that the culture is secular, pluralistic, and changing so rapidly that the perspectives of individual Christians are widely diverse and a common stance is exceedingly difficult to achieve. As a result, efforts in Christian education seem less and less to teach a stance and more and more to accept, even encourage, a variety of perspectives and viewpoints.

There does seem to be an increasing use of position-statements-in-the-making as the focus of educational effort in study, discussion, and reply, and this process is increasingly involving a wider span of interests and ages. The educational program is becoming one with the development of confessional positions.

Educational Ministry—The Result of Shaping Forces

In any congregation, actual educational events and the attitudes and expectations of the people for them are the result of many forces.

1. *Sections of the country*. There is some evidence that Lutheran congregations are more like other congregations in their section of the country than they are like other congregations of the church body to which they belong. The statistics from 4,214 congregations where groups gave attention to the *Report for Study* from the Joint Commission on the Theology and Practice of Confirmation showed a number of regional differences of attitudes and expectations. An excerpt from the analysis:

> Because of the importance of this question, should the Lord's Supper come at an earlier age than the rite of confirmation? The response will be reported and analyzed from several directions . . .
> The highest "yes" regions include New England, Middle Atlantic, Mountain and Pacific.

The highest "no" regions include East South Central, West South Central and Canada.

The highest "of uncertainty" on this issue is in the West North Central.

Another way of analyzing the regional differences is to point out that the following regions gave a *less than 50 percent* "yes" response: West South Central, West North Central, East South Central and Canada. All the rest were over 50 percent "yes". It appears that the tendency is for "yes" to be stronger toward the coasts, and "no" to be stronger in Canada and the heartland of the U.S.[1]

Early findings from the Lutheran Longitudinal Study of 3,000 children in 600 ALC and LCA congregations suggests the possibility of some regional differences in children's beliefs and attitudes—even their beliefs about God. (Reports from this significant study will be available in 1972.)

It seems likely that the general culture surrounding us is more significant in shaping our perceptions and beliefs than we usually acknowledge. The entire educational ministry in a congregation is affected by the culture of the section of the country in which it exists.

Of further interest in this regard is a growing pressure toward greater self-consciousness of geographic regions in Lutheran church bodies. *A Report of the Continuation Long Range Study Committee to the American Lutheran Church, 1970,* says:

> From its outset, the ALC, designed as a nationally oriented church body, felt pressures to decentralize, to regionalize, or to give its districts more power to respond in their own ways to the needs of their areas . . . Rather than to renew its call for mergers into one national Lutheran corporation, the ALC should press for critical examination of an alternative—the development of strong regional Lutheran synods, working together in a common organization operative on a national scale.[2]

A further manifestation of regional or area awareness is seen in the increasing cooperation among local congregations which are affiliated with different Lutheran bodies, and with other denominations, in the development of joint programs, the sharing of specialized personnel, and a more comprehensive effort at ministry to the total community in which they exist.[3] It is possible that there is movement toward a further shift, "in the direction of consciously chosen interest in a given style or type of religious expression."[4]

2. *Pattern in the parish.* There are patterns of belief and behavior in congregations. They have been shaped, in part, by educational efforts of the past, and they now shape the possibilities for educational ministry in the future.

From his studies of Lutheran youth, Strommen has been able to identify belief systems in youth, and also in congregations.[5]

Some congregations are innovative. They are ready to try new ways. Church field staff persons can identify such congregations, and they provide information on them from time to time. Leaders in such congregations are ready to identify them as innovative.[6]

Some congregations are loyal; they feel close ties with other congregations in their district or conference and work to accomplish programs and emphases that are undertaken together. Their educational efforts are strongly affected by what such programs and emphases may be. A significant part of their pattern of life and work is their expectation of participating with other congregations in a church-wide program.

The degree to which a congregation has developed a sense of unity of theme and effort among its own organizational units affects its educational effort.

These and other patterns of attitude and expectation are diffuse and rather difficult to describe with precision. They are, however, very real and they powerfully affect the possibilities for educational ministry to be attempted.

3. *Role of the pastor.* Central to almost all that happens educationally in the parish has been the style and ministry by the pastor. The possibilities of what may happen seldom exceed his vision, ability, or leadership. It is valuable, therefore, to reflect on the extent to which the pastor's role has been shaped and limited by the image he has formed of himself, by his own observation of other pastors, by the expectations others seem to have of him, and by his own preparatory experiences at the seminary. Although these images are undergoing pressures and possibly some change, they still powerfully affect the entire educational ministry in the parish and must be reckoned with. A number of characterizations of such images include:

The answer-giver more than a thought-giver.
The exhorter more than a trainer.
The position-stater more than a theological resource or guide.

17

The priest-maintainer more than a project-innovator.
The teacher of a few separated groups or events more than a leader of the entire educational ministry.

4. *Varied expectations of the people.* In any congregation, even one characterized by an identifiable belief system, there is considerable range of emphasis in matters of doctrinal belief, of ethical judgments, and of social accountability.[7]

Some people in the congregation, therefore, want educational programs to provide much visibility of Bible and doctrinal content. Others want much more emphasis on understanding and dealing with our current situation and the decisions it forces upon us. There are persons looking for educational materials that are easy to teach. There are others looking for challenges to undertake efforts directly relevant to the local situation that must be developed largely by the people immediately on the scene.

There is a double process going in Lutheran church bodies; both fragmentation and homogenization are happening at the same time. The national church body is structured to serve the various portions of the congregation's ministry through a number of national divisions and boards. These national units tend to function somewhat independently and to cultivate their own constituencies of congregational leaders. Considerable fragmentation of emphases and efforts results. But in the congregation a different process takes place: homogenization, sameness. The various tasks undertaken by volunteer leaders tend to meld together. Many persons serve as leaders in more than one task (church school, youth stewardship, social action, evangelism). Many of those tasks have educational aspects, expressing programs that may be based on rather different educational premises, emphases, or assumptions. The leaders and teachers find it difficult to keep the premises of each program separately in mind. The tendency then is to treat them all alike. Consequently, each educational program is only partially effective because it is being used only partly according to plan.

Even the idea of "school" as the appropriate model for Christian education finds people divided into varied opinions and practices. The assumption that "school" is the appropriate model for teaching and learning is now being questioned by theorists' statements and people's behavior. Great dissatisfaction with formal educational systems is a characteristic of our times. In congregations as well, enthusiasm and support for the *schools* of the parish (Sunday church school, weekday church school, vacation church school, choir school) seems difficult to build up and maintain. Weekday school, for instance, which once seemed to offer great possibilities, has *not* been undertaken generally by congregations in the ALC or the LCA.

These varying expectations of the people are a dynamic mixture in every congregation, and they are bound to exert considerable force upon the shape of educational ministry in a given congregation or section of the church.

5. *Recommendations from national boards.* The influence of national boards and their programs upon the educational ministry in a congregation is a fifth magnitude force, of less power than the four forces already considered. A national board can argue eloquently for the importance of more time for Christian education, it can produce splendid materials for use in such additional time, and it can provide events to prepare leaders for the program. But, unless these efforts coincide with the expectations and the habits of people in congregations, the program ends in the statistics of what did not get done, and in the warehouse of unpurchased materials.

On the other hand, a well planned program that meets the interests of people, is compatible with their habits, and follows the dynamics of social change, can significantly mold the patterns of thought and behavior in the parish.

STATING THE OBJECTIVES

Three Central Elements

It is interesting to examine a number of efforts to state a central objective for Christian education in the parish. There is a consistent trinitarian emphasis on knowing God and His Word, on Christ's presence among people, and on one's personal experience and commitment. In 1931 M. Reu wrote:

> The aim is (1) faithfully to imbed and anchor in the INTELLECT of the rising generation all the holy truths upon which the life of the mature congregation fundamentally is based, and by which alone it is constantly renewed, and without a knowledge of which one cannot

possibly participate in its entire life; (2) to stir the EMOTIONS to a vital interest in those truths; (3) to bend the WILL so that it may run in the paths in which the Holy Spirit, turning to account those truths, in His own season, leads to personal faith and participation in the life of the mature congregation.[8]

In 1958 the United Lutheran Church in America and other Lutheran church bodies associated with it in the Long Range Program of the Boards of Parish Education stated a general objective as follows:

> Inasmuch as the Church, as the Body of Christ, seeks to become more effectively that community of believers in which the Holy Spirit calls, gathers, enlightens, and sanctifies individuals in their relationships with God and their fellowmen, the Church's central educational objective, therefore, shall be—
> To assist the individual in his response and witness to the eternal and incarnate Word of God as he grows within this community of the church toward greater maturity in his Christian life through ever-deepening understandings of, more wholesome attitudes with reference to, more responsible patterns of actions with reference to: his relationship with God, his relationship with the Christian Church, his relationship to the Bible, his relationship with his fellowmen, his relationship to the physical world, himself.

In 1961 the American Lutheran Church stated its central objective as follows:

> In accordance with God's revelation in the Old and New Testaments,
> in response to the Savior's great commission, and
> > by the power of the Holy Spirit,
> > in order that men may live with Christ,
> > The American Lutheran Church
> > pledges itself in its program of parish education
> > to teach faithfully God's truth—
> > confronting persons with God
> > > and what He has done for man,
> > nurturing adults, youth, and children
> > > in their continued Christian growth, and
> > guiding the Lord's disciples
> > > in their personal response and faithful witness
> > > in every area of life
> > > as they look forward to His return.

In 1969 the ALC and the LCA stated a central objective for educational ministry in the parish:

> The central objective for educational ministry
> in the American Lutheran Church and the Lutheran Church
> in America
> shall be to assist persons
> to perceive, respond to, and participate in
> God's continuing activity and revelation,
> particularly in Jesus Christ,
> in the human and Christian communities
> as they deal with their continual life involvements of
> being a person,
> relating to persons and groups, and
> living in society, culture, and the physical universe.

In 1970 the ALC and LCA Task Forces striving to prepare proposals for a program of educational ministry, have repeatedly found themselves giving emphasis to studying, belonging, and deciding—acting.

It is of value to align the central words. Each line nearly forms a sentence.

1961 ALC	1931 Reu	1970 Task Force	1969 ALC-LCA	1958 LCA
confront	mind	study	perceive	understand
nurture	emotions	belong	respond	attitudes
guide	will	decide	participate	action patterns

The Situation Now Before Us

From the outset of the joint ALC-LCA effort in 1969, the concept of educational ministry has moved from an awareness that it is time to re-examine the assumption that one curriculum can meet the needs of all situations to the vision of a process by which parishes and church-wide agencies work together to develop parish programs which will meet the educational needs and release the potentials of persons in each individual parish.

The movement of the joint Lutheran effort toward objectives, programs, strategy, events, and resources is a movement which runs with the mainstream of many forces shaping the next decade in these church bodies. It is significant, therefore, to consider carefully the foundational concepts informing that joint work and to assess their adequacy for shaping directions and emphases to be developed in the years ahead.

NOTES AND REFERENCES

1. Joint Commission on the Theology and Practice of Confirmation, *A Report for Study* (Minneapolis: Augsburg Publishing House, St. Louis: Concordia Publishing House, Philadelphia: Board of Publication of the Lutheran Church in America, 1969).
2. "Report of Continuation Long Range Study Committee." Minneapolis: The American Lutheran Church, May 29-30, 1970.
3. Edward W. Uthe, *Social Change: An Assessment of Current Trends* (Philadelphia: Fortress Press, 1968), p. 61.
4. *Ibid.,* p. 182.
5. M. P. Strommen, *Profiles of Church Youth* (St. Louis: Concordia Publishing House, 1963), pp. 55-65.
6. ALC/LCA Joint Task Force, "A Study of Educational Ministry in the Parish."
7. Charles Y. Glock and R. Stark, *Religion and Society in Tension* (Chicago: Rand McNally & Co., 1965). Also John Strommen, *Profiles on Church Youth, op. cit.*
8. M. Reu, *Catechetics.* 2nd rev. ed. (Chicago: Wartburg Publishing House, 1931), p. 280.

Historical Foundations—A Response

WILLIAM D. STRENG

The moment we begin to interpret history we reveal ourselves. For that which, at the moment, has gained priority in our thinking or our faith becomes also the focus of our search as we cull from the past what we consider of prime importance. Historical and contemporary issues constantly intertwine. To be aware of this fact should deter us from believing that anyone or any group—pietists, modernists, traditionalists—has the ultimate interpretation of history's truth.

The intent of this chapter is to be constructively critical and tentatively suggestive rather than to expatiate fully on all issues and to support extensively all ambiguous assertions. My purpose is to react, first of all, to the assertions of Dr. C. Richard Evenson in the previous pages and then to add, hopefully, a few seminal thoughts of my own.

The major thesis of Dr. Evenson, as I interpret it, is that educational ministry throughout our long history has been the result of various forces shaping contours and content in any given period and situation. In fact, in the religious community at one and the same time there has been a diversity of emphases, simply because responses have varied to different situations in which Christians found themselves.

Hence the search for identity has gone on continuously and has never reached complete fruition. "To fail in building the identity of the community," Evenson asserts, "is to allow it to become a community of *different* belief, or to dissolve its very existence." History gives evidence of this truth, especially in the disappearance of those little communities who, in order to maintain the truth as they saw it, severed themselves from the larger stream and stagnated into ineffective little sects. We drive by their settlements occasionally and look at their "museums".

A question arises, however, which has become extremely urgent in our day. "Basic experiences are essential to the formation and continuance of any human community." Right. But how can any community determine what is basic and what is peripheral? History seems to shout that man's propensity leans toward adding to the basics until these are almost obscured by accretions. Always and again the church has to clean house rigidly so that ultimates are not obscured by the dust of the centuries. No effort is more difficult, for it can be painful to slice away one pet theory after another in order to let the true light shine forth in all its radiance.

It is encouraging to note that the bishop of The American Lutheran Church stated this aim at the time of his election: "to help the church retain its identity and mission . . . for the church's chief problem is lack of confidence, which is a general reaction to the rate of change in affairs at the present time . . . There is little doubt that we face problems in our world which dwarf the luxuries of subtle theological distinctions . . . Our basic problem is not our past but our mission to the present world."[1]

Correctly Evenson asserts that God's people have events to remember. Things have happened; the great acts of God are there, simply there. They confront us, crying out for a response from us.

23

"New situations call for new interpretations," Evenson asserts. Once this fact captures us as one of history's clearest mandates, we may find some assistance with our present theological polarizations.

Ambiguity has always been indigenous to the enterprise of theology. From two accounts of creation, each with a different emphasis, through the gulf that has always existed between the prophet who cries for social change and the priest who pleads for return to the time honored foundations, to Paul who asserts that we are justified by faith while James categorically states that love shall cover a multitude of sins, the ambiguity of theology has been entrenched securely.

If new situations call for new interpretations then one of our assignments is to determine when a situation is new. Two major cultural periods have had their day in the history of Western religion—first from the early church to the Reformation, the second from the sixteenth century to our own. Now we may well be beginning a third major cultural style but some are still catching up on the second while others are embarked on the third. Hence the dichotomy of our day in religious circles. But this may also explain new alignments which are no longer determined by denominational loyalties but by "new interpretations" which cross old sectarian borders.

If history teaches anything it ought to remind us that in our new situation, in which we are leaving one cultural period and entering another, we should not be snared by the repristinations of the old nor by the confident assertions of those who stoutly affirm the transitory new as if it answered all the ultimate questions for all times.

The notion that God has yet more light to break forth out of his word, a wholesome Protestant affirmation against a rigid identification of truth and our interpretation of it, does not mean necessarily that there will be new truths revealed or that the gospel will be different. But it does mean that as the Christian community wrestles with the givenness of its foundations, the Holy Spirit will reshape his people. In that process God's saints have always made mistakes—from Abraham to Paul to Luther—but their aberrations have not been as destructive as the mistakes of those who wanted to arrest the light, or who merely repeated old formulations in new situations so that their formulations actually became heretical, while they were trying to stop heresy. The intentionality of a theological event or doctrine must be reinterpreted for each new occasion or else we may fossilize what was intended to give life.

This may explain for us why it is becoming less and less acceptable to appeal to certain periods of history as being better than all others. The Middle Ages had their strong points and their weaknesses, as did the Church of the sixteenth century or of any other. People who would have risked their lives for a facet of the truth, a single accent, may now give their lives not for a new creed but for justice toward the neglected or against participation in a foreign war. In our day it may well be true that the most daring assignment is not primarily to be for justice but to fight injustice.

An this change may help us adjust to the fact that for some time to come we shall not have systematic theologies to give us a well-rounded presentation of the faith. Tillich was probably the last one to attempt this. How this will change our educational materials is already becoming evident in the appearance of many units and modules with little coherence.

This ought not to depress us since Luther, if judged by the usual canons, is certainly not a systematic theologian. Reading him, then some of the systematic theologians of our day, gives one a severe jolt—not only as far as content is concerned but also as far as systematic presentation is involved.

The inevitability and desirability of change rings forth clearly from Evenson's pages. Assertions such as "Successive Ways of Transmitting Beliefs, Evoking Faith", or "Educational Ministry as a Resultant of Shaping Forces", serve as section headings. Cultures, ethnic backgrounds, sections of the country have had far-reaching effect on the theology and hence the educational ministry of the church.

If this is true, if "the entire educational ministry in a congregation is affected by the surrounding culture in the sections of the country in which it exists", then history urges us to avoid the pettiness of parochialism and provincialism through ecumenical contacts and broader dialogue, lest the culture determine our theology. This involves but goes a bit beyond Evenson's suggestion about the "development of joint programs, the sharing of specialized personnel, and a more comprehensive effort at ministry to the total community in which they exist."

Possibly one other conclusion should have been underscored—namely that history reminds us, I believe clearly reminds us, that those who could adjust to change were the most effective in sharing the gospel of Jesus Christ. In the process they had to experiment and to improvise but in the end they were the ones who contributed to the continuity of our historic faith. The church ought to comprehend change better than its secular counterparts.

And if the church's history cries out with any clear voice it is possibly with this plea: be ready to adjust your theology to changing cultures and new situations in order not to lose the one thing needful, the unique contribution of Jesus Christ for all men. One period may stress eschatology, another resurrection, another forgiveness and another social justice, depending upon the needs of men at that moment. One age may speak of justification by faith and another of accepting one's acceptance by God while basically the love of Jesus Christ continues to radiate. In fact, this is a part of the splendor of Christ's church that it can serve in any situation and in all historical changes. Anyone who has been captured by the validity of such a "process theology" will not bemoan the fact that the world is subject to change but will thrill to the fact that our universe, God's universe, is alive to change.

Evenson summarizes his conclusions in the conviction that "a well planned program that meets the interests of people, is compatible with their habits, and follows the dynamics of social change, can significantly mold the patterns of thought and behavior in the parish." This has to be underscored. Man does have a mind, is deeply affected by his emotions, and does not change until his will is reached—hence our educational enterprise must be geared to that kind of human being.

Luther urged the church in his day "to begin from below." He began with the faults and aspirations of his German peasants. Wesley felt the agonies of his contemporaries. Tillich knew that the questions of his generation centered around meaninglessness and attempted to assist them in the ambiguities of their routine lives. The counter-culture is reminding us today that there are problems and concerns to which no one seems to be giving an answer.

The history of the church is a constant reminder that when one "begins from below" one's message gains power and effects change in the lives of people.

Certainly, Biblical history carries the same emphasis. Christ came "deep in the flesh," as Luther asserts, helping and loving the heavy laden. He had learned it from his Father who, back in the hoary past, had assured his people, "I have seen the affliction of my people who are in Egypt, and have heard their cry because of their taskmasters; I know their sufferings" (Exodus 3:7).

Will not such an approach, "to begin from below", dilute the church's message, for how many ask ultimate questions? History seems to say that precisely when God's people were concerned with ultimates their message effected change. Let historical foundations be "foundations". On every page of church history one seems to sense the plea for priorities, a call to stick to essentials.

The difficulty is not so much in the historicity of the events (How long were the days of creation? Who wrote the book of Isaiah?) for these questions can become evasions of the major thrust. The difficulty, rather, is in sensing priorities. Each period in history and each religious community chose its own emphasis. The constant temptation is to get lost in what Luther termed "the caverns of Scripture" and fail to see the lamp which has been placed at the entrance. In fact, with mechanical repetition, those attempting to point to the light were brutally beaten as innovators. The list of martyrs is a long and depressing portion of our history.

It was not the intellectual acumen of an Erasmus but the deep concern of a Luther, not the thick volumes of profound theology but the life-style of a Bonhoeffer, which seem to have warmed more hearts to the call of Christ.

The skill to feel what others feel, history reminds us, may well be the secret of dynamic education for this moment and for the immediate future. Whenever God's people refused to take love with sufficient seriousness and to employ it as the ultimate theological criterion the educational enterprise was off balance. We are here to learn to love. Like good wine this emphasis improves with age.

NOTES AND REFERENCES

1. Kent S. Knutson, "The Response of the Lutheran Churches to the Roman Catholic Church and Theology Today," *Lutheran World*, vol. 17, no. 4, 1970, pp. 330-340.

Chapter II

The Central Objective's Concept of the Church

DONALD R. PICHASKE

The winds of change have been attacking the structures within which men organize their lives with growing force. Nor have they left the church untouched. A goodly number of Protestant theologians are likely to agree with Catholic Archbishop Richard Cushing's statement in the introduction of Hans Küng's *Structures of the Church.* "The chief *theological* concern . . . of all the Christian community today is ecclesiology."[1]

Anyone even casually associated with the church can list a half dozen reasons for these current efforts to reevaluate its traditional categories of self-understanding and restate them. There are the new directions in theology, with a strong taste for process and the secular. There is the predilection for relevance, the sense of need to conceive of the church and provide for participation in it in terms that will be meaningful to modern man. Any institution must attend to maintenance (renewal) functions if only to remain alive. Of course, one hopes that the drafting of a new ecclesiology is also in response to the Spirit's prompting and the laying open of one's mind to the pledge in John 16:13: "When he comes who is the Spirit of truth, he will guide you into all truth" (*New English Bible*).*

Current directions in which such self-evaluation and redefinition are moving have also become quite clear. Whereas, in the past, men

Personally N.B.
Jan 1976

tended to think of the church in ontological terms or even, more recently, in terms of its message (creature, guardian, and proclaimer of the *kerygma*), the drift today is toward definition or description in terms of function or mission. Any number of writings expound the proposition that "the Church is mission." Thus, for example, James Burtness's biblical-theological expositions of the 1970 LWF assembly theme, "Sent into the World" (in itself an indicator of the current trend): "The church is mission. It finds its identity in the fact that it is sent to proclaim that in Jesus Christ all things hold together, in heaven and on earth (Colossians 1:17). . . . The Christian church locates its identity in the fact that it is *sent*. Church is inseparable from mission."[2] The Manifesto attached to the Report of the LCA Commission on the Nature and Mission of the Congregation described the church as "God's people," itself a functional term, as we shall see, "sent into the world to speak his Word and to be his agents of reconciliation." "'People of God' can be grasped as a symbol that directs us to the high calling of the Church to be the new community of love, the obedient servant of Christ, the instrument of the Holy Spirit, the one agency in the world truly capable of reconciling not only man to God but man to man."[3] In his chapter of this yearbook, Reumann allows for this notion in describing the church as "the mission of the people of God." And, of course, the stress on an operational definition of the church explains at least in part the articulation of the ALC-LCA Central Objective for Educational Ministry in the Parish in such verb forms as "perceive, respond to, and participate in" and "being . . ., relating . . ., and living . . ." (p. 31).

For the most part such thinking still focuses mission in what God does through the Christ event, so that the mission of the church in its broadest sense remains God's ministry of reconciliation wrought in Christ. "If mission is basically understood as God working out his purpose for his creation, the church does not have a separate mission of its own. It is called to participate in God's mission. The missionary call is a call to participation."[4] The church knows the miracle of reconciliation achieved by God in his Son. "To be reconciled to God is to be sent into the world as his reconciling community. This community, the church universal, is entrusted with God's message of reconciliation and shares his labor of healing the enmities of mankind. Christ has called his church to this mission . . ."[5]

29

At the same time, however, the current emphasis on the church as mission has its own special set of facets that reflect the context out of which it comes and to which it speaks. We cite here some of the most significant.

1. Primary is the recognition of God's call to the church to serve the world. This is consonant with identification with God's mission. We recognize the fact that God's mission is to the world, that it is God's purpose to achieve reconciliation, *Shalom,* in the world, and that to this end he was, is, and shall continue to be active in the world both within and apart from the church. From this viewpoint the church exists to identify, proclaim, and share in what God is doing in the world.

This "worldly concern" of God has been thoroughly described and its biblical foundations cited in any number of places. Of chief importance here is its reminder that God's activity cannot be confined to the activity of the church. To do so would be to refashion God "in the image of a residential deity" and leave "the world . . . bereft of the divine presence, which is enshrined within and reserved exclusively for the Church."[6] This is a reported reason for Bonhoeffer's giving up his identification of the church with the Kingdom of God. To do so is to recognize a realm where Christ is not lord. This is unthinkable in the light of the New Testament proclamation that Christ is lord of all creation.

2. The current accent of mission is on human need and service as perceived by those in want and in their present, very human, earthly situation. Thus main-line Protestant and Catholic churches have moved into the forefront of social action efforts. Local congregations have sought to identify their mission goals in terms of community needs and have supported a wide variety of community action programs aimed at alleviating racial tension; raising the level of education; improving the lot of the poor; ministering to the sick, the aged, the handicapped, the lonely; attacking corrupt political institutions. The church-at-large has moved in the same directions in funding and promoting national and international programs. Christ remains, even in these activities, the center of mission, but the accent is on that side of him commonly described in the phrase "the man for others." The Incarnation is not neglected, but the stress is on its attestation to

God's concern for man as he strives for freedom and fulfillment in this world. Jesus has revealed not only God but what it means to be fully human, and God's purpose for all humanity.[7]

3. The stress is more on the deed than on the word. It has been said that modern man is no longer searching, like Luther, for a forgiving God; he is looking for a gracious man. Luther found his forgiving God in the pronouncements of the Gospel. The verbal proclamation of God's forgiving, reconciling deed in Christ stressed by his followers has often been regarded as the church's foremost task. Today the accent is on the Christian deed. The characteristic image is that of the servant, tending the wants of humankind and so witnessing to the faith that is in him. This serving, understanding presence has even become the mark of distinction between honest witness and mere propagandizing. Writes H. Hoekendijk, "Whoever pontificates about salvation where soup and soap is required betrays his evangelistic ministry. . . . Gospel news is not a matter of words. It comes in flesh . . . in people. . . . It comes in people in all walks of life who put their bodies on the line and we are invited to join them in our mature worship (Romans 12:1 ff)."[8]

4. Current thinking has the church feeling a strong sense of identification with the world. This is apparent in what has already been said, but it needs to be stated. The boldest, most secularized Christians would erase all distinctions between church and world. Some not quite so radical would distinguish between past models of relationship between church and world and what is needed today in the light of a recovered appreciation of God's presence in and concern for his entire creation. A more tempered view distinguishes between identical to and identifying with.[9]

5. A fifth significant characteristic of the church's current functional view of itself is the abdication of its imperialistic role in favor of seeing itself in partnership with other instruments through which God makes himself felt in the life of the world. "In the ecclesiologies of previous generations, the church was regarded as the instrument or agent through which God speaks to the world. God entrusted the saving message of the gospel to the church, which proclaimed it to the world. Those outside the church had little hope of knowing God unless they accepted the message proclaimed by the church and entered

its fellowship. Those in the church were called out of the world into the church. There was a tendency to regard the church as a colony of heaven, as the kingdom of God, at least in embryo."[10]

We have noted here a different kind of relationship between church and world. An inevitable corollary is that the church does not have the responsibility for creating a Christian society coextensive with the whole world. As one segment of and a part of a larger society, "The function or mission of the church is to serve as one means by which the world may come more perfectly under the rule of God. It serves by articulating and interpreting God's revelation of himself as it occurs in the world, by engaging in dialogue with the world, not by attempting to impose its view on the world."[11]

As part of this more humble, less pretentious approach to its mission stands the admission that any current delineation of nature and function must be just that, temporary, fitted to the times and seasons, a reflection of God's doings and desires among men now. In another day a right goal of the church might well have been the gathering of men into communities where new life is created by the Word embodied in sermon and sacrament. An altered set of circumstances calls for a restatement of the nature and function of the church for our day. And we may well anticipate that present efforts will not be adequate for tomorrow.

A Community of Believers

Entwined in and deriving to some degree from this emphasis on viewing the church in terms of what it does in the service of humanity are a number of other current accents in the church's evolving self-understanding. The functional quality of the use of "people of God" in referring to the church has already been alluded to. The term also underscores the fact that the church functions as a *community of believers*.

The phrase "people of God" has deep roots in both Scripture Testaments. In the Old Testament, Israel is reminded repeatedly that she is a distinctive people chosen to serve mankind on behalf of God through a life of absolute faith and obedience. (See, e.g., Deuteronomy 7:6-11; 14:2; 26:18-19; 28:9-14). The New Testament testifies to the fact that Christ not only assumed in himself this role of God's people but also called a new people into existence, connected to Israel by bonds of promise and faith. 1 Peter 2:9 clearly describes this people with a mission: "You are a chosen race, a royal priesthood, a holy nation, God's own people that you may declare the wonderful deeds of him who called you out of darkness into his marvelous light." Here are the roots out of which developed the church as "the community of the redeemed bound together in spirit in Jesus Christ, and at the same time a visible organized society with rules and founder's charter."[12]

This community is to be seen more as a fellowship of the redeemed than as an institution, although, as we shall see, institutional qualities and practices are indispensable for both mission and continuity. "Koinonia is a kind of community which transcends ordinary human community in that God is present and participates in the community. . . . Thus koinonia is by its nature a community intimately indwelt by the Spirit."[13] This fellowship is held together by a common commitment to a common Lord. Christ stands at its center as both the model of its ministry and the source of power to fulfill it. "He supplies the power which enables the community of believers to grow together into the fullness of humanity which he revealed—to become whole and free, to exist for others, and joyfully to affirm life."[14]

This community is essential to Christianity. It provides guidance, support, the source of renewal of faith for all its members as they honor and grow in a common heritage, seek to respond faithfully to their vocation, and share the hope of Christ's kingdom both present and yet to come. It also provides the instrumentality through which participation in God's mission becomes possible. It is even a means of witness, testifying to the world that God's redemptive act in Christ has changed the human situation. The church becomes a sign of the new humanity.

It is a real community, that is, it has historical legitimacy. The old careful distinctions between spiritual community and institutional form, the "church visible" and the "Invisible church," what the Catholic theologian Rahner terms "the union in Christ by grace of the redeemed" and "the organized society, the Ministry of Salvation"[15] are at least blurred if not wiped out. We recognize that koinonia, Christian community, the experience of the shared life in Christ, the people of God are to be located in the visible, empirical church. That church may be assuming new forms and dimensions and located in unsuspected places, but it is always marked by visible signs and procedures acceptable to their advocates and adherents.[16]

Four More Qualities

Four other characteristics of current thinking about the church deserve at least mention. There has been *a bonding together of worship and social activism* in a renewed emphasis on *leitourgia* as the whole service of the people of God. In its most extreme expression the act of worship involved has been taken out of the church building, but sensitive churchmen still believe that the building can provide "a sacred space" whose consecrating power can reach out "from the altar, from the church, to embrace all other areas, all places in which men live and labor, so that all human effort may become more directly and consciously part of the great act of sacrificial worship."[17] To this end the form of church buildings has changed, and one can see a very contemporary structure with the worship space in the center and meeting and educational facilities surrounding it. This is not viewed as an effort to sacralize the whole of life as its wide breadth of concerns is brought into discussion and planning. Rather it is to symbolize the reality of the situation whereby the Christ whose presence is celebrated in the sacrament and proclamation of the Word is the Lord of all life and always the center.

Second, there is a strong sense of the critical importance for mission of *the ministry of the laity*. To write of the church is to write of its ministry. A ministry to the world is inconceivable without expanding the concept of ministry beyond the ordained clergy and into a variety of forms suited to the places where ministry takes place. "We have indeed to move beyond isolating the present, supposedly single, form of ministry to a more inclusive, flexible, and effective pattern of ministry in terms of innumerable ministries. . . . In a society characterized by differentiation and specialization, the ministry of the whole Church must also be differentiated to engage the world at all its diverse points of need."[18]

Moreover, there is a recognized need to move toward a unified concept of ministry to eradicate the consumer viewpoint most lay people have toward the church and to introduce them to their true role as part of the missionary people of God. Ideally, the church has one ministry which is the ministry of Christ. This need not destroy the significance of the ordained ministry of the clergy. It simply calls for a clear differentation of the varieties of ministry that make up the one.

Third, today's ecclesiologists give greater recognition to *the church as a social institution* and, as such, subject to the interplay of social processes. This results from (or leads to—depending on your viewpoint) the honest effort to find out the relation between the theological statements about the church (prescriptive) and the historical and social forms which Christian communities actually assume (descriptive). It is a recognition of the fact we do not exhaust all that needs to be said in describing the church when we refer to it in terms of such biblical symbols as "the people of God," "the body of Christ," and "the bride of Christ," or even in such a theological formulation as "where the gospel is preached and the sacraments administered." Much of the church's baggage derives from the social fabric of communication and human interaction. This is inevitable to its functioning. To function, a church must become an organized body. As such it has "a structure based upon the division of labor between leaders, officials, and members, the sets of different tasks to be performed, and the apparatus for performing them. A church has an organized round of life which focuses upon its meetings, ceremonies, and rituals. It has a shared body of beliefs and values in the form of creeds, doctrines, and tenets; it has sets of rules and regulations to guide the activities of the people within it. Members have a sense of identity, a feeling that theirs is a religious organization distinct from other churches and groups. A church acts to preserve itself and to protect and advance its interests. Such feelings are found in every religious group, whether it is a primitive sect or a huge, complex denomination. They signify that the church by its very being is a social organization."[19]

Finally, thinking about the church in our time has recognized both its unity and disunity and *the need to strive toward wholeness through some form of oneness.* Strong motivation again derives from seeing the church in terms of its worldly mission. The *missio Dei* can only be fulfilled in ecumenical dimensions. The word *oikumene* in biblical usage means, primarily, the inhabited world of men. It is this which is the recipient of God's searching love and the object of his saving will. The Church is that segment of the world which reveals the final goal towards which God is working for the whole world. Herein is the glory of the Church. But, if it fails to fulfill its missionary commission to the world, it is abusing, for its own benefit, the gifts of God, and God's judgment upon a self-centered world begins with the Church. Disunity becomes not only a scandal but a sturdy barrier to fulfilling vocation. Hence it is to be hoped that "under the guidance of the Holy Spirit, the churches may grow into a charismatic unity, which comprehends differences of language, background, race, sex, generations, and social milieu (Galatians 3:28); it [the church] may grow towards a living interplay of charismatic gifts and ministries and so become a body of congregations that are knit together in the fullness of truth and wisdom."[20]

Reflections of Current Trends in the ALC-LCA Objective

To what degree does the ALC-LCA Central Objective for Educational Ministry in the Parish reflect these current emphases? Before answering the question one needs to remind himself that the statement is an educational objective. One should expect it to be a carefully worked out description of the goal of educational ministry in ALC and LCA parishes. One should not expect a complete definition of the nature and mission of the church.

At the same time, no statement of a church's objective for educational ministry in the parish can fail to include reflections of how the church making the statement views itself. In fact, the very statement of an objective will, of necessity, mirror to some degree how the church sees its task and, so, its nature and mission. Hence, even if we have no right to expect a full ecclesiological statement, we can expect some clean-cut clues. And these we find in abundance.

Under the rubric, "A Concept of the Church," one immediately comes upon all the current terms being used in speaking of the church. It is a community (the term is used five times in the first seven lines!) of the redeemed where mutual love and care are shared. Here God communicates his gifts to all members irrespective of race, sex, or other human divisions. Central in the community is Christ, whose mission defines the church's task and who provides it with its singular hope and new life through forgiveness, freedom, and righteousness. The mission of the church is further elaborated in the statement that it "is seen as a community of faith and love, a self-conscious vehicle of God constantly called into being by the Spirit to confront men with the Word and to minister to human need" (p. 5). Thus, if the opening description appears somewhat limited to qualities indicative of the institutional nature of the church and its internal ministry, the limitation is quickly broken open.

The statement identifies the past accents of ecclesiological formulations and notes the current accent on mission in terms of the service of humanity. Approval is implied of both the emphasis and the underlying concepts of acknowledging the world as the chief setting of God's activity and chief object of his love, viewing the church as a community of faith and love called to witness to the Word and to minister to human need, and adapting a theological posture beamed toward the future and the Christian hope.

There's a hint of bowing to secular theology in the acknowledgment that, "the world is the place in which men find and fulfill his (God's) purposes for all" (p. 5). Recognizing The American Lutheran Church and the Lutheran Church in America as "empirical, historical manifestations of theological concepts of the church" (p. 4) and as "concrete, though incomplete and imperfect, expressions of such concepts as 'the communion of saints' " (p. 4) reveals an openness toward a sociological perspective of the church, a readiness to measure the normative theological statements about the church by its visible, human forms. Worship is tied to study and the preparation of members "for carrying out personal (we might add here "and corporate") ministries in daily life, at work and leisure, in family and neighborhood, as responsible citizens" (p. 5). The same phrases underscore the responsible role of the laity in the life and mission of the church.

But one needs to reach outside the section aimed at explicating the concept of the church to get a full picture. Some of the phrases found there are quite as explicit as those set apart under the special heading. Behind the objective lies: "the biblical descriptions of the church as a fellowship of believers, caring and serving" (p. 2); the fact that "the church is not simply a social institution" and therefore from a sociological perspective it is a social institution (p. 2); "the God who acts" without restriction as to "any specific time, or place, or type of action" and who is "present and active in what takes place in and through religious groups, agencies, or institutions consciously dedicated to carrying out his redemptive purposes" (p. 11) (phrases that seem deliberately to omit specific reference to the institutional church as we know it in its traditional forms in order to open the way to new structures); an acceptance of "the Bible and . . . the heritage and witness of the Christian church" as testimony to the ways God reveals himself in specific events (p. 13); acknowledgment of the church as that community in which God's continuing activity and revelation get interpreted in the light and person of Jesus Christ (p. 13); a readiness to tie the church to non-church structures of society for the achievement of its educational objectives (p. 14) (and so, by inference, other kinds of goals); the readiness to interpret such biblical terms as "body of Christ" and "people of God" in relation to new forms of ministry quite temporary and related to current human needs; (pp. 18, 27) and unabashed recognition that "the church is included within the human community" (p. 18).

The summary statement of objectives (p. 31) must be viewed in the light of these particular accents. In itself it points in general to the contemporary views of the church that have been enunciated.

Other Basic Assumptions

The general objective also makes other basic assumptions. In affirming current insights into the church as *missio Dei* in the world and to its present needs, the traditional biblical and theological concepts of the church are not discarded. Rather they are recognized as valid, informing insights which need to be seen not only in their historical context but also utilized now in man's present circumstances. In this manner they provide a basic framework that has a stabilizing and conserving effect.

It has been estimated that the New Testament contains more than one hundred terms cognate to the basic notion of *ecclesia*, which in itself is quite neutral and refers simply to an assembly of persons called together for any and every purpose. These include the body of Christ, the people of God, saints and sanctified, the vine and the branches, the temple and the cornerstone, kingdom, priesthood, shepherd and flock, new humanity, household and family, bride, and slaves and servants. Paul Minear has arranged a useful set of categories for looking at them in terms of:

1. God's action toward men. The church consists of those whom God calls, gathers, chooses, justifies, sanctifies, glorifies.

2. Personal, communal response to God's action in Christ; those who are prompted by the Spirit to assent in faith.

3. The basic duties such faith entails. The church is made up of servants, witnesses, ambassadors, stewards, soldiers, friends.

4. The people of God, the continuation and consummation of God's covenant community. The community of Christ assumes the identity of God's Israel through promise and faith.

5. Institutions long associated with the history of God's people, e.g., the kingdom of Israel and the Temple.

6. The eschatological gathering of God's people into his household; God's family.

7. Key epochs in scriptural history, such as the Creation, the Flood, the Exodus.

8. A wide range of pastoral analogies evocative of the church's dependence upon God, the responsibility to bear fruit, and the imminence of God's judgment on her.

9. The body of Christ with its key cognate idea of community; the church is made up of many parts but is one through its head, Christ.

10. The new humanity. The church is the beginning, the sign, of a new creation, in which men reconciled to Christ are reconciled to one another.[21]

The list is recounted here only to indicate the kind of tapestry on which the concept of the church in the central objective is woven. Minear is right in insisting that the New Testament does not define the church so much as provide a gallery of pictures. And "none of the separate titles or pictures can be taken as comprehending the total range of thought. None of them can be reduced to objective, qualifying definitions. These words and pictures are channels of thought rather than receptacles of ideas with fixed meanings."[22]

How the process works out when the biblical symbols are used in the light of contemporary concerns in a way that does justice to both is illustrated in Burtness' paper on "Sent into the World" already alluded to. Burtness can resolve the tension between the inherent particularity of the people of God and the unquestioned universality of the Gospel in the identification of the church with the world. The people "finds its identity in the fact that it is 'sent,' that it is given a word to be spoken, a message to proclaim." This gospel "with which the Christian community is sent and in which it finds its identity, includes both word and deed." The Christian community, "if it is to retain its identity, must . . . tell the story, and clarify the claim, and name the Name. . . . In the process of clarifying that claim, the church finds itself identifying with the world." In its present circumstances, "The church finds its identity in the fact that it is sent with this good news, and it is able to identify with the world because it is sent with the good news that God is at work in His world, carrying out His redemptive purposes."[23]

One can make a similar claim with respect to the confessional statements found in the church's creeds and in their explications in theological textbooks. Because the objective nowhere defines the church as "the assembly of all believers among whom the Gospel is preached in its purity and the holy sacraments are administered according to the Gospel"[24] or "the assembly of saints who truly believe the Gospel of Christ and who have the Holy Spirit"[25] or in terms of its traditional marks—"one, holy, catholic, and apostolic," or in the systems of theologians, such as Aulen's differentiation between "the nature of the church" and its "constitutive factors" does not mean that these concepts play no role in designing a contemporary view of the church.

For one thing they stand as that which is over against or in continuity with current statements. If the times call for an operational, missionary definition of the church in terms of how the Christian community relates to the world in fulfilling its commission, this does not negate the fact that the community is still "one" in terms of its mission and Lord, "holy" in terms of its God and the sanctifying power of the Spirit who calls its members together, "catholic" in the light of its ecumenicity, "apostolic" in terms of its message and task. If it be true that we need to structure the kinds of communities of Christians that will make realizable "life together in love," or task forces to testify to the presence of God in the midst of the city, this does not mean these cells or families, or whatever they are will not be organized around the Word and the sacraments and, as Aulen suggests, prayer. This was one of the facts that quickly came to light when a task force working on calibrating the general objective for various age levels convened a consultation to counsel its work. Churchmen from every discipline called for strong attention at almost every point on what we have come to call the heritage of the church, its totality of experience since the days of its inception.

The Concept of the Church and an Educational Objective

How the church is viewed has great significance for the shape of the educational objective that it espouses. This is reflected in other papers in this volume but can be illustrated here as part of that interactive process by means of which we see the church in the objective and the objective in the concept of the church. The following items are more illustrative than exhaustive.

1. The concept of the church opens the way for a stronger emphasis in education on process. This is not the same as saying content is of less importance, or that methodology assumes the chief role. Rather it is to play honest with the acknowledgment that the church is a living community constantly being brought into being, shaped, and renewed by the Spirit. It is also a reflection of concern for the lack of any empirical evidence that the church's educational effort has significantly determined the faith and life of those involved in it.[26] The task calls for an honest boring in on what is happening, how change occurs in persons, and what the church (congregations) can do to nurture change in the direction in which God would move people, while still respecting their freedom.

2. Doors are opened to new theoretical and practical approaches to the educational task. It becomes possible to conceive of "educational ministry in the parish." A significant difference in the central objectives of 1958 and 1969 is the latter's emphasis on the role of the community in the educational process. We have come to the recognition that, "the curriculum of Christian education really resides in all the activities the church provides, uses, or recognizes for guiding the growth of persons in their relationships to God, the church, other persons, and themselves."[27] Here we discover as much about the church as we do about its educational ministry. A special concern arises in protecting the individual (who is always the seat of change and so the focus of the educational process) from the growing concern for the collective body, the welfare of the community. The swinging pendulum needs to be stopped in the middle.

3. The focus must be on finding ways to counteract the traditional attitude toward the church as an institution (fixed, unchanging, cold, authoritarian, clergy-dominated) and to provide for its becoming an open organization which allows for and nurtures personal freedom,

41

participation, and responsibility. Such is, in part, a proposed goal of Lutheran congregations in the 1970s.[28] Implementation of the goal hinges to a large degree on how seriously we honor such slogans as respecting the integrity of each child's participation according to the level of his maturation, youth ministry, and the validity of cultural variations in the educational program of the church. There are real tensions that must be dealt with here, as, for example, in the realization that the church does not exist for the sake of its members and the educator's conviction that the church must respect the person of the child. Structures, including those in and of the church, are not neutral. How far they go toward fixing attitudes and responses may be seen in the current polarization of opinions between those who reject it as totally irrelevant in this post-civilization era and those who call for a stiffening of conservative traditions and characteristics.

4. If "it is the world that must be allowed to provide the agenda for the churches"[29] then the concerns of the world must provide a larger chunk of the content of the educational program of the church. The signs are already present as curriculum focuses on social unrest, world order, ecology, and the technological revolution and uses the media of secular organizations and individuals for study materials. The church becomes the place where the humanization of man is dealt with in all of its phases.

There are some obvious dangers that will arise here as theory gets translated into program, the risks that the church will be identified with the world in an undiscriminating way or that we shall propagate a false theology of the world. But the risks will have to be taken and efforts made to maintain proper balance between worldly concerns and the "Christian perspective" and "theological dimension" called for in the central objective.[30]

5. The fluidity and flexibility in the approach to those accents which mark the church and its mission in our time call for a similar fluidity and flexibility with regard to educational approaches, programs, and materials. If "the needs and potentials of the individual and the congregation are in flux," as a report on an ALC-LCA Task Force for Planning Educational Ministry indicates, it seems quite unlikely that a carefully articulated and graded set of materials and supporting services will match current parish requirements. Like the church, the educational program will require more of a task-orientation of limited time and setting value. We might anticipate decreasing emphasis on

universal agencies and their full-blown administrative and organizational systems and an increasing stress on such things as flexible units, broader patterns of learning settings, more local initiative in deciding settings and choosing materials, trans-generational groupings, a stronger stress on dialog as a form of learning, the recognition of a variety of legitimate Christian life styles and the like.

6. The growing respect for the laity in broadening dimensions of ministry will call for not only a redefinition of leadership and new emphasis on leadership training but also utilization of Christian community groups in new forms and places as seats of leadership development and expression. The dispersion of Christians into the world, of course, makes a similar demand.

7. The groping for unity on the part of the church calls for sharing among the churches in educational planning, design, and production.

8. Finally, the whole agonizing experience of turning itself inside out and refocusing its eyes on the service of others rather than self means for the church a reappraisal of those for whom its educational mission is intended, even on the so-called parish level. The *Age Group Objectives of Christian Education* adopted in 1958 by the predecessor bodies of the American Lutheran Church and Lutheran Church in America stated unequivocally, "All charts are developed with the presupposition that the learner is a child of God through baptism." This was equivalent to saying that he is a member of the church and can be counted on as participating in the agencies established by the church for the nurture of its members. There is no parallel statement in any document developed thus far in the new Lutheran cooperative effort. There is good reason for this if we recognize the changing situation in the church and its changing attitude toward what is transpiring outside its walls. A growing number of churchmen no longer question the mandate of the church to reach outside itself in affecting people and events positively toward its perception of God's purpose for mankind. But the matter of the means and the responsibility of parish education remain unanswered questions.

NOTES AND REFERENCES

1. Hans Kung, *Structures of the Church* (Camden, N.J.: Thomas Nelson & Sons, 1964), p. vii.
2. James Burtness, "Sent into the World: A Biblical-Theological Exposition of the Theme of the LWF's Fifth Assembly," *Ministers Information Service,* June, 1970, LW-7.

3. Donald R. Pichaske, *A Study Book on the Manifesto: God's Call to the Church in Each Place* (Philadelphia: Board of Publication of the Lutheran Church in America, 1967), p. 12.

4. World Council of Churches, *The Church For Others: Two Reports on the Missionary Structure of the Congregation,* The Final Report of the Western European Working Group and North American Working Group for the Department on Studies in Evangelism (Geneva: World Council of Churches, 1967), p. 75.

5. "The Confession of 1967," *The Book of Confessions* (Philadelphia: General Assembly, 1967).

6. *The Church for Others,* p. 17.

7. In all this this-worldly stress, the present has a special significance. Note, for example, Hans Hoekendijk, "Evangelization of the World in This Generation," *International Review of Missions,* vol. 59, no. 233 (Jan., 1970), p. 28: ". . . evangelization is simply a description of the mode of Christian existence . . . In a very special sense Christians are the NOW generation. They realize that '*this* is the hour, *today* is the day' (2 Corinthians 6:2). Of course, the future is opened and we are 'children of tomorrow.' We don't live by the things as we see them. Whatever we are is anchored in the things we hope for or, rather, in the One who promises to come, the *ad-ventus* God. But it is *now,* this hour, today that we appropriate things hoped for."

8. "Evangelization of the World in This Generation," p. 30.

9. The three viewpoints may be illustrated. The extreme is reflected in such a document as the "Report on the Dutch Augustinian Province, November 1, 1969,": "The religious life has to do with the proclamation of the *Gospel,* the coming of the *kingdom of God,* the pilgrimage of the church as the people of God. These are all very lovely words, but many of us are not all that sure of their content. We take offense when our situation is called to these 'sacred' words because they seem to be slogans which easily distract one from the concrete, even brutal, reality of what is going on in the world. It has often been said that sacred words furnish an alibi for those who, perhaps unconsciously, are afraid they are in danger of losing their security.

"Despite our irritation at the facile use of such words as *Gospel, Kingdom of God, church,* and *people of God,* we think it necessary for what regards the function of the religious life, to see these words in the reality precisely where human words, including the most sacred, have their source . . .

"The reality in question is of course man himself . . . They [the words] refer to a future where the accomplishment and achievement of man will be realized . . .

"It is indeed this man, his way of being human, that Christians search for when they search for what is human and believe that such words as *kingdom of God* and *church* have something to say on the subject . . .

"In this context we must pose to ourselves once more the question, What is meant by saying that the religious life has a function vis-a-vis the church and society? What is this function in connection with the Gospel and the kingdom of God, the church and the people of God? "We believe the essence of it is the service that we must offer in the founding of human relationships . . .

"When we lay such stress on the importance of human relationships in the function of the religious life, we hit upon another question, Does the distinction between church and society still have meaning?" (IDOC-INTERNATIONAL, North American Edition, May 9, 1970, pp. 44-46.)

A somewhat less extreme view is reflected in the final report of the Western European Working Group of the World Council of Churches' study dealing with the quest for structures for missionary congregations: "How then are we to define the relationship between the Church and the world? Again we must distinguish between models that have been adopted in the past and the emphasis that is required today. In former times the Church was viewed as an ark, perilously afloat amidst the turbulent seas of this world; outside the safety of this vessel mankind is going down to destruction and the only safety is to be dragged from the deep into the ecclesiastical ship. Or again, the Church has been seen as an armed camp and individual Christian soldiers are members of the army of the Lord of hosts set in the midst of active enemies. From time to time Christians sally forth from their palisades to rescue from the hostile environment as many as they can . . .

"But the Church has to be seen as a segment of the world, and thinking about the Church should always begin by defining it as a part of the world, albeit one which confesses the universal Lordship of Christ . . . We may say that the Church is only required to be separate in order to be prepared for engagement, that is, the Church exists for the world . . . The Church exists that the world may know its true being. It is *pars pro toto*; it is the first fruits of the new creation." (*The Church for Others*, pp. 17-18.)

The third example distinguishes between being identical to and identifying with. This is the line of thought James Burtness develops in his biblical-theological exposition of the LWF theme, "Sent into the World." Since its [the church's] identity is in its mission, it can never be identical to the world. But since its mission is to the world, it not only may, but must, identify itself with the world." Burtness identifies two meanings for "world," its designation of the whole inhabited creation and of the summation of evil. The church is sent into the world in both senses, and it looks upon the world with "hopeful realism." "It looks upon the inhabited creation as *substantially good,* created by God and the object of His redemptive love, but *accidentally evil . . .,* thoroughly distorted and perverted as a result of the creature's rebellion against the Creator . . . "The church itself does not escape this ambiguity. It is a piece of the world. The presence of evil cannot be limited to the world apart from the church any more than the presence of God can be limited to the church apart from the world . . .

"The church is not identical to the world. But it can identify itself with the world because, as a piece of the world, it shares the world's struggles and joys, its problems and cares, its failures and successes." ("Sent into the World," *Ministers Information Service,* LW-8.)

10. Edward W. Uthe, ed., *Theology: An Assessment of Current Trends. Report of the Lutheran Church in America Task Group for Long Range Planning* (Philadelphia: Board of Publication of the Lutheran Church in America, 1968), p. 139.

11. *Ibid.,* p. 151.

12. Karl Rahner, *Nature and Grace* (New York: Sheed & Ward, Inc., 1964), p. 21.

13. Lewis J. Sherrill, *The Gift of Power* (New York: Macmillan Co., 1955), p. 50.

14. Edward W. Uthe, ed., *Significant Issues for the 1970's: Report of the Lutheran Church in America Task Group for Long Range Planning* (Philadelphia: Fortress Press, 1968), p. 24.

15. *Nature and Grace,* p. 21.

16. Douglass and Brunner clearly demonstrate at least the inevitability of visible institutional forms and practices in their analysis of anti-ecclesiastical Christian groups such as the Primitive Baptists. Among these groups the very rules set up to guard against the creation of an ecclesiastical institution became the foundation stones for building just such a structure. "The attempt . . . to conceive of a non-institutionalized religion for modern man is sociologically infantile. It is an attack on rationality and ethical stability themselves. Religion cannot have currency without developing some generalized form, and generalized form implies habits resistant to change which are the essence of institutionalization." See H. Paul Douglas and Edmund deS. Brunner, *The Protestant Church as a Social Institution* (New York: Institute of Social and Religious Research, 1935), p. 15.

17. Godfrey Diekmann, *Come, Let Us Worship* (Baltimore: Helicon Press, Inc., 1961), p. 54.

18. *The Church for Others,* p. 43.

19. David O. Moberg, *The Church as a Social Institution* (Englewood Cliffs, N. J.: Prentice-Hall, Inc., 1962), pp. 4-5.

Moberg presses the point that much of what the church is derives from the efforts of its members to meet the requirements of its mission:

"In meeting the requirements of its life, a church, like other social institutions, must be recognized as an organization made, and continually remade, by men. The inner structure which is formed, the rules and regulations which are established, the means which are fashioned to nurture and sustain religious beliefs, the purposes and goals which are cultivated, the policies and procedures which are devised, and the sense of identity which is developed are all products of collective effort by the people who comprise the church."

For a description of how this tension between theological and sociological concepts of the church was resolved in patristic writings, see Robert L. Wilken's "Speaking Modestly of the Church," *Una Sancta*, vol. 25, no. 3, pp. 52-63.

20. *The Church for Others*, p. 43.
21. Paul S. Minear, "Church, Idea of," in *The Interpreter's Dictionary of the Bible*, vol. 1, George A. Buttrick, ed. (New York-Nashville: Abingdon Press, 1962), pp. 607-617.
22. *Ibid.*, p. 616.
23. "Sent into the World," *Ministers Information Service*, LW-6.
24. "The Augsburg Confession," in *The Book of Concord*, Theodore G. Tappert, trans. and ed. (Philadelphia: Fortress Press, 1959), p. 32.
25. "The Apology of the Augsburg Confession" in *The Book of Concord*, p. 173.
26. The churches have generally steered clear of trying to measure the results of their efforts to change human lives through educational processes on the grounds that this is not a suitable area for empirical studies. Where such small beginnings as the LCA's Continuing Curriculum Evaluation Project series of multiple-choice tests designed to measure growth toward objectives in Sunday (through Grade 12) and weekday church school (Grades 7-9) courses have been used, the results are often both inconclusive and unimpressive. One feels strong sympathy for the judgment of the German Catholic educator Hubertus Halbfass: "Not infrequently is religious instruction a source of endless frustration and certain alienation from the church." Halbfass quotes a fellow churchman (Görres, *Kirches Und Empirischer Katholizismus*, p. 283) as concluding: "Christians of the world exert great effort in the proclamation of the faith. In many countries children between their sixth and sixteenth years receive many hundreds, often over a thousand, hours of nuture in the faith through religious instruction, catechizing, and preaching. Apart from the communist world, no "world view" has comparable institutional possibilities to communicate its teachings to its children. The result of this mighty effort, so far as empirical data can determine, seems to provide little comfort. After a thousand hours of instruction the knowledge of faith that can stand the test of time is small, the understanding of the faith paltry, the decisive faith-stance more the exception than the rule, the influence

on behavior hardly convincing. The large majority of students who receive religious instruction make the end of their school days also the end of their believing." Hubertus Halbfass, *Fundamental Kate-chetik, Sprache und Erfahrung im Religionsunterricht* (Stuttgart: Carl Verlag, 1968), p. 274.

27. David J. Ernsberger, *Reviving the Local Church* (Philadelphia: Fortress Press, 1969), p. 7.
28. *Significant Issues for the 1970's,* especially pp. 33-36.
29. *The Church for Others,* p. 20.
30. Some of these risks will undoubtedly become more apparent as the reports of the 1970 LWF Assembly become available. Attention was given to them in pre-Assembly discussions. See, for example, Frederick Wilhelm-Krummacher's article "Sent Into the World," *Lutheran World,* vol. 14, no. 2, 1967. Krummacher warns against a false theology of the world, one in which we say Christ is latently present and the church's confirming of the world as it is. "One cannot say that today we owe the world encounter and dialog and not the call to rescue and salvation. A dialog with the world which did not call for a return to the hidden Lord of the world would not be an authentic encounter" (p. 149).

Josef Glazik has stated a missionary proposition for the church that can well be applied to her educational task: ". . . the Church must accomplish her task, not by incorporating the world, its people, cultures, and religions to herself, but rather by becoming incarnate within them." ("The Mission of the Church in Today's World," *International Review of Missions,* vol. 56, 1967, p. 316).

* From *The New English Bible, New Testament.* © The Delegates of the Oxford University Press and the Syndics of the Cambridge University Press 1961. Reprinted by permission.

Chapter III

God's Activity

JOHN H. REUMANN

It is a sign of the times that "God's activity" is our theme, rather than the incarnation or the "Christ event," and that this subject is placed between essays on "the church" and "man and his community." It is the same in the guiding statement itself for educational ministry in the Lutheran churches in the years ahead. The central objective in these churches:

> shall be to assist persons to perceive, respond to, and participate in *God's continuing activity and revelation, particularly in Jesus Christ,* in the human and Christian communities as they deal with their continual life involvements. . . .

We are no longer just repeating traditional terms, and the sequence reflects something of the thinking of the day. Yet precisely this poses particular problems. Church, ALC, LCA, seem concrete. Man and his communities are tangible. But people living in the seventies, even convinced Christians, have difficulty speaking articulately about God and identifying his workings. Every word in our section of the statement on objective is under fire: "revelation," divine "activity," even the place and significance of Jesus Christ, to say nothing of whether the term "God" is useful any more.

Yet in these phrases about "God . . . in Jesus Christ" we came to the most obviously Christian and specifically theological part of the whole statement on a central objective for Christian education.

The triplet of infinitives can be paralleled in general educational theory or in the earlier (1958) LCA statement on general objectives of Christian education, or, for that matter—as if to remind us that not all wisdom arises only in modern times—in the formulation by the classical Lutheran dogmaticians as to what "faith" is:

> to perceive, respond to, and participate in; (1969)
> perceiving, behaving, becoming;[1]
> understandings, attitudes, patterns of action; (1958)
> *notitia, assensus, fiducia.*

The phrase about "human and Christian communities"—while it reflects an awareness that the Christian always lives simultaneously in two spheres, the human or the world, and the church or realm of the gospel—could simply be taken as sociological description. Or it might be taken, not as enumerating the arenas where the believer perceives, responds, and participates, but as the locus or places of God's revelation. In that case, in the one instance, humanity, not Christ, would become the sphere of God's self-revelation and, in the other instance, the church becomes itself the revelation. Unless we clearly understand how Christians come to knowledge of God in his world and in the fellowship of his people, respond in that church and by service in the world, and participate in the life of the church community and in the world, we shall be plagued by a confusion over whether "human and Christian" is ascending or descending order, an equation, a tautology, or two realms where God works in characteristic ways.

The same thing is true of the list of continual life involvements in the statement. The three areas of self, personal or group relations, and society/culture/world can be termed plain common sense, or anthropological analysis, or just an outline of disciplines proceeding from the science of the self (psychology) to the sciences of society and the physical universe. Hence many of these life involvements will have nothing specifically Christian about them. They become patently theological only if one adds "under God" as a rubic for each area or unless one views each area in light of God's act in Christ.

Thus most of the central objective could be interpreted simply as educational psychology or social engineering, with a line or two left for "God" where the statement gets traditionally "theological." But I choose to construe these phrases about "God's continuing activity and revelation, particularly in Jesus Christ," not as a sop to tradition or a vestige of past verbiage in an otherwise scientific age, to be interpreted in light of our educational, social, and psychological theories, but as *the central theme in the central objective.*

It is no accident that in a statement of direction for Lutheran parish ministry and its educational task, the word of God in Christ appears at its heart. "God's continuing activity and revelation" is the object of the three infinitives; it is what we "assist persons to perceive, respond to, and participate in." God's revelation in Christ and his ongoing activity are the guide and goal for the involvement of persons we assist. The revelation in Christ and the continuing activity of such a God provide the lodestars for their many involvements in life.

But how does one speak of "God's continuing activity" today or of "revelation" for the seventies and eighties? How does one "apply Christ," as the reformers would put it, to all the areas of society, world, and life? The educational principles, the programming of life involvements at each stage, the improvement of interpersonal relationships—these are, in many ways, but technicians' and craftsmen's jobs —exceedingly difficult, demanding, to be sure, but we do have increasingly the know-how to make advancements here. But how to talk of *God* today? There the computer, laboratory research, tests and measurements, all our usual devices, not only fail to solve the dilemmas but may actually exacerbate the problems.

Reasons for our difficulties in talking about God are apparent at every hand. We live in a post-"God-is-dead" age. Social unrest and calamitous problems make talk about revelation and divine activity seem irrelevant when man has so much to do and old answers do not hold. One does not formulate a new view of the Trinity nor of world history when the whole fabric of society is being torn apart. (Or is that precisely the time to do so Augustine, Luther, and all the other thinker-doers who lived in changing times might ask.) In an age when man has come into his own, why talk of God? Events call for affirmation of the world, the one world in all its plural variety. Why complicate and offend by affirming something "particularly in Jesus Christ"? Even biblical study in the hands of modern scholarship seems to contribute to our difficulties with God-talk by the way it analyzes the Bible critically and suggests almost a "history of God" in Israel and since Jesus Christ.

Our challenge thus is to talk meaningfully to our day about divine revelation and activity, aware of all the changes projected and now going on yet faithful still to the Word of God.

In this chapter, after reminding ourselves of how we have been accustomed to talk of the acts of God in the past (Part I), we shall sketch some of the current developments (Part II) and certain options possible in talking about God and his work with man and the world (Part III). The real task, in many ways, is searching for clues and criteria in how God's people over the years, especially in those key periods of biblical traces, have identified revelation and God's activity so that we may look for it today. The probes in that direction (Part IV) will point towards some conclusions (Part V).

Again, however, the nature of our concern and its difficulty needs to be underscored: "God's activity." the man in the street inevitably shies away from such language, protesting as one factory worker did, "A cup of coffee, I can see, smell, taste, and feel. But God . . . ?" As for "revelation," modern man, we are told again and again, believes only what he can verify. How can he trust the word of an unseen Unknown, transmitted to him at one-hundred-and-third-hand, with a string of confusing interpreters trying to apply it to him? To some, "God" and "revelation in Christ" seem so absurd that they would want to do education and face life's involvements without these attachments. The job of Christian education is to show how these traditions still relate and the God revealed in Jesus permeates all. Else why term it "Christian"?

Before plunging into the topic further, we may find it helpful, however, to note two ways—beyond the reaches of this essay—in which Christian attempts to make God "relevant" have been structured, sometimes with success and sometimes with failure. They continue today as methods, we shall see, and we shall encounter their influences at many points.

The one approach concentrates revelation and God's activity *in the church,* the Christian community very often being regarded as a tight little isle of light and truth, precisely structured, destined to lead a fallen world. The Roman Catholic Church, especially prior to the Second Vatican Council, has at times reflected this mentality. So did the

Qumran community in Jesus' day. So have the Lutherans at times. In opposition to such an outlook, *man and the world* have sometimes been stressed as the locus of divine activity and of revelation. Man is himself godly. All men have the light. "God" is throughout the universe (which is therefore not "fallen"), in many religions, not locked up in a single faith or church. Revelation is identified with things going on in the world today. Historically, Stoics, humanists, pantheists, and many a modern Christian have exhibited some of these views.

Perhaps neither view, as baldly outlined, is appealing. The fact is that each position can quote biblical material and portions of the Christian tradition on its side. Recent developments have stressed the latter approach, even among Roman Catholics. It is well to be aware of how currents are moving, as well as how they have moved in the past if for no other reason that to swim against the stream when the truth demands.

At this stage we must simply be aware of the dangers in compartmentalizing, or equating completely, divine activity and revelation so exclusively in church or world. The church and the world as spheres of God's activity, and man as recipient of revelation, and the community formed by what God reveals are part of our problem in grasping what "God" is about.

I

OUR INHERITANCE: TRADITIONAL TALK
OF GOD'S ACTIVITY

At the outset, let us be clear that two thousand years of Christianity have produced a rich variety of ways of presenting God's revelatory activity. Even the Bible, or the New Testament alone, has more than one manner of depicting how God acts. But taken altogether, the biblical witness, combined, interpreted, and amalgamated into a harmonious whole, has over the centuries been developed into a traditional picture of what God is like, how he worked and works in creation and history, and what he has in store for the future. It is a picture which has proven amazingly useful, not only for the business of systematic theology (which seeks to set forth in orderly fashion the science of God for current times), but also for ethics (how the believing Christian acts), preaching, education, pastoral care, and the development of a satisfying *weltanschauung* for the believer living his life in church and world.

By and large, this traditional, composite picture of the manifold workings of God has concentrated on the past, and specifically on certain great moments or epochs in that past: the history of Israel and the event of Jesus Christ. This portrayal of God's past activity was not, of course, left isolated from present life. The course of divine actions was seen as stretching from the beginnings of creation to the grand denouement at the Last Judgment and coming eternal kingdom. All history was thus encompassed in its sweep. The God who spoke in Genesis continued through all vicissitudes of history to have the whole world in his hand. And if not a sparrow fell without his doing, according to Jesus' teaching, surely all events of history since Calvary were under his control. He who did miraculously at the Red Sea or with a Gerasene demoniac could also deal wondrously with his children in subsequent centuries.

The vision here of God's works whereby he reveals himself and his purpose is almost too well known to repeat. We have heard it from childhood and keep on telling it "like is was," for one dimension of Christian education (and worship) ought to be recounting the tales our fathers told of a God who "made known his ways to Moses [and a host of others, especially in Christ], his acts to the people of Israel" [and all who would subsequently believe] (Psalm 103:7).

This God made the heavens and the earth. Man, his creature, he is with, even after disobedience. God judges justly and can display wrath, but his mercy is great and he chooses men and nations to carry out his plans. While he cares for all men, the focus of Yahweh's love falls on the patriarchs, and then on the nation Israel, whose very nationhood he creates by the Exodus event, his care and guidance in the wilderness (giving food and law), his help in conquering a promised land. Judges, prophets, kings—men whom he calls may fail him, but Yahweh's work goes on, not merely in the sustenance of all life, but in a special way among his chosen people and select leaders. A kingdom, divided, fallen one half at a time; exile, restoration for a remnant; dark days. Time would fail to tell of all those in and through whom Yahweh worked, though a narrowing is apparent in the ranks of those involved. The nation dwindles to a pious few, from whose midst new life springs.

God sent a man named John, much like the prophets centuries before. The forerunner pointed to a man from Nazareth, who preaches, teaches, manifests God's power, and is put to death. Here God's power raises Jesus up; he is proclaimed as Lord, by a band of men on whom the Spirit of God has come. A message of good news is spread. A new community of people who confess Jesus as Lord is born. "The Way" is established and prospered by God.

Jerusalem falls, again, but God's hand can be seen here too, as in past centuries. For the story goes on. God works through missionaries, ministers, all who follow Jesus and receive his Spirit. He is with them through many vicissitudes, some of which are specifically spelled out as warnings and prophecies. Evil will wax strong. The love of many will grow cold. Perseverence is the order of the day. False christs will appear. God will seem far off. Voices of his faithful cry out in despair. But, hold fast to the Word. The Son of man will come, the Christ will triumph. All human injustices will be set right at the grand assize. God's own will reign with God all in all.

Any rapid sketch can scarce do justice to the grandeur of this Christian *heilsgeschichte*—the story of salvation, which is God's proper work and revelation of what lies at his heart, a desire to save and make whole. It has guided believers for centuries, inspired their art, given themes for song, comforted the periods without hope, directed their gaze through the world's inhumanities and beyond, and served as the very lifeblood of the church's faith. Precisely because it was firmly rooted in the past, this view gave a firm base for life in the present. All could be looked at in light of God's activity in Israel and the definitive revelation in Jesus Christ. One knew where and how to search for God because he knew whence he himself had come and somthing of God's plan. The songs of Zion could be transferred to Bedford Green. Our forefathers could sing the Lord's song in a strange land. There was a sensible, comprehensive, and widely shared picture of reality.

This view of God's revelatory activity still continues serviceable today in many ways. It is reflected in a study book in the LCA's curriculum for the sixties, *The Mighty Acts of God*. On the more scholarly level, *The Book of the Acts of God*, by G. Ernest Wright and Reginald Fuller presents this view. The success of the Bethel series and similar Bible study courses testifies to the pulling power that this traditional presentation has in one form or another. Indeed, liturgy and the very church year in its general outline reflect this understanding of God's acts and revelation. Who of us has not been enriched by it? When has a church long flourished with some substitute?

For a time, in the fifties and early sixties, this theology of *heilsgeschichte,* championed particularly by biblical scholars like von Rad and his school in Old Testament studies and Cullmann in the New, bade fair to become *the* ecumenical theology. A considerable amount of World Council and Vatican theologizing reflected this biblical, patristic view of God's plan or "economy," centered in Jesus Christ, flanked on one side by the divine revelation in creation and Israel and on the other by God's ongoing activity in church and world.

It can be claimed that the 1958 LCA statement on the objectives of Christian education rests on this understanding, even if the full design is not spelled out:

> Inasmuch as the Church, as the Body of Christ, seeks to become more effectively that community of believers in which the Holy Spirit calls, gathers, enlightens, and sanctifies individuals in their relationships with God and their fellow men, the church's central educational objective, therefore, shall be—
> To assist the individual in his response and witness to the eternal and incarnate Word of God as he grows within this community of the church toward ever-deepening understandings, more wholesome attitudes, and more responsible patterns of action.

One is, of course, struck immediately by certain similarities with the 1969 statement before us now. The aim is "to assist," in three areas of response: understanding, attitudes, actions. The "incarnate Word of God" (cf. "God's activity . . . in Jesus Christ") is central. Relationships (is "continual life involvements" a *less* personal term?) are stressed.

Likewise one can note changes in emphasis and differences reflective of developments in the sixties or of a deeper understanding of what Christian education ought to be about. No longer is the individual (twice mentioned in the 1958 statement) stressed; rather, "persons," in groups and society (1969). The world gets greater emphasis in the more recent central objective ("the physical universe," "culture") and the church gets less (though more specifically, the ALC and LCA are mentioned; "body of Christ" drops out as a description, "community of believers" becomes the Christian community, parallel with the human community). Language from Luther's Catechism ("calls, gathers, enlightens, and sanctifies") is no longer used. What might be termed "language of efficiency" ("become more effectively," "toward greater maturity," "ever-deepening," "more wholesome," "more responsible") is eschewed (people now simply "deal with . . . involvements"), either for simplicity's sake or because of the view involved of man. There is a shift from a psychological bent to the sociological. Omission of the word "witness" is not strange when one considers what has happened to the outlook in the churches' departments of evangelism in the last decade.

It is, however, dangerous to read too much into such analysis. No single sentence can say everything, and carefully framed as these statements are, they form working statements for a decade, not principles for eternity. We should therefore not be surprised if nuances change. Some of the contrasts noted above are likely mere happenstance.

Nevertheless, it is worth noting several striking points which do emerge.

1. The emphasis on the world and society for the seventies has already been pointed out, along with a lessened stress on church and individual. These shifts are deliberate and can be said to reflect, not just the changing times, but, more important, insights from biblical theology. The traditional picture of *heilsgeschichte* outlined above has, especially in the hands of Cullmann, regularly not ignored the corporate aspects or the world as the stage within which God's saving activities are presented.

2. Both statements are christocentric. That of 1958 uses word-of-God terminology, Christ being stressed, it may be assumed, over a Book-as-the-word-of-God approach. But the 1969 statement lays its emphasis on God, his continuing activity and revelation, with the phrase "particularly in Jesus Christ" added to sharpen the focus. Obviously the intent is to encourage seeing God's work as not merely back there, but "here and now," in line with the stress noted above on world and society. At the same time the revelation in Jesus Christ is made definitive, so as to give a clue and criteria for understanding God's subsequent workings. Two things may strike the reader:

1. In a period when people have been saying "God is dead," the 1969 statement lays greater emphasis on God's working today;

2. In presenting God's continuing activity no reference is made to the Holy Spirit, such as was prominent in the 1958 statement. Granted, the 1958 statement spoke of the Spirit's role in the church primarily, and the new statement is interested in society and world. But the fact remains that the traditional Christian vocabulary about the Spirit for God's ongoing working has not surfaced. One might be tempted to add, "Typical of Lutheranism, never knowing what to do with the Holy Ghost," that underdeveloped area theologically, the Third Article of the Creed! Or, we must ask, Is this connection of the Spirit the Sanctifier with the Church (1958) and stress on God's activity in the world (1969) really a correct reflection of biblical thought?

Our general conclusion is that *both statements owe something to the traditional picture of God's saving acts,* his work from creation to present day, in world and church, even though the two statements for Lutheran educational ministry inflect the proposition differently to fit changing needs. In fact, the 1969 statement on central objective may assume even more the kind of sketch Cullmann has mapped out for depicting God's onging activity. One recalls the "time line" running through history, from creation to consummation, with a series of X's on it where God's acts intersect this line and a revelatory, saving event occurs.[2] God is assumed to be active always, today included, so that his self-revelation is to be seen not only in the eternal and incarnate Word, but also in creation, Israel, church and world history, and the near and remote future. Such a view is true to Scripture. The Bible does speak of the world's beginnings and ending, and not just of "holy history." Most people nurtured on this biblical view do have a sense of God in history and the heavens and earth declaring his glory. Clearly Scripture points beyond its own time to a future consummation. Subsequent confessions of faith and theologizing of the faithful have recognized this grand sweep.

Nonetheless, certain general criticisms of this whole heilsgeschichte view can be made, and have been made in recent years, the force of which sometimes carries over to the way we need to look at our 1969 statment on objective.

In spite of all the emphasis in this approach on "the God who acts" or the claim that "God is what he does," the view which stresses being or ontology survives and sometimes still shines through. Interest continues in metaphysics and God "as he really is," in himself. Not just function, but also form is the concern. His being, and not merely his work, is at issue. Functional statements lead into ontological propositions, as when one says "God is, and can be known." While the tendency is biblical studies and the current mood may be to stress the functional and activity, the old ontological questions have a way of popping up again. What we say about "activity and revelation" might mask a failure to specify what we mean by God. The death of God may reflect a failure to say God "is" as well as that "he acts."

The traditional approach of *heilsgeschichte* forgets that it often involves a *construct*. The "time line" is constructed to connect a series of *Xs,* and the whole is then extrapolated into the present and future on the basis of certain agreed points of revelation in the past. Such an approach runs the danger of forgetting that the revelatory activity as grasped by human comprehension is episodic; we assume we can look at it from God's side, as part of the finished plan. This issue becomes especially acute when one tries to speak of "ongoing activity and revelation." How does one verify where the *Xs* occur *in our day?* Is Che Guevara, Malcolm X, the Six-Day War, or the achievements of Women's Liberation an expression of divine activity? On which side was God at the Kent State massacre in May, 1970? (The ease with which students and law-and-order people answer that question, in diametrically opposed ways, ought to give us pause). How does one identify, let alone verify, an action of God today?

Along with such questions as the meaning of "God" and how we identify his acts—places where the traditional view is still useful but not clear or conclusive today—there is the danger that the *heilsgeschichte* view will degenerate, as it sometimes has, into a biblical ghetto, where God is confined to the past, or that his work will be seen in static, "church only" categories. Any dynamic relation to the world or church today will be lost. This is especially true when the German word *heilsgeschichte* (which we have been treating as an English loanword, as now in Webster) is translated as "holy history" (as if one pocket or one line only of history were God's) or even as "salvation history" (with the possible misinterpretation that history, rather than God, saves).

The variety of views of *heilsgeschichte* in the Bible itself is ignored sometimes. In the New Testament, the view in Luke-Acts (perhaps the one that became normative for the church) is not the same precisely as that in Revelation, Paul, or even Matthew.

The trinitarian view of God implied in *heilsgeschichte*—as Father, who created and was active in Israel, as Son who redeemed at Calvary, as Spirit active ever since—may not be fully true to the Bible (the Son also creates, the Father continues to exercise his rule, etc.) and can lead to misleading systems of dispensationalism, departmentalizing history and God. (In neither the 1958 nor 1969 statement, it may be added, is a trinitarian understanding of God spelled out). Questions may be asked whether our way, traditionally or in our statements, is the best way of handling the "God question."

Two final terms in our statement on central objective call for comment against the background of the traditional view. The one is *revelation*, "God's . . . revelation, particularly in Jesus Christ." Christian theologies have always been built around the idea that "God reveals . . ." All sorts of theories have been advanced as to how and when and where. The deity is held to manifest himself; he speaks. The Revealer reveals himself in Christ and the Spirit helps man to appropriate the revelation, in personal and sometimes propositional terms, and so respond and participate. Thus, the traditional view.

Along with this understanding of revelation and its centrality, obviously assumed in the 1969 statement, there has been traditionally a distinction between "general revelation" and "specific revelation." "General revelation" is that knowledge which God has imparted, including perception of his deity and power, in the world generally, the world of nature, the world of men, quite apart from any Christian scriptures or witness of the Hebrew Bible or testimony of the church about what it has experienced in *heilgeschichte*. What God has plainly made known to all (Romans 1:19 ff.) and everything that man can search out (Acts 17:24 ff.) is subsumed here. Above and beyond this is the special revealing of himself or particular manifestation of his actvity God has granted in Israel and "particularly in Jesus Christ"—revelations of his ultimate design and clues for measuring all that he does.

This standard view of general and special revelation (some prefer "natural" and "revealed theology") offers a firm basis for anchoring the 1969 statement. It permits God's activity both in biblical times and our contemporary world. God can be present and at work in any time or place. He can be active not merely in groups dedicated to his redemptive purpose but also, to use biblical examples, in a non-believer king (like Cyrus, who is even called Yahweh's Anointed, Isaiah 45:1) or Balaam's ass (Numbers 22:28 ff.). He can be seen as working in all sorts of world processes, at least according to the witness of faith. (Actually the biblical expressions vary: sometimes it is the Father who works, John 5:17; sometimes it is Christ who is in the midst of believers, Matthew 18:20, 28:20; sometimes it is Yahweh present as spirit who is involved. Cf. 2 Corinthians 3:17 ff, in light of Exodus 34:29-35—the statement sums all this ups as "God.")

But is *all* this working to be termed "revelation"? Here caution is in order. The traditional view always granted that God gives knowledge of himself in all sorts of ways, but held these "general" revelations were to be understood in light of the special revelation, "particularly in Christ." God's world gives men the possibility of knowing him. But as what? Paul's answer was as power, but scarcely as love or saving righteousness; that comes only in Christ (Romans 1:20; cf. 3:21 ff.).

Nowadays we are living in a period when people wish to stress more the contemporary ("the relevant"), the revolutionary—sometimes not merely alongside the past and its definitive landmarks—but actually replacing the old with "new revelations." Thus, in one of the deliberations in the Consultation on Christian Unity, it was proposed that that the ministry in a pan-Protestant merger would be not so much to proclaim the work of God revealed in Christ as to identify what God is doing today. The "age of the Spirit" in the world is taken as the key. The text is emphasized, the Spirit "will guide you into all truth" (John 16:13), without citing John's insistence that this Spirit who is to teach all things will bring to remembrance what Jesus had already taught and what has been revealed by God in Christ (John 14:26, 16:13). Thus, in stressing the contemporary, we run the danger —like the sects which purport new revelations—of exalting something new in place of what the Christian heritage had designated as central, and we force the difficulty of identifying *which* trends in the world today are God's and which are not.

The other phrase has to do with *God's activity. Heilsgeschichte's* notion of the acts of God, ongoing, is still useful. The 1969 statement assumes it and, indeed, wants to stress the contemporaneity of such

61

acts, both in the sense that God's past, decisive saving acts still have meaning to be appropriated today and in the sense that God still is at work. The real hitch is in appropriating for our lives what God has already done, and in identifying something today as an action of God.

The statement suggests a clue which is quite in harmony with *heilsgeschichte's* approach: what happened in Jesus is particularly decisive and a key to how and where we may see redemptive divine action today. To emphasize this Christ event is not to deny God's working in Israel, or at creation, or since, or today, but it is to affirm Jesus as the clue as well as the Christ. That is very much what many a modern inside and outside the church is saying. The current mood—the "New quest of the historical Jesus," hippie quests for new life styles, liberation movements' embrace of Jesus, "God is dead" but Jesus is his son"—all reflect what one Presbyterian said, "Theology is a shambles; Jesus is the 'Saving Certainty.' "[3] We turn now to survey "the shambles" and current trends, seeking which alternatives to the traditional view with its strengths and weaknesses may be posed.

II

THE CHALLENGE: CHANGE AND DEVELOPMENTS TODAY

It is true that the 1960s have been a time of rapid change. Everything indicates change will accelerate in the seventies in many ways. In a sense, there's nothing new about all this. Adam, leaving the Garden, is reputed to have remarked, "Eve! It's a changing world." But the acceleration in the last decade has been breathtaking, and change has even, in a way never talked of before, gotten to God.

Generally it has been assumed that change is good. Churches and their ministry have been called upon to become "agents of change." That particular phrase, first popularized by the group dynamics emphases in the mid 'forties, has again come to the fore in the black revolution. For some churchmen it has implied riding with, or riding out, the tide. Others see Christians as the prophetic vanguard for revolutionary change. Sometimes there is a notion of skilled managers steering recalcitrant rank-and-file. Sometimes it is the average member pushing the church leaders on. Change is envisioned in world, culture, society—and church. The central objective statement points to the church's educational ministry assisting persons in such a time.

But in what direction? Amid all the currents of change, which are the ones that God inspires? In a time of many revolutions—black, red Indian, the third world, women's lib, students—it is to the credit of many of those Christians who advocate some role of constructive leadership for the church and for Christians in the movements of the time that they recognize the need to ask, Which change? We are in for a time of desperate searching for criteria to guide us in an age of ferment.

All too often, of course, all change has been viewed as bad. It is no accident that one Christian hymnwriter laments, "change and decay in all around I see." But it is no solution to baptize all changes. At the least, some are contrary to others, and certain ones are perverse and retrogressive. So we need measuring rods, but at a time when even our models of the universe of reality seem crumbling. The older model often viewed God as addressing through the church the world to which he might wish to speak. The modern reaction is often to see God working in the world to address the church. The alternative and antidote to both of these is to see God speaking through both world and church, in complimentary ways, now here, now there. Even the model needs careful analysis, and perhaps overhauling, to get straight on God's activity.

Space does not permit tracing out all the types of change in recent years or the recent developments which made it more difficult to speak to God's activity or even to presuppose a model for the way he works. One need only recall the achievements of science whereby many traditional traces of divine activity and proofs of the deity have died by inches or space miles. God cannot be "out there" (Sputnik says). He cannot be "within" (the biologist and analyst aver). He is hard to locate in historical or natural process. One is reduced to keeping silent about God in traditional or in scientific (verifiable) discourse. Hence the suggestion, even by theologians, for a moratorium on "God talk."

Yet, we have already indicated, the central objective for the seventies speaks more specifically than the statement ten years before of "God's activity." No capitulation here to currents of the day. But what does "God" mean (that nagging question)? And how to speak to him?

Before sketching some lines of interpretation which recent theologians have prepared as substitutes for the classical, traditional view, we may find it helpful to enumerate with some specificity the failings of the traditional view (beyond the general criticisms already enumerated above), failings of which our statement is not unaware and sometimes seeks to correct.

We have already referred to an emphasis on community in the 1969 statement, needed to balance the overemphasis on the individual which appeared in some traditional presentations.

There is a criticism that all forms of *heilsgeschichte* focus too narrowly on Israel and Jesus. Such a focus, it is said, is inexcusable in an age when one world is more than a figure of speech, and a host of world religions are on the march and in our midst in a pluralistic society. We have tried to show that *heilsgeschichte* can be put into a universal setting, and that general revelation allows room for insights from outside the canon. The central objective (1969) seeks to give place to this by the prominence it gives to God's continuing activity, to the human community, society, culture, and the universe, while still holding fast to Jesus as the ultimate, in whom God's revelation comes particularly. But there are still problems here. Posed in terms of John 1:9, is it that everyman coming into the world has the true light, or that Jesus had more light than other men, or that he alone is the light of the world, other men being in darkness?

The traditional view stresses the church too much, it is said. Israel was too pretentious; Christians claim revelation and truth too exclusively. Hence the emphasis on the world, the secular city. If God is "in all," why not meet him everywhere? Our 1969 statement accepts some of this criticism and opens the church's educational ministry more than ever before to God's world. But how far can "church" go here and still remain the body of Jesus Christ? Has the church (for whom we plan our educational programs!) been simply dull, wrongly structured, and status quo, or has it actually been disloyal to God and apostate to his activity? Is it beyond hope for use by God?

While it need not be true of *heilsgeschichte,* traditional views have all too often ignored creation, the world, as if it were not God's; nature, in favor of history. The Bible abets this, for while the Old Testament refers to creation as in Genesis 1, the primary emphasis is put on the history of salvation. The New Testament, even worse, has less to say on creation. Such a concern can be gleaned from our central objective statement best by reading it in, under "God's activity . . . in the physical universe."

Verification of propositions has become an issue for some. *Heilsgeschichte* and traditional theology have tended to put their truths into propositions, appealing to history and often to Scripture for verification. The cry today is for personal relationships, not propositions, and against appeal to an authoritative book for proof. The historical critical method has removed many of the old means of appeal, and "scientific man" refuses to believe in what he cannot verify.

The contemporary has been exalted in our day, at the expense of the past stressed in the traditional view. On these last two points the 1969 statement is open, stressing "continuing activity" and life today, and striking a rather modest stance on asserting verifiability for Christian claims.

The future imagery found in traditional views—about the Second Coming, judgment, eternal life—has been attacked as irrelevant. It is in many places tacitly dropped or ignored. Neither LCA statement, one may note, directly reflects the future hope, and eschatology must be read in under some other terms. (The ALC general objective, 1960, concluded, "as they look forward to his return.")

All this looks like good reason for scuttling the traditional view. But before listing the alternatives, a moment of rebuttal.

First, it may be said that all our talk of "modern man" or "scientific thought today" is something of a chimaera. There is no single view of "modern man." Secondly, the scene in the seventies is tremendously complex and by no means a clear, unilateral development. Consider these conflicting currents:

1. Some people today are concerned with the cosmos or universal, some are probing deep within themselves individually. To play off "world and community" against "individual" is a dichotomy untrue to current trends. Both are in today's picture.

2. To ignore Israel and Jesus is to ignore two phenomena of our times: the rebirth of "Israel-consciousness" among Jews (and elsewhere) and the quest for a Jesus-figure to bear the weight of modern dreams.

3. We live in a time when traditional churches may be ignored, but new church groups, often very conservative so far as biblical outlook

goes, are growing rapidly and all sorts of fellowship groups (*ecclesiolae*) are springing up.

4. As for the God question, while he has been declared dead again and again, there persists a desire to find him in all of life. Men may discern no God in history, but sometimes still they demand one—a cosmic deity, at that!

5. While the tenor of the times is to salute man and search for genuine humanity in the world community, some, even outside the church, find a clue in Jesus. Many more are suspicious precisely of the greatest achievements of man, in science, government, social welfare, as "establishment" or "anti-human." Just as man is emerging as more powerful than ever, fear of his power grows.

6. We are in a period where "relevant" is a magic word, yet some, even among the young, want to retreat from a world where all must be relevant, and cop-out from the "time of achievement" that is dawning.

7. Just at a time when traditional future imagery is being discarded, there has been born a "theology of hope". We are told to view the world from the future. That is what counts.

8. Some, for all the future-orientedness of our society, are content to settle for the now. They are a "now generation," uninterested in the past or the future.

To this list could be added much more. At a time when the autonomy of man is stressed, there is more talk of the lordship of Christ than ever before. When opportunity for biblical and theological study is greater than ever, there is perhaps less clear knowledge mastered than has been for some time. In a scientific age, many college students are open to religious, even superstitious, cults of an exotic kind.

It's a complex age in which we live, and the currents are conflicting. The church needs more guidance than an accurate reading of one of the winds of change or even of all of them. When you use the world of man and his communities as foundation, it's a conflicting picture!

IV

ALTERNATIVES FOR TALKING ABOUT GOD TODAY

With this picture of conflicting trends in mind, and remembering that the old traditional view no longer packs the popular punch it once did, it is now time for us to ask what alternatives recent theologians have been advancing to the classical concept of Christianity. Needless to say, ideas here are as numerous as theologians. At risk of over-simplification we shall limit our presentation to three. The first can be called a more *cosmic* model, emphasizing the world. The second deals with the individual and is more subjective; it can be termed *existential*. The third is a *tradition-history* approach, stressing a theology of the Word. The first has great vogue today. The second, ironically, has seldom received much conscious endorsement in official Lutheran circles. The third is only beginning to be worked out educationally.

These three models for talking about God's activity need not be regarded as mutually exclusive. At points they share insights. The 1969 statement could be developed compatibly with any one of them as well as with the traditional view.

A Cosmic View of God's Activity

Even though men are saying God is dead and some decry any imperialistic claims for Jesus Christ in a pluralistic world, some theologians have boldly been reiterating that the only proper sphere in which to speak of God's work and rule is the whole wide world. This claim is advanced not merely for God, but specifically for Jesus Christ. He must be lord of the earth and the heavens and the galaxies—or he is meaningless.

While Christians have for centuries proclaimed Jesus as Lord, certain historical factors in the present century have elevated this theme into prominence. The worldwide missionary movement early in the century set the stage—"the world for Christ in this generation" (a magnificent evangelism goal which failed). The Barmen Declaration against the Nazis in 1934 rejected any notions of a non-public, pietistic Christianity, by declaring that Christ is "God's mighty claim on our whole life," and that there are no areas in life where we do not belong to Christ. Karl Barth's theology, stressing God's sovereign reign, set forth the rule of Christ, now, in the world, as well as in the church. More immediately, Joseph Sittler brought "cosmic Christology" to the fore in ecumenical discussion with his 1961 speech to the World Council of Churches at New Delhi where he sought to "claim nature for Christ" as well as history. Churches in the sixties, seeking to be rele-

67

vant to God's world, took up this theme. It is, therefore, commonplace to insist that the entire cosmos must be the scene of Christ's lordship, not at some future parousia, but now.

The approach unquestionably picks up valuable themes which many Christians had forgotten. It is tremendously useful in getting our thinking about God out of sanctuaries and holy-history ghettos. It inspires Christians with a new vision of what God is about. It encourages links with other Christians who have been similarly moved by this ecumenical development, and produces openness to other cultures and religions of the world.

In spite of such advantages to the cosmic approach to divine activity, there are some problems, however.

1. This assertion of Christ's lordship over all the world does not seem to produce any sort of missionary impulse as it did in John R. Mott's day. Is our statement that Christ is already lord of all men, in fact, an all-too-simple way to get ourselves off the hook for having failed to move those men to his gospel? Is it a way of talking universally about what we have not experienced personally?

2. The exegetical basis for asserting Christ's present cosmic lordship, especially the "Christ hymn" at Colossians 1:15-20, is, when examined by biblical scholarship of the last decade, somewhat tenuous.[4]

3. The lordship of Christ in the world has often been exaggerated, for example, when the universe is made the primary place of God's activity and love. Does one speak of the world as a revelation of God's love unless the point has been extrapolated from its manifestation in the cross, the way Colossians does (the reconciling blood of the cross causes redeemed and baptized men to sing that Christ is "first-born of creation," just as he is "first-born from the dead")? One dares to say God loves the world (John 3:16) only in view of the demonstration of it when the Son laid down his life (1 John 4:9 ff.).

4. The verification problem is even more acute in asserting the present lordship of Jesus Christ, than for asserting God as lord—for Jesus of Nazareth was a mortal man who once lived on earth. One is tempted to suspect that, in an age when God is said to be dead, Jesus is being asked to carry the freight which the deity once did. Critics ask, Is this but one last desperate gasp to save the whole theological structure by speaking of Jesus as the world's lord, instead of God?

5. If we are to see God and Christ at work in revolutions, how do we tell which revolutions?

6. The cosmic Christ threatens at times to lose the features of Jesus and becomes a rather vague force. If "Christ figures" can be found everywhere, why bother anchoring Christ "particularly in Jesus"? Pantheism has become pan-Christism, all men are declared "anonymous Christians." Either Jesus Christ becomes indistinguishable from the spirit of the age, or assertion of his lordship (that of the crucified Jew) is an affront to a pluralistic world.

In spite of all these dangers and unsolved problems, we can record our gratitude for this model and must keep it in mind in doing Christian education in the years ahead. It is reflected in other sections of this yearbook.

An Existential Approach

While the cosmic model seeks to claim all the world for Christ, other theologians have long since been aware that divine activity—by God or Christ—in the stars, or seasons, or world history is unverifiable. They suspect that it all may be simply a hangover from rather pretentious past views when men thought there was a God "out there" who ran the universe and especially history. This second approach is much more modest and is content to speak of God only in the individual's existence, at times in the lingo of existentialism.

At first glance, this approach may sound like a step back to the past —individualism, with the corporate ignored. But the intrepid thinkers here are not retreating to the past. Quite the contrary. They are preparing positions where, in their opinion, Christianity, if it is to have any meaning in life, can take up a stronghold in the decades ahead. As these theologians read the history of religions, we have come to another crucial turning point. The ideas of ancient man can no longer be ours. But that does not mean "sack the past entirely. For in ancient literature like the Bible, its revelation and myth, there is still something of permanent import: a way of understanding life.

These theologians have, of course, given up as no longer tenable many of the features of traditional Christianity. The second coming of Jesus, for example, simply did not occur as Paul and other early Christians expected, in their day. It is foolish, such theologians say, to go on assuming after 2,000 years that the parousia may happen at any time. At best it is a symbol of hope and a reminder that Christian life in our world has not arrived at fulness or consummation. The stories of creation and the fall? These, too, are ancient stories, not literal history but profound insights for human existence, for they describe how man is, what life is like.

All this is to say that the Bible, myths included, just as all ancient myth, enshrines a view of man and concept of existence. It is not "man's theology" but "God's anthropology," a definitive (for Christians) insight into existence. God, miracles, even Jesus' resurrection—these are not things to be validated, but parts of the ancient story, which tells us how to look upon ourselves, come to decision that we cannot exist on our own.

By now, presumably, every reader has guessed we are describing the program of Rudolf Bultmann and his followers and others like them, for "demythologizing" the Bible and translating its meaning for men today into existential terms. Deliberately we have tried not to use all the characteristic phrases or make it too definite, to allow for the fact that this approach takes many forms, and has adherents far beyond admitted Bultmannites. Indeed, every person who asks what a miracle story or saying of Jesus means for him is going part way with this approach.

It remains to be added that this approach, which may or may not employ the language of the existentialists, has been developed in new ways in the past few years. Rightly it has claimed that in the Bible every statement is (also) a statement about man. At least, the statement "God is holy" implies "man is sinner." But some go further. What if we boldly admit, as many do in practice, that a traditional God "beyond the heavens" does *not* exist. Cannot, then, man be God, and all statements about God really be anthropological?

This particular development is exemplified by the theologizing of Herbert Braun. Claiming that even Christology in the New Testament is a variable, with many forms, but that anthropology is the constant, Braun has gone on to talk of "God" in terms of man—not as an incarnate deity from beyond, but in terms of men who heed Jesus and see in life a system of coordinates of "I may" and "I ought," a complex of what has been graciously given and what is demanded of me, of my being taken care of and my obligation. "God" is then "the whence of my being taken care of and of my being obliged," but can be spoken of only anthropologically, since it is through my fellow men that I am taken care of and for them have obligations to discharge. "God would then be a definite type of relation with one's fellow man." The atheist is not one who misses God but misses his fellow men![5]

This proposal to speak of God in so baldly an anthropological, existential way is probably a shock to most Christians. But a few theologians are moving in just that direction. Probably many more persons use snatches of language and thought from this model, or some form of it, without realizing it.

Though few people doing curriculum in the ALC or LCA would openly espouse so radical a position, note these points:

1. If in our objective statement, "God's continuing activity and revelation" in the human community and the world is made the emphasis, and particularly if reference to Jesus Christ is minimized, one of the options is to speak, as Braun does, of "God" at work in our fellow men. Or, more accurately, of what man does as the *theos* we encounter.

2. The existential approach takes many forms and has wide adherence—with or without jargon terms, with or without Bultmann's method of rigorous critical scholarship.

3. The model, emphasizing internalizing the message subjectively, "for me" (*pro me*), has features which make it attractive to some of the currents at work in the seventies. In particular it can be argued that this approach is doing what Scripture itself sometimes intends. In Romans 8, for all his talk about the whole cosmos (vv. 18-25) and cosmic powers (vv. 38-39), Paul is concerned with the believer's existence now in Christ. The model gives us a way of talking meaningfully about biblical truths today.

4. Some scholars and preachers have hooked this approach up with the new quest for the historical Jesus, and made the aim recovery of Jesus' view of existence. Of course, preachers, taking the post-Easter gospel stories at face value, have long undertaken that. Only here, in a highly sophisticated way and in light of modern critical research, what Jesus brought to pass in what he said is the aim today, through our words.

The pros and cons of this approach are so well known we simply list some here:

—Strong on the personal meaning, weak on the corporate, social, cosmic side;

—Emphatic about the word speaking now but forgets its past, historical content;

—Does not wrongly objectify history or claim too much can be verified, but removes all myth, which even modern man may need;

—Emphasizes life now, but often minimizes the historical Jesus;

—Grasps the role of our presuppositions in interpreting Scripture, but avoids "sin" or future-fulfillment language.

I do not see how we can fail to employ in educational ministry some of the insights of the existential approach, without, however, buying all of its assumptions or conclusions.

The Tradition-History Method

We use the phrase "tradition-history method" to cover a variety of approaches. In common they emphasize history as a vehicle of God's revelation. These approaches do not necessarily exclude nature or world; they simply say that it is in history that the decisive revelation has occurred. There is likewise an emphasis on "tradition," meaning the handing on of the report that "God is alive" and has done this or that. "The Tradition" often denotes what we have been accustomed to call Scripture. The idea is that Scripture's reports and interpretations about God represent a "handing on" process, not just in biblical times, but also down to our day.

Intertwined with these emphases on history and "traditioning the Tradition" is a concern for the historical-critical method and theologically for the Word of God. As in the other models and, perhaps even more so, practitioners of this view press for careful examination of "what happened," and, since we cannot always tell that very accurately, more important, how was the account developed and interpreted? Assumed regularly is that God speaks to men in words. The word, not theophany, is the chief means of divine encounter. Words are the way in which we express and convey experience about such a reality as God.

As is apparent, this approach roots not merely in the Bible but also in the Reformation and owes much to the development in the nineteenth century of critical-historical method. It seeks to show how the biblical data continues to be living and to speak, in spite of critical dissection. For it is precisely through such hermeneutical analysis that we ascertained what God's activity meant when it occurred, and at certain checkpoints through the centuries down to today. The view can, of course, be hooked up with a concept of *heilsgeschichte* or with existentialistic interpretation today, but it has taken a distinct enough shape at the hands of Gerhard Ebeling or the Pannenberg school to be accounted a movement of its own, with its ways of speaking about God.

Here it is taken very seriously that language is "the house of being" in which man resides. We are, in a sense, what we say. Reality resides in linguisticality, in "word-events" (*Wortgeschehen, Sprachereignisse*). For God to come, is to have his word come, the word of God which comes onto the scene, revealing, and comes into words as proclamation, with faith its goal. If God was once enthroned "in the praises of Israel," so today he is where he is confessed, and brings love, e.g., to bear on a situation, when someone ventures to risk existence in words, as Jesus did.

If the approach of Ebling and Fuchs and the New Hermeneutic, as just indicated, seems at all limiting, one also has the much broader approach begun by Wolfhart Pannenberg and a group of theologians around him. They owe something to traditional *heilsgeschichte*, the Bultmann school, and contemporary hermeneutics, but also react against all of these and seek to do justice also to the Old Testament world history, and philosophy. On such an immense canvas their picture is painted. God's revelation is not (as traditionally) to be seen directly, in manifestations, but only indirectly through history. It is there, however, for anyone to see, universally, though it is grasped only at the end of history (as if eschatologically we could look back across its sweep and thus know the turning points). But a clue, the clue, proleptically can be grasped in Jesus of Nazareth, especially his resurrection. This Jesus climaxes God's dealings with Israel and becomes the content of new, even non-Jewish, ways of talking about revelation. But it is in a process of promise, instruction and reports about God's doing that the revelation goes on, unfolded over the years for God's people.

It is possible for the Christian who wants to do justice to the word-of-God quality to Scripture and yet desires to keep honest historically and on the verifiability issue to get quite excited about this approach,

73

particularly when it is given so broad a setting as tradition-history implies and some of the implications of a theology of hope. Here God is not the beginning of a process, or occasional intruder into history, or cosmic lord, or key to existence, but the "power of the future," yet fully to break through. It must be admitted, though, that this model has scarcely been worked out in its implications for, or applications to, Christian education. Perhaps it is too encompassing to be.

We have now examined three types of model for speaking about God's activity, apart from the traditional classical view and the options of giving up talk about God or indiscriminately identifying him with everything that happens in the world today. Each of these approaches has some claim to biblical and legitimate theological roots. Each of them has something to offer. Each of them has some compatibility with the traditional views. Perhaps we need not be exclusive, choosing only one, nor need we bind ourselves to the current vogue or be prisoners in God-talk to whims of the day.

V

CLUES AND CRITERIA

When Christians talk about God, it is primarily to Jesus Christ they look for some standard of what God is about—and what man is meant to be. Jesus Christ is the heart of *heilsgeschichte*; lord of the cosmos; the crucified one proclaimed as risen, who brings man to authentic existence; the model for understanding the "may" and "ought" of life with fellow men; the one whose words told men it was a time for faith and love, so that we still expound his parables in the hope of bringing into speech what happened with him. What is more, for all our emphasis on relevance and God acting today, we still, all of us in the Christian community, derive our background for talking about God from the accounts in canonical scripture. If we say he is love, or lord, or creator and preserver, or even the revolutionary force in life making for God's future, it is because the Bible said these things or can be interpreted to imply them.

Unless we posit new, definitive revelations superceding, or on a par with, those at Sinai or Mt. Calvary—and that is an option which Mormons, Christian Scientists, and other groups have adopted (Pentecostal groups are a different case, for, while claiming widespread work of the Spirit, they are also firmly anchored in an often literal understanding of the Bible events)—unless we mean to jettison the biblical and historic Christian heritage, we must look for clues and criteria about God primarily in the biblical witness to measure what is going on today. There, in Scripture, is the norm—without stultifying God as if he could speak only in ancient Hebrew today or be revealable solely in terms of a three-story universe. There is the standard for judging future manifestations and statements and acts purporting to be from God.

To be honest with our Lutheran heritage, we must add we hold not merely to the Bible as norm in revelation, but, within Scripture, to Christ as the key. Over the book towers the Word. At the center of all the "Word of God" activity (a shorthand phrase for all God says and does) is the Word, Jesus, God's incarnate representative in the world. Over all, in all, and through all is God—but as Lord, not simply a process or diffused animating spirit.

Scripture, in this view, is revelation in that it records events where God has spoken and interprets them. It has been precisely the vehicle for proclaiming God; it is, as word-event, a locus where he speaks again.

God, in this view, though "hidden" and unknown, is the ultimate who has become known in his world, his works, his revelatory actions in Israel and Christ, his ongoing self-expression among men, the clue to which is that supreme encounter through Jesus, and the prior history of Israel which led up to it. While all men make gods of various sorts, this God and Father of the Lord Jesus Christ and of the people to whom he has given new birth is one we do not invent but whom we identify, so that the test of Christian experience is to be able to say, "This is that . . ." (Acts 2:16). This experience of mine comports with that which the Christian community over the centuries has confessed and which once came to expression in Israel or in the Jesus-event. What God is now doing agrees with that in its shape and direction.

Space does not permit a spelling out here, with many illustrations of how the Bible presents God or how men fruitfully talk of this God today. But a few examples of how the Scriptures go about this task may be helpful, and be suggestive for today.

Strangely enough, study of the term "activity" in a biblical concordance will do little good; it does not occur that often in standard translations. Nor need we list here all the traits of God which can be compiled in biblical theology; many good books and articles do that.

What is helpful is to examine how Scripture talks about God's working in some significant cases. Some of them can be developed from study materials already available in courses for Lutheran Sunday church schools, so that this way of seeing God's activity is nothing new.

Take the Exodus from Egypt as an example.[6] We know that Israel looked back on the happening at the Red Sea as a constitutive event, when Yahweh delivered a band of slaves from captivity under Pharoah. What actually occurred is open to a host of opinions and interpretation. The oldest account is the poetic Song of Miriam: "Sing to the LORD, for he has triumphed gloriously; the horse and his rider he has thrown into the sea" (Exodus 15:21). Somewhat later came a longer poetic account, the Song of Moses (15:1-18), beginning "I will sing to the LORD . . .," and praising God with concepts from the "Holy War" motif. Later still, various Israelites retold this glorious tale, often using earlier traditions. Then came an editor who put it all together in a book for us, and there followed centuries of telling and reliving the experience, for Jews and Christians, so that the exodus theme and God's deliverance as a base for life became a theme by which men have found hope again and again.

The resurrection of Jesus could be traced out in a similar way: the stories of how he appeared after death to men who became witnesses that he was alive and let loose in all the earth; the empty tomb with its hint of the numinous; the confession that God had raised him from the dead; a band of people who staked all in this Good News; the growth of a church based on the avowed presence of the Risen Lord.[7]

We can attempt to trace out how a miracle story has been told over the years. "Go home to your friends, tell them how much the Lord has done for you, and how he has had mercy on you" (Mark 5:19) is the way the account of how Jesus healed the Gerasene demoniac comes to a close. As it stands, there is some question as to whether "the Lord" means Jesus Christ (as usually for Christians) or God (as it would have in Jesus' day). There is the fact that the advice makes sense for all believers, and it has no doubt been reapplied to many subsequent experiences. Since it also differs from the usual Markan emphasis that the person healed shall keep quiet about the event ("the Messianic secret," cf. 1:44, 5:43), we can assume the story in its present form is earlier than Mark, perhaps part of a collection of miracle stories about Jesus as a wonder worker. How much of that emphasis is part of a christological portrayal and what actually originally happened is again open to debate.

Exodus, resurrection, miracle story—in each of these instances, the sequence unfolded like this:

1. Something *happened*—Israel or an individual experienced deliverance, though we cannot always describe precisely what occurred.

2. This event was recounted as something *the Lord* had done, attributed to his mercy, prowess, and intervention.

3. The earliest recounting was often in the form of *praise* to God for his goodness, in poetic hymn or confession of faith, or response of service.

4. Subsequent *retellings* expand, add, explain.

5. Each one of these retellings becomes *itself an event*, where God speaks to later hearers.

6. The *aggregate* of these accounts, edited in the biblical books, becomes *the Tradition*.

7. This biblical Tradition itself makes waves, and in its retelling and *reapplication* becomes a vehicle for *praising* God who has done these things, extending witness to him on to the *present day*, and serving as a *touchstone* for identification of God's further activity.

We take one example each of how the basic experience of God's redemptive activity was extrapolated in order to speak about other works of God—in one case, his prior activity in creation, in the other the end of things. The Bible, arranged as it is with creation first and the last things in the closing book of Revelation, gives an impression that all was written in a neat logical and chronological progression. Actually these statements about creation and the future are outgrowths of Israel's (or the church's) primary experience of being redeemed. It is as if from the Exodus or Christ event lines were extrapolated in each direction, to speak about the beginning and the end.

With the creation stories in Genesis 1 and 2 it is apparent that men of faith in Israel took stories abounding in their day, from Babylonia and elsewhere, and used them to confess their belief that their God who had acted in the exodus was the creator too. To the praise of Yahweh, his work in creation was told, retaining the details of the how from *Enuma elish* or other foreign religious literature, purging from these pagan stories elements of the who and why which did not fit with the character of the Lord Israel had come to know.

It is not different in Christian times. Jesus who was confessed as lord of the life of believers whom he had ransomed, it was soon apparent, must also be acknowledged for the part faith sees he played in creation and the role he has alongside God's. Hence, even before Paul wrote 1 Corinthians, prior to A.D. 50, some Christians had juxtaposed their slogan about "Jesus Christ the Lord" alongside the Old Testament credo concerning the "One God" (Deuteronomy 6:4), adding typically Greek phrases to create a balanced formula for faith: "for us there is one God, the Father, from whom are all things and for whom we exist, and one Lord, Jesus Christ, through whom are all things and through whom we exist" (1 Corinthians 8:6).

The situation is not dissimilar in statements about the future. Note the sequence of redemption experienced by pagan converts, a new life style of service, and a future hope: "You turned to God from idols, to serve a living and true God, and to wait for his Son from heaven, whom he raised from the dead, Jesus who delivers us from the wrath to come" (1 Thessalonians 1:9-10). From here it was but a step to more detailed statements and whole books about the future hope amid judgment and for deliverance.

Not every story that was told about God's activity or Jesus in biblical times got into biblical books, of course. Many perished because they were duplicates, or fell by the wayside because they were not as good or fitting accounts or could be misleading. We all know there were stories about the boy Jesus making clay birds which flew away, stories which never made it into any canonical gospel. There were times, too, when prophets misread signs, and that what must have been touted as a sure and certain example of God's activity proved wrong and was discarded.

All this is worth remembering in our day, that not everyone who says "God is doing this" is accurate, and not every claim of "Here is Jesus at work" is of God. The problem is how to arrive at criteria for applying our biblical clues. Fortunately, there are some standards already in the Bible used to test the authenticity of events there which I suggest have value for ascertaining "God's ongoing activity" and testing for revelation today.

C. F. D. Moule, of Cambridge, once proposed three tests for weighing the miracle stories of the gospels.[8] The first was that of *sources*; the second, *probability*; the third, *congruity* with the known character of God and Jesus. It seems to me that these standards and two more related to them are pertinent and helpful in talking about God's activity in the past or today.

1. The test of sources and the testing of sources. For many, the limits of the canon have often provided parameters for God's acts, but we have seen that God's working, in the biblical view, extends beyond the scriptural ages or geographical area of Palestine. The Holy God works outside the Holy Land. Furthermore, the historical-critical method of Bible study raises question about some items already within the canon. Our first test implies that *all* claims about divine activity must be vetted as to the source of the claim at least as carefully as modern scholarship has subjected the biblical witness to it. It would be a cheap way out if Christians abandoned biblical revelation because of supposed problems about it, and then brought uncritically modern claims of revelatory activity.

2. Whether we like it or not, most people work with degrees of probability in mind; some miracles seem "more likely" than others. Such a tendency no doubt operates with regard to measurement of God's activity: we see what we like and designate as divine what we regard as likely. The revolutionary finds God marching with those in revolt; the law-and-order man sees God working through structures and orders. It is natural enough to employ probability in measuring even God. At the least, this test of probability can be a warning not merely to accept what we or our age prefer as probable. On a higher level, it ought to make us allow for the improbable in history at times. Even the secular planner sees "surprise" as one of the norms in the years ahead (the "impossible dream"). Above all, it raises the question, Probable by whose times? That brings in the issue again of what we mean by God.

3. Congruity with the known character of God and Jesus therefore becomes the acid test. Is this action consistent with what we know this deity to be like? The traditional view gave a clear picture of what God

is like—perhaps too clear! Moderns seize on Jesus or the revelation in Christ as a clue. The question, Which Jesus is to be answered only by careful historical scholarship and attention to the Tradition and traditions about him with which historians must work. I venture the opinion that we know enough about Jesus as one who viewed life as being under God, who spoke of grace and judgment, freely welcomed all people, rebuked sin, declared God's love, pointed to new meanings for life, and gave himself utterly, that we can find here a usable standard. And I find it hard to deal with Jesus' outlook on man and life apart from his penetrating, filial concept of God as lord and father.

4. I add the fact that an identification of God's activity must be one which arises out of more than individual, momentary conviction; it must rather persuade a community of believers and stand the test of time over the years. There must have been dozens of cases in primitive Christianity where people said, "Lo, here is Christ" (Matthew 24:5), but the "revelation" proved erroneous. There have been claims about God which have not perdured over the years. This test serves to remind us that Christianity has a long history, the biblical faith a longer one, and God a history centuries long. The latest supposed mutation may be dead as the dodo bird a decade hence. Truth can and often does arise in a minority, but the failure of a truth to endure over the long haul or to appeal generally, can be applied as a rule of thumb to God-concepts, proving them ephemeral. Such standards have long been appiled to the Tradition (in scripture); they ought to be applied to current claims of divine activity. Has the item measured up, in value for the people of God and their wholeness, in their opinion, over the years?

5. Finally, and somewhat related to the congruity issue, is the matter of a central theme, by which Scripture and subsequent activity by God are measured. We have admitted that Lutherans look at the Bible and all revelation christocentrically. They have also been accustomed to look at revelation and scripture in light of justification or the righteousness of God (though we must not simply play off righteousness against grace or mercy, for it can be "saving" as well as judging and preserving). We could just as well, in Pauline terms, substitute "reconciliation" or "grace" (God's love in action) as a central theme. We could also propose the rule or reign of God, his "kingdom," provided we remember it is a sovereignty which creates and preserves on the

one hand and also saves on the other. "Salvation" and "redemption" likewise have long been presented as central themes.

My own feeling is that all these themes associated with God and his work intertwine. Understand one, the others follow. The point is, this God whose work we seek to trace, must be understood in terms of some effect or function, so that we have some idea what to look for and how to assess what we find.

VI

TOWARD CONCLUSIONS: GOD AND HIS ACTIVITY IN THE YEARS AHEAD

The net result of all this is to suggest that we have a variety of ways available to talk about God, helpful clues and criteria from the Christian tradition for assessing what we choose to confess as divine activity. We, thus, have a viable inheritance, alive today and open toward the future, even amid the changing developments of the seventies.

My guess is that, in the years ahead, many Christians will find the traditional picture of God still usable, especially if its full resources are exploited. Others will find this option or that sketched above preferable as models. Most will combine strengths from each approach. Thus we are likely to—and this may be the best strategy for spelling out and implementing the central objective statement—trace out a *heilsgeschichtlich* pattern of God's activity, in an ever broadening setting of the world, helped by the tradition-history approach. The cosmic emphasis will be helpful for expanding our God-concept to the necessary breadth, and the attempt to see God working in the world will keep the church from looking inward too much. Many will find the application to existence primary, even though they are also, by this very understanding of God, motivated to apply themselves to ministry in the world. A few will frankly opt for "God" only as a term to cover interpersonal relationships, and a number will find God of greatest meaning in the linguisticality of life—expression words which are at the heart of living.

The following points need to be stressed:

1. All talk about God's activity arises out of a (saving) *experience* of him and this represents an *affirmation of faith*. Needless to say, di-

vine actions can be experienced in a number of ways, as sketched above, and may be negative or positive. Faith rests on a positive (saving) experience.

2. Such affirmations can be *extrapolated backwards* (to creation), *forward* (to the future, including judgment and life eternal) and *into the world* around us, life now, and throughout all history. Such affirmations can even be extended cosmically, but they remain a confession of faith, not verifiable ontology.

3. The Christian tradition is clear where the saving experience is *anchored, in Jesus Christ.* The primary requisite is to make one's own today what God has done for us in the man of Nazareth.

4. In *Jesus* and the whole *Tradition* therefore is the clue to *revelation* and God's continuing *activity.* Jesus measures the biblical witness, the biblical witness measures subsequent revelation and divine activity. But God has not stopped with the Bible or Jesus. It might be helpful to remember that, while all of God's activity reveals something of himself, "revelation" as a term might be used in the special sense that adheres to God's most significant self-expressions, in Israel and Jesus. We believe God is still at work. We do not suggest he will countermand the revelation in Jesus Christ. I personally would prefer to speak of "revelation in Jesus Christ" and "continuing activity," but avoid "continuing revelation" if that suggests Jesus does not represent ultimacy and a word of finality from God.

5. This emphasis on God's ongoing work and our present realization of what he is and has done in Christ should not blind us to the fact that God's people are ever only "on the way" and have not arrived. The *future* looms large; *fulfillment* is not yet; life is marked by *hope,* not attainment to God, or a deity who is in our grasp and under our control.

6. This picture sheds some light on the phrase "human and Christian communities." Every man belongs to many groups. Christian education today has the task of helping the believer to be fully human and to participate to the utmost in God's world, but it is also committed to the distinctiveness of the church, where the reign of God and ultimacy of Jesus Christ are confessed, and to participation in the mission of this people of God.

7. An implication of this is that Christian education has a role to bring men to *decision,* to move them to greater commitment, in God's

world, but also to decision, commitment, and response for Jesus Christ. The believer's affirmation must be reaffirmed, the consequences drawn anew, the meaning of the Christian anchorage applied *pro me,* the way opened to more effective involvement in church, society, and world.

8. Finally, if we take seriously this involvement in both world and church, if we recognize that we are human beings who have confessed Christ, if we work together with people who may believe in him or may not, then our involvements in life (the *life involvements of the Christian*) will sometimes directly be able to pick up biblical, traditionally Christian qualities and values. They will sometimes show God's will and way on the human worldly level. Sometimes the two will intertwine. For it is not at every point that "Christian" and "human" differ if the same God is at work in both, but differences there are, if his revelating action in Jesus Christ is the touchstone. It is the willingness to praise and confess this God which marks the Christian, not just his actions and attitudes.

God will continue to be enthroned most of all in the praises of his people, in church and world.

NOTES AND REFERENCES

1. Cf. *Perceiving, Behaving, Becoming: A New Focus for Education* (Washington, D.C.: Association for Supervision and Curriculum Development, 1962).
2. Cf. Oscar Cullman, *Christ and Time: The Primitive Christian Conception of Time and History,* trans. Floyd V. Wilson, rev. ed. (Philadelphia: Westminster Press, 1964).
3. *New York Times,* May 21, 1970, reporting on the address by the Rev. George E. Sweazey, moderator of the United Presbyterian Church to that body's convention.
4. Cf. the examination of Colossians 1:15-20 in *Christ and Humanity,* ed. Ivar Asheim (Philadelphia: Fortress Press, 1970), pp. 96-109.
5. "The Meaning of New Testament Christology" in H. Braun *et al., God and Christ: Existence and Providence,* Journal for Theology and the Church, vol. 5 (New York: Harper Torchbooks, 1968), pp. 89-127. Also "The Problem of a New Testament Theology" in James M. Robinson *et al., The Bultmann School of Biblical Interpretation: New Directions?,* Journal for Theology and the Church, vol. 1 (New York: Harper Torchbooks, 1965), pp. 169-183, quotes from pp. 182ff.
6. Cf. Foster R. McCurley, Jr., *Exodus,* LCA Adult Christian Education Series (Philadelphia: Lutheran Church Press, 1969).

7. I have attempted to sketch this in *Jesus of Nazareth: Son of Man, Son of God*, LCA Sunday Church School Series (Philadelphia: Lutheran Church Press, 1966) and more fully in *Jesus in the Church's Gospels: Modern Scholarship and the Earliest Sources* (Philadelphia: Fortress Press, 1968).
8. *Jesus in the Church's Gospel*, pp. 202 ff.

God's Activity—A Response

HENRY J. BERTNESS

First of all, what business do I have writing about this topic? I am not a theologian. But then, I do have ideas, attitudes, and interpretations, all of which affect behavior. So, a bit of personal commentary.

As Christians, do we testify to God's activity, do we question that God is active, or do we actually question the existence of God? I do not question the existence of God, but I really do question the apparent emphasis of the Christian church on God's activity in the past to the virtual exclusion of his activity in the present. Certainly, commenting on the present is risky, but it does seem to be evident that God is working. If there is a risk in claiming this, then perhaps we ought to take that risk.

We can go to scripture to read about God's working in and through His people in the past, but we can also extrapolate the life of Christ into the present to comment on the probable workings of God today. In fact, if our faith is to be real and alive, we must do this.

Christ spoke of love of God and love of neighbor as being the greatest of all commandments. Sometimes it seems that we have over-emphasized the first of these. It does not seem right to talk only about love of God. These two commandments seem interdependent, with the second, love of neighbor, being the logical and necessary behavioral outcome of the first. Look at today. There is visible evidence of love of neighbor. It is happening, and it seems that this is the greatest indication of God's activity among us.

GOD IS WORKING EVERYWHERE!

A long time ago I was taught that God is present everywhere and that all of creation is His doing. To this day this is easy for me to believe, but it seems that some Christian people are denying God's presence everywhere and denying all creation being His. There is too much separatism going on, too much talking about we and they, ours and theirs. So when we look for God's activity, we may look back into the days of the Old and New Testament, or we may look within our own congregation. Both of these may be fine to look at, in fact may be necessary, but they are not sufficient. Maybe we are looking in the wrong places if we are interested in seeing God's activity today.

For some years I have read a church periodical with a section entitled, "Dear fellow workmen in the King's business." I think I know what that means and I take no offense, but it does seem to illustrate a point of omission. What King's business? Is not all of creation the King's business? And what fellow workmen? Should we include only those who are directly connected with the organized church in some salaried way, or perhaps all of us? God is everywhere and working everywhere and everything is His business. Let us look at some familiar and at some unfamiliar events.

Recently, a series of articles dealing with the existence of God has appeared in some newspapers. One article examined the assertion and belief that God exists because man seems to know there is a God. Something within man seems to tell him that there is something beyond him, something greater. It is contended that this phenomenon occurs in all mankind, wherever men, women and children are found. Strange? It does seem to be an indication of God's activity.

Christmas is a particularly warm and human time of year, and yet some Christian people say that Christmas is not what it used to be. Probably Christmas now is more like what it was intended to be way back when. The goodwill that is expressed among people and the good feeling are really samples of what it is like to be a Christian the year long. Those who are not Christian and who do not see the Christ in Christmas do experience the feeling of love during the Christmas season. So, without knowing the theory, they are experiencing the practice of Christian love. This love feeling and action is most pronounced at Christmas time, but it can be sensed during other holiday seasons

85

as well. Is this a subtle God-directed phenomenon which helps people experience what love to neighbor is really about?

We can consider women. Women are our neighbors and have been ever since the beginning. Women, however, even to the present, have been second and third-class neighbors. It does seem to be a modern phenomenon that women are being accepted as a part of mankind, as neighbors and as persons, each of infinite worth. Something has happened here. I choose to believe that, again, it is God at work over the centuries and man gradually catching on to what God has meant all along. There is more respect for women, wives, and mothers today than ever before, and part of this has been pretty tough going. It is easy to honor someone who stays in her place, but now we honor women as individuals with all rights of the human being regardless of what they do.

Children are our neighbors and are to be loved. There is more intelligent concern about children than ever before. The handicapped child no longer is left unattended, cast out, and left to die. The child no longer is considered a miniature adult and expected to perform as an adult without any of the privileges of adulthood. This concern for children is not only in our immediate society but extends throughout the world. Certainly this concern is not fully universal nor is it sufficiently comprehensive, but it is there and it is growing.

Children are dealt with differently in our courts and in our schools today. Again, no big revolution has taken place, but it has begun. People are saying, and the courts are insisting, that children have rights, so children are being treated as individuals, as neighbors. There will be struggles in families, schools, and courts during this development. The result will be the realization that children, too, are individuals of infinite worth and with rights. We will discover them to be our neighbors. We will love them in enlightened ways.

It has taken a long time, but children are being discovered. Some would say rediscovered but that is stretching. Children are being discovered as neighbors whose very being and development are a reflection of how neighborly we have been to them. This has been expressed in many ways in the past and in the present. Recently, Dr. Angelo Giaudrone, Superintendent of Schools, Tacoma, Washington, gave a short address in which he expressed this developmental notion beautifully.

Anyone who has worked closely with youth for 35 years is not unaccustomed to change and revolt, but the events of the past few weeks have given me cause to wonder what it was I used to worry about. It is pretty hard to "keep our cool" when our concerns are so deep and so serious. It's frightening to see changes come so rapidly and young people, too, are frightened . . . and they are as impatient as they are scared. They want so desperately to be involved at such an early age in the complexities of life.

How to describe today's youth? Do we dare try?

First of all, they are our kids. They haven't come to us from other parents on another planet. They're ours. They've had many different teachers—their parents, their church, their school, the community, television, and, possibly most important, their friends. Sometimes I think we've all done a pretty good job of teaching because they are pretty much what we've taught them to be.

We said to them, "Stand up and be counted"—and they are! They're taking unbelievable risks where our generation played it safe.

We told them "all men are created equal," and they believed this too.

We said, "Peace is better than war," and they learned that also.

We said, "Money isn't everything," and they've turned their back on the business community. They've even joined the Peace Corps and Vista.

We said, "Be your brother's keeper," so they're deeply concerned about the impoverished, the hungry.

We said, "We must conserve our natural resources," so they're angry about pollution of the environment.

(If only they would spend their energies on planning for the Junior Prom, or electing a Yell Queen—we'd feel so much more comfortable.)

Just to make their lives even more frustrating, our youthful society, like our adult society, is harrassed by fringe groups pressuring them into irresponsible and violent action.

Would you want to trade places with our young people today? Probably not. What we really want is to know how we can help them. The best way seems to be to "put our creed into our deed," to believe, really believe, all the things we have taught them, so they will see no hypocrisy in us, but instead, some good examples of responsible human behavior.

Let's not give up on our youth—they are all we have!

Some would say this attention to children is a simple part of the evolution of man. Man has come to see that this attention to children is to his own benefit. Again, we can ask ourselves, is it not possible that man is finally seeing and implementing what God had intended all along?

Consider the possibility that public education in the United States is a part of God's activity. What a notion! What a fantasy! Yet take a look at it. In spite of its many failings, in spite of not reaching every stated goal, there is probably more love of neighbor expressed in American public education than in any other institution throughout the world. Public education is a huge enterprise and attempts to minister to all children. With the possible exception of some hospitals, public schools were the first to claim all the children as their clients regardless of race, creed, sex, or condition. We are pretty much over the sex hurdle in public education today. Girls are receiving almost as appropriate an education as our boys. We are gradually overcoming all kinds of discrimination barriers, including the artificial barrier of race. We are gradually overcoming the various barriers of handicapping conditions, and now have seen and demonstrated the educational possibilities even among the most severely handicapped of our children. Love thy neighbor? Well, this is it! Love must be more than a feeling, it must be action. Public education is one of the actions of a society concerned for her children, and it is all children, not just those who deserve attention or who are eligible for attention, it is *all* children. Children are our neighbors; love thy neighbor.

There is another large category of human conditions which is being looked at differently today than was the case yesterday. Some of the issues include what a person looks like, drug addiction, alcoholism, unwed mothers, abortion, birth control, juvenile offenders—the list could go on and on. It may be that young people with long hair, beards, minis, maxis, and boots have finally broken through to us with the lesson they felt was so very important to them. "The hair is not me," they said. "My appearance is not me. I am something else, I am more. You look at me and you don't see me, you see my beard and you are turned off." The lesson we are learning is that the person is not his appearance but what he is within. We have learned that these, too, are our neighbors.

Take the drug scene. A lesson is being learned very slowly, but it is being learned. Many are calling for drug education and saying that children should know more about the danger of drugs. The children themselves, however, are saying and demonstrating that they do know about drugs. Lack of knowledge is not why some children and youth go the drug route. Rather, it is that life has become less satisfying to them than they would wish. In fact, life has become intolerable. We will find this out when we start listening to children and youth talk about drugs. It will come when we discover that the drug child is our neighbor. It will come when we start listening to him. It will come when we start caring for him.

Have you noticed what has been happening to unwed mothers? Not too many unwed mothers are being branded and sent away anymore. We have finally discovered the person of the unwed mother, her worth. We have finally separated the person from the condition. This is an intelligent act, but it is also an act of love. We have discovered another neighbor.

Our society is experiencing heartache and concern about birth control and abortion. Curiously, more attention is being given to the person in need once more. Very difficult decisions are being made but increasingly these decisions are being made out of love rather than judgment. Love thy neighbor!

It seems that God is working on the war and peace front as well. In the past, both people at war and people at peace have claimed to have God on their side. Now technological development has placed man in a position capable of total self-destruction. Finally, mankind may realize that peace and love are the way. Is this another mysterious work of God?

Almost in the same vein, we see the impact of population explosion on man. So, through his contemporary miseries of war, threat of total destruction, and overpopulation, is man finally understanding what God has conveyed all along and man has not understood or refused to understand? Love thy neighbor!

POSSIBLE IMPLICATIONS

Perhaps the implications are self-evident. Perhaps the thoughts are self-evident. Perhaps it's all been said before many times. A bit of restatement and emphasis may be appropriate for, while the ideas may be familiar, the implementation seems scanty!

God is working everywhere, and we see his work primarily through the increased implementation of the commandment, "Love thy neighbor." The first implication for us in Christian education, therefore, is to recognize and to publicize this very thought.

We should follow the lead of many and see the sanctuary as necessary, but certainly not sufficient. We should avoid any advocacy of separatism or isolation. We should avoid any advocacy of superiority or rejection of certain people because of who they are or what they do. We should live the commandment, "Love thy neighbor," with full acceptance of the fact that everyone is our neighbor. "Everyone is beautiful in his own way."

Slowly, education is learning that human variability is the richest seedbed for learning. Variability should be encouraged and singularity should be abhorred. One of the greatest human gifts is this magnificent variability. We have learned that when this variability is accepted and nurtured in learning, each child learns more and becomes more variable at the same time. Implications are numerous here, but the prime implications concern attitudes. First we must treasure variability. We must love our neighbor even though he is different, for he will be different.

Better a theologian should write on these matters! It does seem, though, that the implementation of love thy neighbor is being found more generally and in some of the strangest places. This seems to be God's work. So, in the eyes of one observer, God continues to work in all creation, especially mankind. And, God does not seem to be confined by our thinking, nor by our traditions, nor by our institutions.

Chapter IV

Man and His Community

ARVID E. ANDERSON

At one time the theological foundations of education in the parish were limited primarily to Bible stories, church history, and doctrine. More recently, man and his community was considered an appropriate subject for study and important as a sociological and psychological foundation. The central objective for educational ministry being developed for the mid seventies and eighties views man and his community as a theological foundation as well.

This chapter will discuss man and his community in three sections: (1) influences toward broader theological foundation, (2) man and his community in the biblical witness, and (3) man and his community in the program of educational ministry.

INFLUENCES TOWARD BROADER THEOLOGICAL FOUNDATIONS

Theological foundations for the church's educational ministry and objectives are broader today than they once were. Theological thinking has been influenced by present day human problems and social movements. Theology today would be incomplete if its foundation were limited to God and the church, as central as those foundations are.

This concern for man and his community is not a detraction from the creative and redemptive work of God in Christ, and its spoken and written record. It is a way of linking the action of God and the human setting of that action, so that theology does not take flight into abstraction. Christian theology has as its center the incarnation of Christ in the human situation, and the mission of the church cannot be thought of apart from the people in society or from the community of believers.

Theology today is taking seriously the historical and the social aspects of life. Man, his environment, and his community are thought of as the setting where God and the Christian faith have meaning. Roger Shinn described the dynamics of theology this way:

> Of course, Christian faith has qualities of constancy and continuity; otherwise, there would be no possibility of distinguishing Christian thought from whim or idolatry. But even in its constancy the accent that is appropriate to one time may be unheeded in another . . . theology is a human activity. Like any human activity, it is partly an expression of the particular human culture in which it develops. It is also a response to that same culture. As an expression of culture it tends to follow the experiences and moods of its time and to say what the culture is saying. As a response to culture it seeks to change the ethos and thinking of its time and today what the culture neglects to say or prefers not to hear.[1]

The linking of God and man and his community in the theological footings of educational ministry is an important step in the Lutheran church. In the past, theology has at times concentrated only on the historical confessions and traditions without adequate attention to the contemporary society in which the message is applied. Without this relevant application, the church has no real mission in the world. Fortunately, in the current social revolution, theology does at times have a relevant prophetic voice. One example, frequently cited, is the relationship between the current ecological interest in the natural world, stimulated by the problems of air and water pollution, and the theological basis for approaching such problems so clearly announced by Joseph Sittler in 1961 at New Delhi. Referring to the Christ hymn in Colossians with its words, "All things were created through him and for him," (1:16) Sittler called for "a doctrine of the cosmos, the theatre of man's selfhood under God, in cooperation with his neighbor, and in caring-relationship with nature, his sister."[2] In a similar way, man and his community is a kind of prophetic theological emphasis for the church's educational ministry in the mid seventies and eighties.

A comparison of the central objectives for Christian education in several Lutheran bodies written in 1957 for the sixties with the central objective written in 1969 for the late seventies indicates a significant shift in the "man and his community" emphasis. The 1957 central objective was:

> . . . to assist the individual in his response and witness to the eternal and incarnate Word of God as he grows within this community of the church toward greater maturity in his Christian life through ever-deepening understandings, more wholesome attitudes, and more responsible patterns of action.[3]

The 1969 central objective for educational ministry in the parish:

> . . . shall be to assist persons to perceive, respond to, and participate in God's continuing activity and revelation, particularly in Jesus Christ, in the human and Christian communities as they deal with their continual life involvements of being a person, relating to persons and groups, and living in society, culture, and the physical universe.[4]

The 1957 objective sees the individual as growing within the community of the church; the 1969 sees him as perceiving, responding to, and participating in God's activity in the human and Christian community. The community is the setting for God's action in a more direct way according to the latest objective.

The 1957 central objective for Christian education viewed man in terms of an individual who is a member of the church and who has various life involvements of a personal, interpersonal, and impersonal nature. This emphasis may have reflected the theological emphasis of the post World War II era when existential and individual aspects of life were strongly emphasized. The objective focused on the individual with less emphasis on society.

The 1969 central objective for educational ministry has a somewhat different focus in terms of man and community. The concern is for "persons," because no individual lives independently. He lives in the "Christian and human communities."

This broader theological base with its stronger emphasis on persons and society grew out of an effort to discover the most relevant emphases for educational ministry in the mid-seventies. A task force spent two years investigating the social, theological and church trends in preparation for formulating a plan of educational ministry. The conclusion of the task force was that the basic issues for the 1970s were likely to be: "The challenge of participating responsibly and communicating Christian faith within the community of believers, and the challenge of participating in the human community in order to enhance the chances for survival, social justice, and human fulfillment."[5]

This study of social change, theology, and church life, with parallel and equal emphasis on each aspect, implies a view toward the foundations of educational ministry which is not narrowly limited to traditional confessional doctrines. Studies related to social change included a wide variety of areas: nature of social change, government and politics, economic trends, natural sciences, health and medicine, education, religious institutions, American family, art, literature, and mass communication. Studies related to theology included: theological responses to the present challenge, biblical interpretation, Christian ethics, ecumenism, history and tradition, and the church and its mission. Trends in church life were investigated through a broad survey of Lutheran congregations. The significance of this approach to building foundations for educational ministry in the future is not only in the content of the findings, but in its inclusiveness of many areas of life. It means, in fact, that the Christian community is looking far beyond itself as it seeks to understand its purpose and plan its work.

It is in this context that man and his community becomes an essential theological foundation in the current era. The central objective clearly reflects this viewpoint when it says that persons are to perceive, respond to, and participate in God's ongoing activity and relavation, particularly in Jesus Christ, in the Christian and human communities.

The thrust of this objective is that the community of man, the believing and human communities, is the setting in which God's activity and revelation take place. Man can perceive this action of God, respond to it, and participate in it. One cannot speak of God's action or revelation outside of community and the persons which comprise it.

MAN AND HIS COMMUNITY IN THE BIBLICAL WITNESS

The current emphasis on man and his community as a foundation for educational ministry is not a new way of thinking theologically. It is basically a reaffirmation of biblical thinking from which theology has sometimes departed. The inevitable result has been the dichotomy of the secular and sacred, and the divorcing of faith from everyday life.

The biblical description of God's action is basically a recounting of how the people of God saw the historical events of their time. The biblical account is an account of history, as seen by the people of God, not a fantasy of some other world. Even the apocalytic elements of the biblical account are primarily an extension of history as seen through the eyes of faith, not a denial of human history.

C. Ellis Nelson describes it this way:

> Revelation from God is not the result of speculative intelligence. God did not set forth a series of ideas about himself nor did he seek to prove his existence. Rather, he elected to show himself to men through the events that made up their *communal life*. The Bible is a description of these events; and although we might call them "holy" because they communicated the meaning of God for the life of his people, the events themselves are not "special" to others who lived at the same time. The events were often quite ordinary, but to the person who was God's chosen interpreter the events were charged with special meaning.[6]

This is not to say the Bible contained only descriptions of historical events. Much of the Bible describes the common human problems and situations which are man's concern in every era. These include the problem of suffering and evil, the question of death, the experience of sin, and the wondering about how the world began. The poetic writings of the Psalms, the Book of Job, the creation accounts of Genesis, and the Book of Revelation, are of this kind of writing. Nevertheless, even these writings emerged out of a historical context in which interpreters lived.

Man and his community was the setting for God's action in the biblical period. Man and his community included the political life of the people, so evident in the period of the kings in the Old Testament, and in the struggle for power among Judah, Israel, Egypt, Babylon, and Assyria. In the same way, the various other aspects of man and his community are an integral part of the biblical story: family life, economic problems, social justice, personal morality, religious traditions, and cultural forms and expressions.

God communicates to man in the midst of social and cultural forms. God is neither a prisoner of culture, nor an enemy of culture. Rather, it is a matter of God's purposes being worked out in the human situation. James Gustafson describes it this way:

> What purposes of God are being realized in the existence of men in community? We have in mind all three aspects of human community: cultural ethos, interpersonal relationship and institutions. My answer to this question hinges on a number of verbs: God creates, sustains, restrains and makes possible better qualities of life through the existence of men in all three aspects of community.[7]

The biblical account witnesses frequently to the action of God in the context of man and his community. For example, the Genesis accounts of the patriarchs, are inextricably bound up with their family and tribal life. It does not enhance the biblical message to overlook or deny the traditions and behavior of the patriarchs which seem incongruous with a puritanical western view. This distortion has been common in parish education in the past. It is only when we accept the human setting of the Genesis stories as being the context for God's activity and revelation that we begin to acknowledge that the human situation is a part of the theological framework.

Abraham was a man with a culture, a family tradition, and a social pattern. He was a "man in the community." For example, he knew how to work compromises in social situations. To his wife he said: ". . . When the Egyptians see you they will say, 'this is his wife;' then they will kill me, but they will let you live. Say that you are my sister, that it will go well with me because of you, and that my life may be spared on your account" (Genesis 12:12-13). This astuteness in the interest of self-survival apparently is not offensive to the Lord (even though the Pharaoh was critical) and did not detract from the quality of the covenant which the Lord made with Abraham. The social setting of Abraham involved many forms strange to some western traditions, including tribal life, mistresses, nomad hospitality, human sacrifice, and burial rites. It is precisely because the human situation, in its total dimension, is integrally bound up with the covenant message in the patriarchal stories that the message carries historic authenticity and can be interpreted for the present day historical situation.

Another central event in the biblical record is the Exodus and God's covenant with Moses and his people. Interpreters of the record see primarily the salvation story, symbolized in the Passover meal and Exodus. This is the central meaning for the people of God. However, the Exodus event cannot be separated from the total human situation in which God acted redemptively to free his people. The believing community was enmeshed in the political, economic, and cultural situation of Egypt. Moses was very much involved in the political and economic communities under which the people were oppressed. The biblical message can best be understood when the context and setting of the exodus is seen. The religious events again are inextricably bound up with the struggle for political and economic freedom. The Passover and Exodus account includes this significant description of the social situation:

> Now there arose a new king over Egypt who did not know Joseph. And he said to his people, "Behold, the people of Israel are too many and too mighty for us. Come, let us deal shrewdly with them, lest they multiply, and, if war befall us, they join our enemies and fight against us and escape from the land." Therefore, they set taskmasters over them to afflict them with heavy burdens; and they built for Pharoah store–cities, Pithom and Raamses. But the more they were oppressed, the more they multiplied and the more they spread abroad. And the Egyptians were in dread of the people of Israel. So they made the people of Israel serve with rigor, and made their lives bitter with hard service, in mortar and brick, and in all kinds of work in the field; in all their work they made them serve with rigor. (Exodus 1:8-14)

The Passover observance was called for by the Lord: "You shall observe the feast of unleavened bread, for on this very day I brought your hosts out of the land of Egypt: therefore you shall observe this day, throughout your generations, as an ordinance for ever" (Exodus 12:17). This religious ceremony arose out of political, economic, and social conditions. The action of God which brought the people to the promised land took place within the arena of human suffering and struggle.

The concept of God's involvement in the total community of man is clearly seen in the Old Testament prophets. Here the biblical witness is to the lordship of God over man in every area of life, not just the "religious." Social justice for all people is central in the message of several Old Testament prophets. Man as an individual does not exist for himself alone, but is responsible for the community, of which he is a part. Amos and Micah, for example, witness to the inseparability of all areas of life—religious, economic, political, social—and of the individual and his community.

The New Testament builds upon and expands the Old Testament's witness of God's action in the human situation.

The covenant community is called into being within the human community. "Once you were no people, but now you are God's people" (1 Peter 2:10). By no means, however, is the covenant community, the fellowship of believers, considered to be totality of God's rule and object of love. This love of God is expressed to the whole world. "God so loved the world that he gave his only Son" (John 3:16) expresses the overarching doctrine of grace from which all action of God stems.

Viewed from this center, there is no aspect of man and his community which is outside of God's holy love and judgment. Our purpose here is not to survey the New Testament teaching of the church as the believing fellowship and its relation to the world. However, there has been a tendency for the church to dwell upon thinking about itself to the neglect of its relationship to the total human community, which is equally the object of God's love. Julio R. Sabanes has called attention to this matter in this way:

> At certain epochs in its history, the church has stood at the crossroads, and some doctrine has provided a clue to an interpretation of the Christian message, a kind of master key to open the way to a new understanding of Christian theology and mission. During the Reformation era, this role was played by the doctrine of justification by faith or the priesthood of all believers. Dare we say that today the Christian doctrine of community has become the main focus of theological thought, and that it is of decisive relevance for the Christian approach to society.[8]

The New Testament in no way denies the human community within which believers find themselves. Nor does it naively accept the human community as capable of Utopia. The New Testament witness is that all men should acknowledge God in Christ as Lord of the whole world and of all people. Jesus' ongoing conflict with the religious people of his time regarding his association with the sinners, tax collectors, and Samaritans is related to the issue of breaking out of the narrow interpretation of God's love. "Go into all the world . . ." (Mark 16:15) means that the world is God's and that he loves it.

The hymn of grace in Colossians (whether by Paul or by later edition) expresses this view of the world and all mankind as being under the loving and just lordship of God in Christ. ". . . for in him all things were created . . . He is before all things and in him all things hold together . . . For in him all the fulness of God was pleased to dwell, and through him to reconcile to himself all things, whether on earth or in heaven, making peace by the blood of his cross" (Colossians 1:16-20). St. Paul had a universal view by which he saw all of history as leading to the ultimate fulfillment of God's purposes through the Gospel. He saw the whole creation as groaning in travail along with man for redemption (Romans 8:19-23).

In Romans 13, the political powers are recognized as legitimate rulers for believers because rulers are from God (1–3). The misinterpretation which has at times been made of this passage in support of tyrannical government does not nullify the basic fact that political, economic, and social systems are as much under God's lordship of justice and judgment as the church is under his judgment and love.

William Lazareth has described the nature of man from the biblical view in this way:

> Man is simultaneously an earthbound part of creation in temporal community with his fellow creatures. In this civilly horizontal dimension of his experience, man is created in loving interdependence with his differently gifted companions. He is to love his neighbor as himself (Leviticus 19:18), sharing with him a responsible stewardship over the natural resources of sea and field and the wealth of personal gifts and talents with which God has blessed him (Genesis 1:28). These social, political, and economic relationships are meant to constitute a human society which reflects the joyful love of its members' religious communion with God and which is sustained and nourished by that love. The Lord requires of each man that he do justice, love kindness, and walk humbly with his God (Micah 6:8).
>
> Community-in-love, both Godward and neighborward, is what human life is created to be, but never is. Every man is guilty of trying to live in rebellious separation from his God and his neighbors (Romans 5:15). In pledging allegiance to rival forces of evil, man rebels against God's universal command to love. He does so only at a frightful cost to himself and to all those who depend upon him. In attempting to wreck God's created order, he succeeds only in destroying himself.[9]

In summary, the interpretation of the Bible which sees man and his community, as the setting for God's activity and revelation, is the view which the central objective for educational ministry seeks to develop as one of the theological foundations for education in the parish.

MAN AND HIS COMMUNITY IN THE PROGRAM OF EDUCATIONAL MINISTRY

How will man and his community, as a theological foundation in the central objective, effect the directions of the program for educational ministry? Will the two major issues for the seventies—participating responsibly in the community of believers and enhancing the chances for survival, social justice, and human fulfillment in the human community—be reflected in the actual ministry among people?[10]

These emphases are finding shape and form as the planning for educational ministry progresses. Several developments indicate how this is happening.

1. *There is a balance between the "person" and the "community."* The continual life involvement concept which is used to relate the central objective statement to the life of the individual describes his total life experiences in three areas: (1) being a person, (2) relating to persons and groups, and (3) living in society, culture and the physical universe. The interrelationship of these life involvements can best be described in the model of three dimensions:

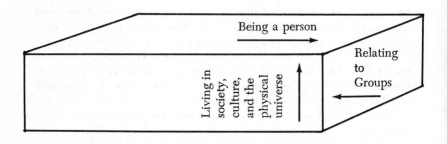

Because each of these dimensions is a part of every person's existence, no one dimension should be thought of apart from the others. If the Gospel is to be communicated to the individual, the groups and culture in which he lives must be taken into account. The individual is influenced through his relationship with others and through the fabric of his society, including the believing community of which he may be a part. At the same time, the worth and identity of the person must be valued and respected because he is unique and created by God.

Earlier parish education efforts have tended to stress the individual and his influence upon community, without emphasizing the inter-action of the individual and society. The central objective for the seventies and eighties gives a more balanced place in the educating community in which the individual lives. On this point, the theological thinking has profited from the social scientists. Ellis Nelson suggests:

> The clue that we obtain from these social scientists is the power of the human group, tribe, or subculture to form the basic personality structure and the way the social-interactional process among adults formulates questions about, and supplies answers to, the meeting of the past (history), and present (morals, customs, beliefs) and the future (end of history and life after death) . . . (they) help us . . . by showing us that the unit of reality with which we must work in order to understand a process of faith-communication, is the group to which a person belongs.[12]

Evidence that the balance between "person" and "community" is shaping educational ministry is seen in the development of age level objectives for early childhood, elementary school age, youth and adults. As the planners have struggled in stating objectives, they con-tinually asked the questions, What are the implications for the con-gregation and family of this person? What is required of the facilita-tors who are to assist the person in reaching the objectives? What kind of climate must there be in the congregation for the educating process to occur? In these questions is an exciting possibility for educa-tional *ministry*—person to person, group to person, and congregation to community. This view is in harmony with the report of the commission on confirmation and first communion, in which confirmation is defined as an educational and pastoral ministry involving the child and the total Christian community.[13]

2. *All dimensions of life—being a person, relating to groups, living in society—are seen in light of God's ongoing activity.* The central objec-tive for educational ministry assumes the basic Christian doctrines, even though they are not spelled out in the document: the doctrine of creation, in which all of nature and society is under the lordship of God; the doctrine of sin and evil, that all of life is affected by sin and, therefore, is under the judgment of God; the doctrine of redemption,

that God seeks reconciliation and salvation for all men and creation.

The way in which these basic theological foundations are related to the educational program is through the continual life involvements. These are basically a description of what is common to all humans: *being a person, relating to others,* and *living in society and the universe.* These continual life involvements are then viewed in "Christian perspective," which is basically interpreting life in light of the Gospel. Every continual life involvement is restated in "Christian perspective."[14]

A new approach to educational ministry is being shaped through this pattern. In essence, no area of life is being labeled as "Christian" rather than "secular." To the contrary, every area of life is viewed as basic to all human beings. The Christian perspective comes in the *interpretation* which comes in perceiving, responding, and participating in God's continuing activity within these areas of life.

In this view, the human and Christian communities are not interpreted in the traditional "two kingdom" form.

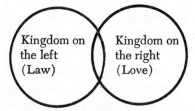

Rather life is viewed as a whole in which both the society and the believing community are created by God through his grace and justice.

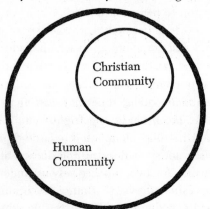

Within the continual life involvements there is no area of life to which the Christian is not related. The Lutheran church has sometimes tended to include only the individual, family, and the congregation within its sphere and concern for Christian education. These are the continual life involvements of (1) being a person, and (2) relating to other persons and groups. However, it is a somewhat new theological interpretation to view living in society, culture, and the physical universe as an area where the continuing activity of God is to be perceived, and entered into. It should be emphasized that revelation is to be understood "particularly in Jesus Christ."

Living in society, culture, and the physical universe, the third section of life involvements, includes the following "Christian perspective" statements, given here as illustrative[15] of how educational ministry is to be concerned with these areas of life:

"perceiving the interrelatedness of everything in God's universe."

"evaluating the place of individual freedom and social conformity in light of God's purpose for human community."

"appreciating the values in other cultures as a means of expressing and experiencing the wholeness of mankind."

"participating in political processes on the basis of one's own ability and sense of purpose, so as to contribute to the well-being of persons and society."

"using economic systems and structures as means for establishing equitable distribution of material goods as an expression of God's justice and love."

"evaluating all religious and philosophical systems and structures in the light of Christian heritage and witness."

These kinds of statements about society and the physical universe must be properly understood as the valid and vital concerns of the Christian community. Too often we get frightened off by these "social" statements for fear that the church has confused law and Gospel. However, the church today cannot retreat under the guise of self-protection of doctrine. As two theologians are quoted in the *Yearbooks in Christian Education—II:* "There is no point in giving the sacrament of Christ's body and blood for the forgiveness of sins when what the man needs is first of all the sacrament of food, clothing, shelter, so he can stay alive and be human. Then the time will also come when only the sacrament of 'God's blood' will satisfy.' This can be done "without compromising the uniqueness of its task in the proclamation of the Law and Gospel."[16] ". . . The church in large measure receives the substance of its teaching material from the world. The church contributes the Gospel and the will to apply it. The world is the arena."[17]

The central objective and its statements about living in society, culture, and the physical universe commits the educational ministry program of the church in the seventies and eighties to a concern for persons' involvement in all areas of life. Even the earliest stages of program development, based on the central objective, indicate that the whole range of society will be taken into account. For example, the social issues of population control, pollution, racism, war, as well as personal problems, are being seen as clearly appropriate areas of study and action.

3. *Man and his community is basic at every age level.* In order for a program of educational ministry to be effective, it must be consistent in its interpretation of the gospel to children, youth, and adults. Man and his community, as a basic theological element, must be related to each age level in a relevant way. If this is not accomplished, it remains a theoretical formulation rather than a meaningful experience.

Program planners sought to relate this, and other basic themes, to each age level. A brief description of how this was done at one stage in the planning process is given here. Planners analyzed each of the continual life involvements as to its degree of importance at a particular age level. Some of the continual life involvements are particularly connected with the theme of man and his community. Similarly, other themes such as God and the church are particularly connected with certain life involvements, with some involvements connected with several themes. It is through the objectives and programs to be developed around particular life involvements that man and his community, for example, will become basic educational experiences.

Beginning in early childhood and continuing with increasing emphasis in elementary school age, youth and adults, man and his community is an important element in the educational ministry. What the "community" means varies with the age group. It starts with the fam-

Continual Life Involvement   *High Degree of Importance*

	Early Childhood	Elementary School Age	Youth	Adults
I. Being a Person				
A. Personal Identity	X	X	X	
B. Dealing in Givenness and Inevitables	X	X	X	X
C. Dealing with Ultimates		X	X	X
II. Relating to Persons and Groups				
*A. Other Individuals	X	X	X	X
*B. Family	X	X		X
*C. Small Groups	X	X	X	X
*D. Large Groups		X	X	X
III. Living in Society, Culture, and Physical Universe				
A. Physical Universe	X	X	X	X
*B. Society		X	X	X
*C. Culture			X	X
*D. Political Processes			X	X
*E. Economic Processes			X	X
*F. Religious and Philosophical Processes			X	X

*These continual life involvements are particularly related to man and his community.

ily in the earliest period of life, but soon expands into the congregation and various groups, as well as into social, cultural, political, economic involvements.

Each succeeding stage of the program implements the basic directions of the previous stage. Therefore, educational ministry in the ALC and LCA in the late seventies and eighties can be expected to give significant attention to man and his community because this is clearly a part of the educational and theological foundations from the outset of the planning.

SUMMARY

1. Man and his community has become a basic theological foundation in the planning of educational ministry for the late seventies and eighties. This results from theological emphases which see the total life of man and all aspects of the human community as belonging to the lordship of God in Christ, and because contemporary social problems and issues have heightened the need for strengthening the life of the Christian community and enhancing the life of society as a whole.

2. The emphasis on man and his community is consistent with the biblical witness of God's action within history and among the people in everyday events and experiences. The community of the covenant and the community of society both belong to God, and exist through his grace, shown particularly in Jesus Christ.

3. Directions in educational ministry are being influenced by the emphasis on man and his community. Evidences of this influence include:

(a) The balance which is being made between the "person" and the "community" in the central objective, age level objectives, and program design.

(b) All aspects of man's continual life involvements, including his relation to others and his life in society and culture, are being interpreted in light of God's ongoing activity. The human community, as well as the covenant community, are seen as the setting for God's activity.

(c) Man and his community is being related to every age level—children, youth, and adults—in order that this basic foundation might be followed consistently in the program of educational ministry being designed for all members of the Christian community.

In conclusion, it seems that man and his community will be a significant new emphasis for educational ministry in the parish in the decade ahead. Man and his community is a prophetic theme which can call the church to its mission of service and involvement in the world. Stating the theological foundations for educational ministry is only one step in planning educational ministry. The real challenge to the Christian community comes in carrying out its mission in society, a society which in many ways is alienated from God, who nevertheless continues to create and sustain his world.

NOTES AND REFERENCES

1. Roger L. Shinn, *Man: The New Humanism,* New Directions in Theology Today, vol. 6 (Philadelphia: The Westminster Press, 1968), p. 15.
2. Quoted from Philip J. Hefner, ed., *The Scope of Grace* (Philadelphia: Fortress Press, 1964), p. vi.
3. Long Range Program of the Boards of Parish Education, *The Objectives of Christian Education* (Philadelphia: Boards of Parish Education of the Lutheran Church, 1957).
4. *A Central Objective for Educational Ministry in the Parish: ALC and LCA* (Philadelphia: Board of Parish Education of the Lutheran Church in America, 1969).
5. Edward W. Uthe, *Significant Issues for the 1970's: Report to the Lutheran Church in America Task Group for Long Range Planning* (Philadelphia: Fortress Press, 1968), p. 5.
6. C. Ellis Nelson, *Where Faith Begins* (Richmond, Va.: John Knox Press, 1967), p. 84.
7. James F. Gustafson, "A Theology of Christian Community?" in *Man in Community,* ed. Egbert DeVries (New York: Association Press, 1966), pp. 178-179.
8. Julio R. Sabanes, "Biblical Understanding of Community" in *Man in Community,* ed. Egbert DeVries (New York: Association Press, 1966), p. 168.
9. William H. Lazareth, "Christian Faith and Culture" in *Life in Community,* Christian Social Responsibility, vol. 3, ed. Harold C. Letts (Philadelphia: Muhlenberg Press, 1957).
10. *Significant Issues for the 1970's,* p. 5.
11. *Central Objective.*
12. *Where Faith Begins,* p. 18.
13. Joint Commission on the Theology and Practice of Confirmation, *A Report for Study* (Minneapolis: Augsburg Publishing House, St. Louis: Concordia Publishing House, Philadelphia: Board of Publication, Lutheran Church in America, 1970).
14. *Central Objective,* pp. 37-43.
15. *Ibid.,* p. 40.
16. Gustav K. Wiencke, ed., *Christian Education in a Secular Society,* Yearbooks in Christian Education—II (Philadelphia: Fortress Press, 1970), p. 30.
17. *Ibid.,* p. 31.

Man and His Community—A Response

LOREN E. HALVORSON

At a time when life together has become problematical for the human species, it is encouraging to note that Christian educators are placing a major emphasis on "community." The theme of community has been central to a number of modern theologians. The young Bonhoeffer chose it as his doctoral dissertation and later pioneered new forms of communal life. Emil Brunner also used "community" as a major organizing concept for his theology. These men witnessed the breakdown of human communities and institutions and likely felt compelled to address themselves, therefore, to this issue.

The apparent breakdown of established communities in America may well explain our belated attention to the human and social content of Christian nurture. Today the foundations upon which society has been established are being radically questioned. Experiments in new life styles, international communities, togetherness, and interpersonal relationships reflect both the rejection of old forms and a fascination with new possibilities for human societies.

In the light of the above I am pleased with the *Central Objective for Educational Ministry in the Parish: ALC and LCA* when it argues for an educational ministry which "helps persons see that God is involved in all life everywhere" and is even willing to consider the possibility that this means working through non-church structures. My comments here intend to reenforce this stated objective, but also to add some critical comments on the specific theological and practical aspects of the Christian understanding of community. These comments take the form of a series of theses following the outline of Arvid Anderson's chapter.

1. *Christian education must be located in the context of human communities.* The task of nurturing Christian growth belongs between the altar and the street, not in some protected hothouse behind the sanctuary. As stated in the *Central Objective*, "a Christian perspective . . . sees Christ precisely in the center of the tensions and forces of society"

(p. 28). The church needs a ministry of a sufficiently hearty variety to thrive in the changing and harsh climate of society. The proper context, therefore, to determine maturity in the faith is not how well the species thrives in the protected household or greenhouse, but its performance outside.

For a number of reasons, a contextual approach has proved necessary and healthy for the church. She has discovered in "outside" encounters that she needs the world for her own healing, that it is not only the reverse that is true. To engage in dialogue with a protagonist and to explore new ways of encouraging dialogue has proved beneficial to the church for several reasons. Exposure for a confessionally-oriented religion is a good thing. In the confessional the church learns to become "question-able", to share its embarrassment of ignorance and failure with others.

Such risk-taking ought to come naturally to the Christian church whose very posture before God is one of confession. Having been radically placed in question and accepted not on the basis of his moral "brownie points" but on the basis of forgiveness, the Christian ought to be the most open person of all. Whatever the ills of society, the church stands not above them, but in their midst, involved and responsible. The words of truth despite all their exposure are necessary for the healing of the church as well as society.

> If prophecy puts itself above history it becomes, in Luther's expression, "a theology of glory," (*theologia gloriae*) which leads to an arbitrary interpretation of events from a fixed position to which the observer has isolated himself. The theology of prophecy must be a theology of cross and shame (*theologia crucis*) where the reality of history can overcome that use of words which seeks to escape the judgment of history.[1]

The concern for a more contextual approach is being recognized in both secular and theological educational circles. Universities, colleges, and seminaries are seeking ways to break out from single track academic syndromes and enrich the learning process by exposing students and faculty to a wider range of human experiences.

Urban training centers are springing up to augment seminary education. Such innovations are far more promising in revitalizing both church and society than the domestic parlor games of rearranging existing furniture in most efforts at curriculum revisions. The "University of the Streets" and the "Street Academies" of the Urban League are additional examples which bring a much needed educational perspective into the learning process by placing education in its immediate human context. Even the old pietists of the seventeenth and eighteenth centuries saw the need for the contextual approach to the study of theology. From them has come the admonition, "The best way to study scriptures is to have the Bible on one knee and the daily newspaper on the other."

The revitalization of education by becoming more contextual points up one of the reasons why the adult education classroom efforts have by and large failed to attract significant numbers or to generate much action. This has certainly been true in the church's experience in seeking to attract adults into educational programs through handsome materials and often very competent coaches. Upon completion of these courses it has been obvious that the players have not rushed out of the classroom and torn up the turf.[2]

2. *Christian education is personal and not individual centered.* It may be true that in recent years social crises have shifted our attention from the individual to corporate and political considerations. But we may be faced with a radical swing back to the individual and his consciousness (cf. Charles Reich, *The Greening of America*) either out of despair of changing society or out of the realization that the transformation of society has its roots in personal values. The pervasive sense of powerlessness felt by all segments of our society has contributed to the former, but longer range analyses of the dynamic of institutional and societal change reaffirm the latter.

To avoid a disastrous swing back to an individualism which seeks religious fulfillment in the cultivation of interior feelings while ignoring the needs of our brothers, it is necessary to distinguish between "individualization" and "personalization." Christian education deals with that kind of knowledge which places the individual in a new relational grid: confrontation with God, with neighbor, and with himself. The new self-awareness which these confrontations produce does not create an *incurvatus se*, but a deeper and broader sense of responsibility.

What is taking place in the disinventing of the established systems or "institutions" is a shift in authority which places far more freedom and accountability on individuals than ever before. That awesome freedom and responsibility, however, could produce a more personal self, keenly aware of the corporateness of existence.

Dietrich von Oppen in his provocative work, *The Age of the Person,* interprets current shifts as reflecting the revolutionary transformation of the individual first articulated in the Sermon on the Mount.

> Man is now addressed as a person and is called on to act responsibly. New powers, hitherto dormant, are awakened, and he is translated into a new status. This status, however, is not that of an isolated individual but of one who stands before God, responds to God, and is answerable to God—answerable, indeed, for his neighbor and for himself. By outlining the individual's relationship to God, to his fellowmen, and to himself, the Sermon on the Mount outlines the structure of personal action.[3]

I would argue that knowledge, whether religious or secular, does not become personal but remains individualistic until one's private convictions are understood in the public context. A religious faith, for example, which is confined just to the private sector (the last fortress where some believe it can best be preserved) becomes, in fact, nonpersonal, indeed apersonal. The separation of religious faith from the public sector eventually impoverishes both. The biblical test of faith in terms of serving one's neighbor attests to a wholistic view that keeps the private and public dimensions of life inseparably together. There is no individual or private life for God's people. But there is a profoundly personal one if personhood is understood in its full sense as involving all human relationships.

In the present decade, as the church is hard pressed to assert her integrity and to articulate the meaning of the gospel in the light of a whole new range of issues, it will be necessary to guard against a new individualistic piety. One way to prevent this is to see Christian education within the context of the public education and socialization of church members. The relating of the Christian community to the larger human community is, therefore, not an issue of secondary importance, but central to our understanding of Biblical faith. The shift in the 1969 central objective must be seen as something more than just a minor and mid-course correction.

3. *The denial of the Biblical view of the wholeness of life leads to pathological forms in religious and social behavior.* God's actions in the context of man and his community mean that both reason and

revolution are necessary for the theological education. One of the weaknesses in theological education (whether at the seminary or parish level) in America is the too frequent isolation of theological research and reflection from secular institutions and activities. As Lutherans we have labored faithfully, and rightly so, to accurately convey the traditions of the faith from one generation to the next. Education has been a very high priority. But we are perplexed when our theological graduates have difficulty relating the faith to everyday affairs and when our best youth test out in careful research to know the form of the faith but not the substance.

The problem does not seem to be the lack of Christian training in the traditional or technical sense, but the failure to integrate such training in the context of today's society. My thesis is simply that the relation between church and society is the necessary matrix for equipping the Christian ministry. The failure to so locate theological reflection and training can lead to pathological conditions.

In reviewing the history of the science/theology debate, for example, it is clear that we are dealing with a credibility gap. I would describe this gap in terms of the polarity which has been developed between "confessionalism" and "professionalism." Or, in very much oversimplified terms between faith and facts. Where the integrity of both is recognized and honored there is no necessary conflict, but rather a complementary relationship.

The sixteenth century reformers would have used different language. Their polarities would have been "special" and "general" grace, or "faith" and "reason," or the "Kingdom on the Right" and the "Kingdom on the Left." The demands that theology and science make on each other are very similar.

Abraham Maslow in *The Psychology of Science* says: "Both orthodox science and orthodox religion have been institutionalized and frozen into a mutually excluding dichotomy . . . One consequence is that they are both pathologized, split into sickness, ripped apart into a crippled half-science and a crippled half-religion. This either-or split forces a kind of either-or choice between them."[4]

A similar observation to that of Maslow could be made regarding religious education. The suffering in the professional ministry, theological schools, and parishes is due in part to "mutually excluding dichotomy." Too frequently they fail to be healing communities. In terms of what is needed in educational reform today perhaps a more satisfying model would include the goal of becoming a healing community rather than simply an academic one.

The obvious lessons of the past decade and one of the clear insights of the astronauts who looked back to earth from the location where modern technology had placed them., is that we stand at the end of single track systems. No single institution of our society can adequately deal with the problems any more. We have been driven relentlessly by the technological progress and social revolutions to the realization that we must work together. We shall achieve a cooperative world not because we are so wise and obedient to have thus appropriated God's purpose, but because survival demands it. There may be higher motives for working together, but none is more effectual than survival.

The end of single track systems means for Christian education that the day of theological isolationism is over. It means that we recognize in the diversity of our society and our religious traditions not the occasion to operate independent of one another but the basis of enlivening interdependence.

Our very life depends on openness to each other. It is only as we are exposed to the insights, resources and experiences of other parts of the human community that we can fulfill the educational tasks of the church. Exposure need not destroy us. Indeed, it can enrich us. What appears to many to be the breakdown of American society may be the breaking open of our institutions, people, and beliefs to fresh and new relationships.

Just prior to one of the most profound changes in the life style of Israel, Moses was taken to a mount and given a vision of the future. What has transpired within the last years may be something like that. An unprecedented view from outer space as well as a fresh perspective through the confrontations on this planet have given us a new vision of the destiny of this ancient piece of cosmic gravel.

Exposure is essential in revitalizing church and society because words and ideas become impoverished when they become separated from reality. Partners in a meaningful dialogue must know firsthand the actualities of what they are discussing. As long as words are used as smoke screens or abstractions from historical reality, they become unbelievable. Therefore, so much of what the white society has tried to say to the black, or the church to society, or Americans to the rest of the world has become "unbelievable." Too many of these words have been out of context and thus impotent. Until that context is shared, until the feet of discussion partners are on a common ground, words will have little authority.

History teaches that periods of hardships can be healthy. Such moments place people on common ground. Just such times help men to reestablish their roots, traditions, and essential goals. When these become radically placed in question, they must be lecated again. The church may well function more faithfully under such conditions than in a comfortable and congenial climate. Robert Ardrey in his book, *African Genesis*, suggests that the human species emerged during a period of climatic upheaval: "Change is the elixir of the human circumstance, and acceptance of challenge the way of our kind. We are bad-weather animals, disaster's fairest children. For the soundest of evolutionary reasons, man appears at his best when times are worst."[5]

For the soundest of theological reasons the church is most responsible in her mission and most accurate in her words when she seeks not to impose her ideology on others from a position of cultural privilege but when, from a position of weakness, she asks radical questions about herself and the world. Or, in theological shorthand, when the church lives by grace alone. This is the significance of a recovery of the Biblical emphasis on history as the locus of revelation. This means that our present history must be the context for education in the faith.

4. *The Christian view of man and community is stereo and not monaural.* The 1969 objective employs the term "continual life involvements" to refer to what I understand as the older concepts of orders of creation, mandates, or social orders. It is noted that the three dimensions of person, group, and society are all interrelated and interdependent. I would like to suggest a somewhat altered model to make it clear that the movement is not just the Christian bringing community to human society but also the reverse.

I would suggest at the outset that part of our difficulty in conceptualizing the relationship of the church community to the civil community arises from our historical perspective as "free" churches (or "sects" in Troeltsch's typology). That is, we view the movement of God's grace primarily, if not exclusively, from the private experience of faith through the corporate church and out into the public sector.

In a culture where organized religion is legally if not ideologically confined to the private and corporate sector, a clockwise understanding of grace seems most appropriate:

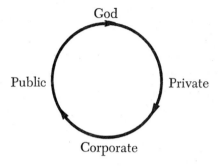

The way Protestants have approached the fundamental theological question also locates the initial experience of grace in the private sector and proceeds clockwise to the corporate (i.e., the community of believers where the individual's faith is nurtured and directed outward toward the neighbor) and finally to the public arena where ministry to the "least of these" is service to the Lord. This, at least, in theory is how the full sweep of grace is conceptualized. There is, of course, more than sufficient evidence that Christians have most often confined their energies to the private or corporate sectors.

Luther's question, How can I find a gracious God? is cited as proof that the life of faith finds its original impulse in a private experience. This may not be an entirely accurate reading of Luther's view of grace, but it seems clearly to be the way much of Protestantism in America has operated. The great revival movements of the nineteenth century accentuated this view by awakening a profound sense of the individual's relation to God. According to the religious understanding that has dominated in America, the way you change society is by converting the individual. Religion is primarily a private affair!

In Christian education as reflected in the central objectives in the past, this has meant that the individual's nurture in faith has been the primary goal. Those who despair at the effectiveness of religious education should realize that the church has been tremendously successful in achieving this objective. Most people within as well as outside the church see religion largely in private terms. Religious institutions have been established with the same objective in mind. Their function is to nurture the individual's faith and to strengthen the community of believers. A quick glance at any church budget makes these priorities perfectly clear. The earlier objectives seem to have been achieved all too well. And that may be our problem.

The understanding of what God is about is being challenged today by another breed of believers whose initial theological question arises not out of private questions, but rather out of public ones. Overwhelmed by the upheavals in human communities, social revolution, and injustices, sensitive spirits probe the question of what God is about with the question, How can I find a gracious fellow man? Their search is for signs of grace within the human community, so they bring an entirely new set of priorities to the corporate structures of the church and rearrange the individual's self-understanding by emphasizing his rootedness in human community. God's actions are conceptualized in a counter-clockwise motion.

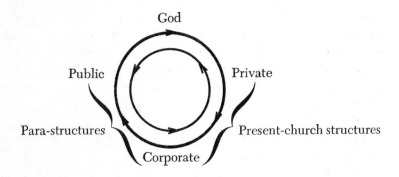

The questions of one's relationship to God, according to this second view, have quite a different thrust. The criterion for faithfulness becomes one's relationship to the neighbor. Gifts are abandoned at the altar and moratoriums on religious assemblies are declared until one is reconciled with his brother. The context for religious education in this second view is the public arena. The exegesis of contemporary history is viewed as essential for the exegesis of the past acts of God, which also occurred in the historical and "secular" affairs of men.

There are clearly two breeds of Christian in every congregation, denomination, and even family. This debate in the religious community threatens to polarize churches into two camps each armed with sufficient Biblical and theological ammunition to guarantee a very long war which neither side can win. One side shouts, "The world needs the church for the healing of the world." The other side replies, "The church needs the world for the healing of the church." The clockwise types steal some weapons from their protagonists by quoting the Kerner Report to the effect that the root cause of social injustice lies in the "heart, mind and spirit" of individual Americans. The counter-clockwise types fire back with weapons from their enemies' arsenal by quoting Martin Luther King, Jr. who is reported to have answered critics of his poor people's march on Washington, D.C. by saying, "We have brought Lazarus to the rich man's gate in order to save the soul of the rich man."

This kind of thing can go on endlessly and probably will until we recognize that God's gracious work is stereo and not monaural. However we distinguish between general and special grace, law and Gospel, preservative and redemptive work, justice and love, the central point is that they both are seen by biblical faith as God's activities. A stereo approach to truth need not split up reality into hopeless contractions. A deeper, richer, more exciting and wholistic understanding may result.

5. *Community provides the middle ground for relating church and society.* It is of course possible and inevitably necessary to interpret the doctrine of justification by faith in terms that deal with sanctification, ethics, and mission, but there seems good reason to employ another organizing principle for theology in today's educational task. The concept of community is useful because it bridges the civil and religious communities. It provides a common ground for a stereo system where the "traffic of God's grace" can flow both ways.

The use of "middle principles" as heuristic tools to bridge the gaps between theology and other disciplines is well known in apologetics and social ethics. What is needed, however, in such applied fields as Christian education is not a middle principle but a "middle form" or common ground as the matrix to relate faith to everyday life. Only rarely are such "middle forms" found in the present structures of the church. Let us return for a moment to the Private–Corporate–Public Diagrams to illustrate.

117

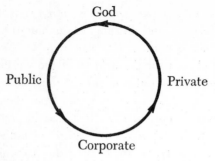

The present church structures produced in the free church tradition in America have been established almost exclusively along the private–corporate segment of the track. Furthermore, they have been largely monaural in the clockwise direction. Traffic has not been flowing both ways. The parish has been identified with the congregation, not the entire community. Denominations have developed their own schools, universities and hospitals.

Present church structures were designed to serve the private and corporate manifestations of the church, but not the public. The widespread frustration experienced by church leaders in responding to the "national crisis" has demonstrated this fact. Existing church structures have programmed the average member to grasp quite well the church as the communion of saints (the church in its most private and mystic mode) and as the gathered community of believers (the church in its corporate mode). But it seems very difficult to convey to the average church man the concept of the church as God's people scattered in the world and functioning within secular occupations and communities.

I would like to suggest that this pedagogical failure is closely related to the absence of functioning models of middle forms of community where religious and secular roles are related. The present models of what it means to be the church are too narrowly restricted to clergy and "pastorized" laity. What is critically needed today in Christian education to realize the objective of man and his community is a new model of the "stereo Christian" for whom the faith is a private, corporate *and* public affair. I believe the educational enterprise of the church will have more vitality, lucidity, integrity, and stability when it is established on this trinitarian base.

One segment of the track remains to be constructed. And that is to attach to our present private and corporate oriented structures new ones which relate the church to the public sector. Provisional bridges or "para-structures" will have to be created to link the religious and secular communities. These are already emerging almost spontaneously here and there: community organizations, multi-congregation parishes, team ministries, action groups, urban training centers, experimental communities, coalitions, consulting firms, and consortiums. Perhaps the time has come to shift our energies from drawing up objectives, issuing policy statements, writing theological responses, developing long range studies and holding more conferences to launching operational models of para-structures which bridge the corporate and public sectors. We need to do more than, as Anderson suggests, "consider an educational ministry that is able to work through non-church structures of society." Such efforts already exist. New ones ought to be tried. Experimental probes more than study papers are the way this generation of pioneers will shape the future.

6. *The exploration of man in this community must also be based on a new understanding of "natural theology."* The 1969 central objective underscores the need to consider the theme of man in community "particularly in Jesus Christ." Since human community is the focus of the approxriate context for Christian education in the 1969 objective why not root this in the First Article of the Creed rather than the Second? Perhaps one of our difficulties in understanding man in community has been our understandable eagerness to Christologize. Sittler's "cosmic Christ" and Chardin's Christo-centric evolutionism are stirring and helpful efforts in this direction. But in dealing with the human community as such there is solid ground for proceeding on the basis of reason. It seems to me we must first acknowledge the integrity of creation through the honest use of reason, and without apology to the categories of faith but in service to them. There is also important apologetic ground for employing the doctrine of creation or nature in exploring the theme of "community." The context for such an exploration is, after all, a world profoundly influenced by science and technology: REASON writ very large.

The old superstitions have been destroyed, or perhaps we might say flattened out. An age dominated by scientific research and technological development pays scant heed to transcendent claims, metaphysical speculation or even poetic insights. The "mystery" has succumbed to empirical analysis. In protest a case must be made for the poets, theologians and philosophers to ply their trade, but I want to move on to another point—the healthy desacralization of nature at the hands of science.

Today the discussion centers on such terms as "secularity," "legitimate profanity" and "holy worldliness." These terms will attest to the liberating of reason from enslavement to political, social, or religious tyranny. In fact, Gogarten and others have argued that Christianity gave birth to a world view which de-divinized creation and made it the proper arena for reasonable investigation. Luther worked hard to free the orders of creation (the realm of God's masked activity, where God rules with his left hand) from ecclesiastical control. Where he thought men were honoring common sense in the management of creation, even though they might be pagan, Luther did not hesitate to call them "Christian" or God's "miracle men."

The distinctions between the functions of faith and reason, between Luther's two kingdoms or Calvin's "special" and "general" grace have led unfortunately to separation. Theological education has been removed from the great university. Church and state operate in a "cold war" climate. Religion gets assigned to the private sphere and legally kept from the public sector. The result of this separation is the impoverishment of both church and society.

The distinction between faith and reason is necessary so that the integrity of each is preserved. Dialogue between them is necessary, however, for keeping each honest. Science's contribution to theology is to protect the integrity of the created world. Perhaps science's desacralization of creation will make it possible to recover a "natural" theology. Such language has fallen into disrepute at the hands of Barth and others, but the "natural" seems to be reasserting its claims in modern theology.

The environmental crisis may provide the matrix for a restoration of the concept of "natural" or at least common sense to theology. It is universally obvious that we have violated the natural environment by ignoring the ancient mandate to "care for the earth." We are realizing anew that there are mandates "built into" nature which cannot be ignored without catastrophic results. These mandates must be seen in dynamic and not static, fixed terms. The categories of "orders of creation," while having a poor history in the way they have been used to prevent change, are not so old fashioned as we might have imagined. In fact, only as we comprehend how creation functions, only as we honor the integrity we find in nature, can we change our environment without destroying it.

The religious question for many today, therefore, may not be How can I find a gracious God? or even a gracious fellow man, but the one Professor Toedt asked at Evian at the Assembly of the Lutheran World Federation: "How can God get His creation back?" A closer partnership, therefore, between science and theology, between reason and faith, is not only desirable, it is inevitable. It is along these lines that our examination of man in community must also proceed.

7. *The context for Christian education is man in his broken communities.* Not enough attention has been given in either the central objective or Mr. Anderson's paper to the pathological condition of man in community. While the point is acknowledged—"community-in-love, both Godward and neighborward, is what human life is created to be, but never is"—it is never pursued. The fact that the Christian does view community in terms of its illness is of paramount importance.

The location of the Christian community within the larger context of the human community can be misleading. It is too easy to presume that the Christian community serves as some kind of ideal model for the rest of society. (Cf. Karl Barth's *The Christian Community and the Civil Community.*) Such a claim has little chance of surviving empirical research, especially in such areas as social justice and prejudice. A more fruitful line of solidarity between the Christian and human communities is their common brokenness.

When the Christian uses the term "community," he speaks of broken relationships restored. The church is not an ideal community in the Greek sense of perfection, but in the Hebrew sense of wholeness which recognizes the alienated and discordant aspects of life. The church is best understood as a community of sick who have found their physician. At the heart of this community is forgiveness, self-giving love, grace. Such a picture of the church places it not above other communities but, in the sense of servanthood (*kenosis*) and *disponibileté*, beneath others.

What is "common to all humans" is broken community, sin. Our approach to community, therefore, is not to point up anything superior in the fellowship of believers as a model for human community, but to share the healing of the Gospel with others with whom we share the solidarity of sin. And there is something peculiarly "Lutheran" about an approach which begins with sickness, with life as it is.

> In depicting as a battleground on which two kingdoms are engaged in combat, Luther seeks to show that the human predicament is not what Erasmus conceives it to be. Man is wounded in the depth of his being and is in search of healing. Growth into humanness takes place as a transition from sickness to health, as a deliverance of conscience shackled by the powers of condemnation into freedom to hear the speech of life, as a transformation of the web of guilt into the fabric of grace.[6]

A view from the "bottom" of human community frees the church from fear of life as it is. Rather than fleeing the points of crisis and conflict the church identifies herself with them as the moments (kairoi) of the deepest disclosure of meaning. As Eugen Rosenstock-Huessy has pointed out, the reality of human life is cruciform.[7] Therefore the church need not panic in the face of social upheaval. The apparent breakdown of institutions, persons and value systems are viewed by those who live by grace as the breaking open of institutions, persons, and value systems to each other in new and potentially healing ways. Perhaps the only unique feature of the Christian community within the human community is the profound sense of hope precisely where others despair. The uniqueness of the church, therefore, is not one which separates her from the human community, but deliberately identifies her with it. The church does need the world for her own healing.

In the light of the above the identification of the Christian community with the successful, affluent, good, and righteous is disastrous. When the church whose Lord immediately identified with the outcasts, poor, sick, and impure becomes the citadel of respectability and a closed community of the "certified" she has failed to grasp the heart of the Gospel. The purity of doctrine goes much deeper than accurate formulations. The implications of this for Christian education are paramount:

> It is apparent that outside of theological study, rather than in theology itself, one finds more of the kind of "theological" elucidation of the nature of divine humanness, of the basic associations of life and

their fragmentation, where conceptual analysis is not predominant but where methods are shaped by a concrete encounter with man.

A theology which concentrates primarily on conceptual analysis has only remote contact with the dynamics of personal experience and thought. This is illustrated by the fact that Protestant theological education, for the most part, is training solely for conceptual analysis and verbal communication. There is an obvious discrepancy between academic learning and clinical experience.[8]

8. *The survival of the human community requires a global, symbiotic society.* There is mounting evidence of the interrelatedness or interdependency of all things. No single system, institution, academic discipline, hypothesis, culture, profession, nation, theology, or whatever, by itself, can deal with the complex, interlocking issues facing man. Certainly the ecological crisis makes it clear that the strongest part of a system is dependent on the weakest. All must be protected and interfacing for the healthy functioning of the whole. Ecologists call this *symbiosis*; theologians call it *koinonia*.

In the vision of that strange poet-scientist-theologian, Pierre Teilhard de Chardin, there is the idea of the eventual global community, the hominization of the planet, called the Noosphere. Teilhard describes the discovery of the interdependence of all of life in terms of "complexity consciousness." That everything relates to everything else may be too dizzy a view to grasp except in moments of poetic imagination. But that here is something central to the current crisis of man and nature, I have no doubt.

Ian Barbour comments on man's interdependence with nature:

> Man is part of a larger whole: his loyalty must be to the community of life, not to mankind alone. We live in subtly balanced systems, and the efforts of our actions reverberate throughout the created order. We must recover a basic respect for the value of all living things, a sense of wonder and reverence for life. Nature has not usually been included in the sphere of ethics; today we need an ethics of nature as well as a theology of nature.[9]

Max Weber was correct in seeing the coming disenchantment with nature at the hands of scientific investigation. The sense of awe and mystery, certainly of superstition at least, seems to be a casualty. But Weber may not have seen far enough. Mystery and wonder may well return in larger dimensions when, at the point of our individual failures and poverty, we experience something akin to ecstasy, when we discover that interfacing with other parts of the system enriches and empowers us. The whole is more than the sum of the parts. The isolation of the parts whether into specialties, racial groups, denominations, socio-economic classes, ideological camps, or international blocs ultimately impoverishes the whole and leads to sickness. The empirical and spiritual discovery of interdependence is a moment of enormous significance for church and society.

Because of modern technology we are now aware of the scope of the human crisis. Some things have to be drawn to the right scale in order to get a proper perspective. The crises facing church and society in America in the 1970s require a global scale. At stake is not simply the health of one world power, the leadership of a single nation, or the political system of one branch of the human community, but the very survival of life on this planet.

We are coming with incredible speed to the end of the "First Settlement" of this planet by man. The appearance of the human species is a relatively recent phenomenon compared to other forms of life. Perhaps older animal species took some pride in the emergence of nature's latest offspring, *homo sapiens*. Man was, after all, the culmination of a long and painful struggle of primitive creatures for self-consciousness. But the appearance of man with his enormous power over other forms of life and the way the human creature set about subduing the earth was hardly the source of continued celebration for the other species whose very existence was placed in jeopardy.

The physical environment intended as the womb for the human community has been so abused that it may now conspire to become mankind's tomb. Suddenly we are confronted with the harsh reality that the earth does not have unlimited resources. It will not endure continuous misuse. We live in a closed ecological system which requires wisdom, delicate care, and the recycling of basic supplies.

Subduing the earth has meant, unfortunately, the exploitation of nature and it has brought us to near catastrophe. It is obviously dangerous for the earth's survival to place in man's hands the complex tools of technology without sufficient wisdom, to trust to man's control the frightening powers of matter without adequate moral responsibility, to allow individuals to accumulate enormous wealth without an accompanying sensitivity for the neighbor, and to clutter man's brain with more and more facts without developing his feelings and conscience.

The first settlement of the earth is approaching an end point. In a closed system options are running out. The great experiments to establish new societies (America in the West and Russia in the East) provide us with little comfort that wisdom will prevail over weaponry or humane aspirations over national power struggles. Perhaps our only hope is that the threats of catastrophy will provide the forge for the fusing of the human community, that the eleventh hour may break open to new relationships, that the eve of Apocalypse will prove to be the matrix from which is born a new epoch. Perhaps in the terror of judgment, in the collapse of pride and confidence, perhaps in a "confessional" of global disaster, men may hear another word and discover another possibility; perhaps in a moment of honest repentance another force may appear on this planet, a new generation pioneering the "second settlement of earth."

The present stage in the emergence of the human species is unique. Man is for the first time consciously determining his future evolution. The first settlement of earth has clearly demonstrated that man's development has been his own doing. No magic intervention from above, no pre-established fate from below can be blamed for the present condition of the world. Mankind faces the awful realization that the course of human society may be in human hands. We are free but responsible for our own future. We are free to create or destroy, free to subdue or renew creation. We are free to pursue our own selfish ends or seek the welfare of all of life. The realization of that unprecedented responsibility and freedom has been flung with such force onto the human species that it just might shock us into responsible behavior.

The second settlement of earth begins with the realization that there is no longer any escape from each other to new continents, to separate and isolated cultures, to independent national existences. Spaceship earth is a closed ecological system whose inhabitants must coexist, learn to handle their restricted supply of resources with care, and restore what they consume. All systems are dependent on each other. The second settlement requires a new set of priorities, a new breed of pioneers with the commitments and skills not of exploitation of new lands, but of creating a world community, facing each other

125

in this crowded complex, interlocking, planetary society. The second settlement of earth means the creation of a "symbiotic" world community where rich diversity is treasured as necessary for the health of the whole, where the weak and frail are protected because the functioning of the total environment depends on healthy subsystems. What is necessary is a community of interdependence based on mutual respect. We are not our brothers' keepers, but under God, our brothers' brothers! This is the scale and the urgency by which Christion education must deal with man in community in the 1970s.

NOTES AND REFERENCES

1. Aarne Siirala, *The Voice of Illness: A Study in Theology and Prophecy* (Philadelphia: Fortress Press, 1964), p. 123.
2. For an enlarged discussion of the argument in these paragraphs, see the author's chapter, "A Call for New Pioneers," in *The Continuing Quest*, ed. James Hofrenning (Minneapolis: Augsburg Publishing House 1970), pp. 131 ff.
3. Dietrich von Oppen, *The Age of the Person* (Philadelphia: Fortress Press, 1969), p. 19.
4. Abraham Maslow, *The Psychology of Science* (Chicago: Henry Regnery Co., 1966), p. 119.
5. Robert Ardrey, *African Genesis* (New York: Dell Publishing Co., 1961), p. 336.
6. Aarne Siirala, *Divine Humanness* (Philadelphia: Fortress Press, 1970), p. 97.
7. On Cruciform Reality, cf. Eugen Rosenstock-Huessy, *The Christian Future or The Modern Mind Outrun* (New York: Charles Scribner's Sons, 1946), pp. 167-71.
8. *Divine Humanness*, p. 139.
9. Ian Barbour, *Science and Secularity* (New York: Harper & Row, 1970), p. 75.

Chapter V

Educational Foundations

EDWARD W. UTHE

"Educational foundations," as the term is commonly used, includes a variety of subjects related to the theory and practice of education.[1] Some are derived from independent disciplines which offer insights that can be applied to education. The discipline of philosophy is regarded as a possible source for insights about such matters as the nature of knowledge and the fundamental purposes of education. Psychology supplies principles about learning and learners that can be applied in designing and implementing educational activities. Sociology is a source of information about the social systems which are the settings for education—the nation, the community, the school, the class. The fields of curriculum and instruction have developed a body of guiding principles and conventional wisdom used in planning and implementing educational programs. Past and present educational policies and practices, the organization and administration of schools and educational programs are examined and interpreted by historians, political scientists, and economists.

Foundations for a central objective for the church's educational ministry include all these disciplines, with the insights they bring to bear on education in general and on education within the church in particular. An additional foundation of great significance for the church's educational task is theology. In this yearbook, there are extensive considerations from these separate foundational disciplines. Therefore these subjects will receive minimal attention in this chapter.

In formulating a central objective for the church's educational ministry in the parish, contributions of all the disciplines mentioned above must be taken into consideration. There must be recognition that each field of study offers insights that are helpful at many points in the overall process of developing and implementing an educational program and that some insights are more pertinent than others at particular points in the overall process.[2]

Formulating a central objective involves making choices from the range of guiding principles offered by the various foundational disciplines. Some choices are made on the basis of appropriateness or suitability, for not all guiding principles are equally appropriate for all situations and subjects. There are differences between teaching analytic philosophy, governmental organization, cabinetmaking, motor vehicle operation, musical composition. There are differences in the institutional settings in which education takes place. There are differences in the motivations which lead persons to participate in various types of educational programs. Therefore, the formulation of a central objective must take into account what is to be taught, where and under what conditions is it to be taught, and who is to be involved in the teaching-learning process. It must utilize those guiding principles which are appropriate.[3]

The guiding principle of appropriateness is helpful because insights offered by various foundational disciplines are not always consistent with one another. Psychological studies which identify desirable teaching strategies and sociological studies that identify feasible teaching strategies sometimes produce different recommendations. Even within a single discipline there are divergent and sometimes irreconcilable viewpoints. In the field of educational philosophy it is difficult to resolve the differences between the idealist and the pragmatist schools without doing violence to one or both. Such dilemmas are sometimes resolved by recognizing that different viewpoints may be particularly appropriate for given situations.

In the formulation of a central objective, there must be awareness of major contributions from various fields of specialization and identification of their contributions which are most relevant. A central objective must make use of contributions which (1) help to develop a concept of educational program, (2) help to develop concepts of the nature of learning and teaching, (3) help to identify content to be included in an educational program, and (4) help to identify an educational strategy which makes content meaningful to learners at various stages of development.

In the present chapter, an attempt will be made to limit the discussion of educational foundations to those which are not dealt with in other yearbook chapters and which are especially relevant for educational objectives. The four items listed in the preceding paragraph provide criteria for selecting content for this chapter. First, there will be offered descriptive *definitions* of the elements which enter into any discussion of objectives. Second, the *functions* of a central objective will be identified and *A Central Objective for Educational Ministry in the Parish: ALC and LCA*[4] will be examined in light of those functions. Third, there will be a consideration of techniques which can be used in the *validation* of a central objective. The closing section of the chapter will deal briefly with the place of a central objective in the overall *process of developing an educational program.*

The text of the chapter will attempt a straightforward discussion of these four topics without examining in detail their many facets and ramifications. Discussion of such considerations will be incorporated in footnotes. Extensive quotations from pertinent sources will likewise be relegated to footnote status. Readers who have a special interest in topics discussed briefly in the chapter text are encouraged to look to the footnotes for detailed information and for sources of additional information.

Definitions

An educational program's central objective is not an isolated entity. It must be seen in its relationships. It stems, presumably, from a concept of education. It is meant to guide an educational program. The program normally will provide for instruction or teaching and, it is hoped, will eventuate in learning. Since these terms will be used in the discussion that follows and since it is possible to interpret them in various ways, they require definition at this point.

"Education" is a term which has a wide range of meanings.[5] Often the word is used in a way that equates it either with schooling or with learning. Education includes more than schooling and it does not include all learning. Education involves some intentional focusing of attention and is thus distinct from accidental or incidental learning. It involves some structurnig of experience with a view to developing desired understandings, attitudes, or skills. One unabridged dictionary defines education broadly as "the act or process of providing with knowledge, skill, competence, or usually desirable qualities of behavior or character or of being so provided especially by a formal course of study, instruction, or training."[6] A broader and more functional definition of education might be: conscious efforts to develop in oneself and in others understandings, attitudes, and skills which are believed to be of value.

"Christian education" is also defined in a variety of ways. Some examples: the teaching ministry of the church," "the education of Christians," "the communication of the gospel," "the transmission of the Christian heritage."[7] There are different answers to the question of what is *Christian* in Christian education. Is it the content? The style? The intent? The persons who are involved? The sponsoring institution? A combination of these? Here the term Christian education will be used to refer to attempts by persons to develop understandings, attitudes, and skills which they believe to be related to Christian faith.

In these definitions of education and Christian education, the emphasis is on the person who is learning. The definition of "educational program" places approximately equal emphasis on the activity of the learner and the activity of the institution (or persons) who design and provide educational program. "Curriculum" is a synonym for educational program but is not used here because in its popular usage in the church "curriculum" is often equated with materials. Educational program consists of the total combination of elements (objectives, resources, teaching, procedures, persons) utilized by an institution to implement its educational objectives.

Teaching or instruction is normally a component of an educational program.[8] It should not be thought of as any single technique of teaching (such as a lecture or self-instruction)), but rather as the structuring of environments with a view to facilitating learning. Teaching or instruction is based on objectives (either explicit or implicit), and has a plan for helping learners make progress toward the objectives. It can take place only when learners assent to it.

"Learning" may be defined as any change in behavior.[9] The change may be desirable or undesirable, depending on the criteria used to evaluate it. Learning may be conscious or unconscious, manifest or latent, intended or accidental. It may be produced by instruction or by random experiences. It occurs because it has some utility for the learner.

An "objective" is an intended outcome of instruction of an educational program. The actual outcome, of course, may be quite different from the intended outcome. Objectives may be stated on several different levels of precision.[10] They may be stated as broad aims or goals, as a central objective for an educational program. They may be refined and stated more exactly for major elements of a total program, for units of study, or for single sessions.

It is desirable to state objectives in terms of observable behaviors, but it is not always possible to do so. Any statement of a broad aim implies a repertoire of a great many behaviors. An analysis of the broad aim should yield a specification of observable behaviors. Vernon Anderson's chapter in this yearbook discusses formulation of specific behavioral objectives and suggests references dealing with objectives at this level. Some of the major concerns of Christian education deal with matters that are not subject to observation, since they lie in the realm of the relationship between the person and God. Of objectives in this realm, the most that can be said is that certain observable behaviors are more likely to be associated with them than are other behaviors.

Functions of a Central Objective

The basic function of a central objective for the church's educational ministry is to provide a foundation for an educational program, to provide guidance for decisions which must be made as an educational program is developed.[11] In order to perform this function, a central objective must (1) articulate a concept of educational program, (2) articulate a concept of the nature of teaching and learning within that program, (3) provide a touchstone for content to be included in the program, and (4) identify an educational strategy which makes content meaningful to learners at various stages of development. *A Central Objective for Educational Ministry in the Parish: ALC and LCA* will be examined to discover how it performs these functions.

The statement begins with the phrase, "The central objective for educational ministry in The American Lutheran Church and the Lutheran Church in America . . ." (p. 31). There is a clear identification of the educating institutions which are to provide an educational program based on the objective, namely the corporate bodies known as The American Lutheran Church and the Lutheran Church in America, and, by implication, parishes of these two denominations.

The phrase "educational ministry" is essential, for it articulates a concept of educational program. The document containing the central objective devotes several pages to an explication of the concept of educational ministry. "Educational ministry is viewed as one aspect of the total work of the church; it should strengthen that work and enhance the life of the church . . . Educational ministry is concerned with the growth of persons in Christian faith and life. Organizationally [at present], no one unit of the church has responsibility for the total educational ministry of the church" (pp. 2-3).

Educational ministry presents a holistic concept of educational program. It is the sum total of all the educational activities of a congregation. For this reason, the program is to be integrated rather than fragmented. Various elements of the educational program are to be designed and implemented in relationship to one another. By designing a total program, it should be possible to avoid competition and duplication and to bring a greater degree of coherence and cohesiveness to program implementation.[12]

The educational ministry concept recognizes the powerful influence of the social system (the congregation) in which Christian education takes place. It recognizes that objectives of the educational program can be reinforced when the congregation as a whole, in the many-faceted aspects of its life and work, is guided by convictions and values which are consistent with the educational objectives. It recognizes that a style of congregational life which contradicts the educational objectives can nullify efforts in Christian education.[13]

Articulation of a concept of the relationship between learning and instruction involves a concept of how learning takes place, a concept of the role of instruction in the learning process, and a concept of the qualitative nature of learning. The relationship between learning and instruction is expressed in a short phrase in the central objective. "The central objective . . . *shall be to assist persons* . . ." In other words, learning is done by the person. No teacher, no institution, no group can do it. Learning is change in the behavior of an individual. It may take place in a group context. It may occur nearly simultaneously for several persons in a group. However, the criterion by which one judges whether learning has taken place is whether there is a change in the behavior of the individuals who make up the group.[14]

Instruction, or guidance of learning activities, takes the form of assisting persons to learn. Again, learning is something done by the learner. Those who accept some responsibility as leaders within the educational program can do no more than help the learner to learn. To phrase objectives in terms of assisting learners is to place learners at center stage. This is quite different from phraseology which puts the spotlight on the teacher or on the educating agency.

The qualitative nature of learning is identified in a further phrase in the central objective: ". . . to assist persons to *perceive, respond to, and participate in* . . ." Learning is action and process. The objective is to help persons become involved in a continuing process rather than to help them acquire a fixed repertoire of behaviors.[15]

Guidance for content to be included in an educational program must be provided by its central objective. Such guidance is provided by the explicit theological reference: ". . . to assist persons to perceive, respond to, and participate in *God's continuing activity and revelation, particularly in Jesus Christ, in the human and Christian communities* . . ."[16] The statement is Christocentric and theoultimate. God's continuing activity and revelation is the reason for being of the church's educational ministry. His activity and revelation is perceived and responded to in the context of the realm of creation (the human community) and in the church, the Christian community of believers. The community of believers also exists within the realm of creation. It has within the context of creation, a distinctive mission and way of life.

The norm for perceiving and responding to God's activity and revelation is none other than Jesus Christ. His life, death, and resurrection express most clearly God's relationship to mankind. In order to perceive and respond to God's activity, Christians must be familiar with and able to interpret the biblical witness and the way the church has interpreted it. In order to perceive, respond to, and participate in God's activity in the Christian community, Christians must participate meaningfully in the life and work of the church. Thus, some elements of content central to the church's educational ministry are the redemptive work of Christ, his life and teachings, the witness of the Bible, the teachings and heritage of the church, the contemporary life of the church.

Providing an educational approach that makes content relevant to learners at various levels of development is the fourth function of a central objective. An educational program can reach learners only if they perceive that it deals with matters that are significant to them.[17] The central objective proposes an approach which assists persons to be involved with the content of the program ". . . as they deal with their continual life involvements of being a person, relating to persons and groups, and living in society, culture, and the physical universe." The concept of continual life involvements provides a point of contact between content and the learner's experiences.[18] The continual life involvement concept originated in inter-Lutheran educational planning done in the late 1950s by the predecessor bodies of the Lutheran Church in America.[19] Since that time it has been used in curriculum development by Lutheran churches in several different countries. Experience has demonstrated its usefulness for curriculum development. Its validity is being evaluated in the Lutheran Longitudinal Study of Religious Development. The findings of that study are to be reported in a fourth Christian education yearbook. (For a more complete description of the concept, see pp. 19-29 of the central objective document.)

Continual life involvements are aspects of human experience which a person encounters by virtue of the fact that he is a human being in contemporary North American society. The three major dimensions listed in the central objective are divided into thirteen areas and fifty-four subareas. For example, the areas under the major category of relating to persons and groups are: relating to other individuals as persons, relating to one's family, relating to small groups, and relating to large groups. The area of family relationships is further divided into subareas of role differentiation, levels of affective relationships, and empathy and compassion, tension and conflict. (See pp. 33-36 of the central objective document for a complete outline of continual life involvements.)

Continual life involvements are lifelong. Their manifestations change and responses to them change, but the area of experience or involvement is inescapable under all but the most extraordinary circumstances. Relationships with one's family, for example, change in relationship to one's age and with the various factors that affect family life. They are different for the childless couple than they are for the couple who have many children. They are different for the unmarried adult (who still has a family of origin, more limited immediate family relationships, and perhaps surrogate family relationships) than they are for the married person. They are different for the infant, the child, the youth, the parent, and the grandparent. Yet the family area of life is inevitably present and calls for involvement.

The central objective document includes both an outline of continual life involvements and an outline which states points of Christian perspective on each involvement. The Christian perspective outline is the first step in indicating points of contact between life experiences and the Christian witness. To illustrate: the first subarea life involvement in the dimension of being a person is "developing a sense of personal identity, which involves self-image" (p. 33). The Christian perspective for this life involvement is "developing a sense of personal identity in the light of having been created in God's image, which involves regarding oneself as a child of God." This basic statement of Christian perspecitve provides a foundation for the educational program at various age levels to deal with the Christian perspective on the continual life involvement.[20] (See pp. 37-43 of the central objective document for a complete outline of continual life involvements in Christian perspective.)

Validation of a Central Objective

Validity of a central objective is established by using external criteria to test the adequacy of what it purports to do and to be.[21] There are three aspects of validation: (1) validation in terms of function, (2) validation in terms of substance, and (3) validation in terms of structure.

Validating a central objective in terms of function is the process of

135

ascertaining whether a central objective in fact does what it is designed to do, and how well it does it. The questions to be asked are: Does the central objective provide a foundation and guidance for decisions required by subsequent steps in program development? Does it present a concept of educational program and to what extent can that concept be implemented in program design? How adequate is its concept of the nature of learning and teaching and to what extent can that concept be implemented in program design? Does the central objective in fact provide guidance concerning content for educational program? How well does its strategy for making content relevant to learners' lives at various stages of development operate? Validation in terms of function is measured empirically by the experience of using the central objective as a basis for program development (process evaluation).

Substantive validation of a central objective is more difficult. It can be done empirically by ascertaining the effects of the program developed on the basis of the central objective and determining whether the effects are consistent with the content of the objective. Such a procedure requires several assumptions which may or may not be justified: that the program developed on the basis of the objective is in truth an unfolding and implementation of the objective, that the program has been adequately and properly implemented at the local level, and that evaluation instruments provide valid and reliable measures of the extent to which the central objective is realized in the lives of learners. This is the approach of product evaluation.

Another approach to content validation hinges on the assumption that a central objective should express the most commonly held convictions and values of the educating community, which in this case consists of members of congregations of The American Lutheran Church and the Lutheran Church in America. This, in turn, requires prior assumptions that educational decisions are essentially value decisions and that they ought to be based on the prevailing sentiment of the educating community. The first of these assumptions is supported by the fact that educational discourse for the most part has a "should" or "ought" quality which expresses value judgments.[22] The second assumption is supported by the fact that educational priorities historically conform to the dominant values of the educating community. Educational ideas and practices inconsistent with prevailing values receive limited acceptance and implementation despite the strenuous efforts of their advocates.[23] The way to measure the content validity of a central objective is to have a representative cross section of persons (or, perhaps, of leaders) in the educating community study the objective and indicate the extent to which they are in agreement with it.

Structural validation of a central objective can be performed by means of philosophical analysis.[24] This involves a linguistic analysis which determines whether the terms used in the objective are unambiguous and whether the statements made have meaning and are verifiable. It also involves a logical analysis which determines whether conclusion-type statements contained in the objective are supported by the premises (implicit and explicit) and whether the premises themselves are justified. Another type of structural validation could be performed by identifying the assumptions (about man, education, the educating community, and the Christian life) imbedded in the objective, evaluating the validity and consistency of those assumptions, and determining whether the objective is an adequate unfolding of the implications of those assumptions.

Clearly, validation of a central objective is an imposing task. Of the various approaches, process evaluation is perhaps the most necessary, the most useful, and the most possible. Procedural difficulties make product evaluation extremely difficult. Content evaluation and structural evaluation may yield contradictory results, because the convictions and values which permeate the educating community may not meet the structural evaluation requirements of logical clarity and consistency. Application of both these approaches is clouded with procedural difficulties.

The Process of Program Development

Formulation of a central objective for educational ministry in the parish is one step in program development. One way of attempting to create a valid objective is to lead up to the formulation of the objective with an examination and analysis of factors related to its content and substance. The major factors are emphases and trends in the life of the church (congregations and the church-at-large), emphases and trends in the interpretation of the gospel (theology), and developments in the environment in which the church and its members live (society). The study of these factors should yield an identification on concerns and emphases which should shape a central objective. Such a study was conducted prior to the formulation of the central objective and its findings were used in the process of formulating the central objective.[25]

Several sequential activities are required for the development and implementation of a program based on a central objective.[26] The first of these is expansion of the objective with specific reference to the persons to be served. An inclusive program will attempt to serve groups of persons who can be identified and differentiated on the basis of their dominant characteristics. If the program envisions serving persons of all ages, one useful method of identifying major characteristics and of expanding the central objective in terms of the person to be served is to develop age-level objectives on the basis of the central objective.[27] This has been done in the ALC-LCA program development project. If the population to be served contains groups that can be distinguished from one another on the basis of such factors as socioeconomic situation, mental or emotional limitations, theological and social viewpoints, strong and distinctive subcultural characteristics, then consideration should be given to expanding the central objective with specific reference to these various groups. It is anticipated that this will be done in the ALC-LCA project to the extent that resources are available and that there is justification for making such distinctions.

Moving from statements of objectives to program design is the next step in the program development process. It involves further refinement of objectives, identification of learning experiences or processes likely to contribute to progress toward objectives, and identification of settings or channels which are (or may become) available as program elements and which offer potential for utilizing the desired learning experiences and processes. At the time of writing, the ALC-LCA project is engaged in this step of program development.

Steps which lie in the future include an analysis and specification of leadership needs of the program, identification of services and resources required for implementation of various channels to be used in the overall program of educational ministry, preparation and production of required services and resources,[28] cultivation and preparation of congregations for a progam of educational ministry, introduction of the program, and evaluation of the program.[29] While it is necessary to build program in this step-by-step fashion, there must also be a recognition of the need to make modifications in the program at any time when the need becomes evident.

NOTES AND REFERENCES

1. Several contributors discuss "educational foundations" in *Teachers College Record* vol. 71, no. 2 (December, 1969). The focus of their discussion is the place and organization of courses in educational foundations in programs of teacher preparation. Several of the contributors deal specifically with the problem of integrating psychological foundations and social foundations. One contributor moves the discussion forward by giving a functional definition of educational foundations as "policy-oriented knowledge" and a "sense of responsibility for disciplined use of such knowledge." He makes a distinction between normative or value issues on the one hand and means issues on the other. (James J. Shields, "Foundations of Education: Relevance Redefined," pp. 193-194).

2. Textbooks in the field of curriculum planning indicate referents for the term "educational foundations" in curriculum planning. The table of contents in the text by Saylor and Alexander includes chapters on "Curriculum Practices in American Schools," "Basic Issues in Curriculum Planning" (including philosophy), "Forces that Influence Curriculum Planning," "Social Aims as a Factor in Curriculum Planning," "The Learning Process and Curriculum Planning" (J. Galen Saylor and William M. Alexander, *Curriculum Planning for Better Teaching and Learning* [New York: Holt, Rinehart & Winston, Inc., 1954], p. iv). Smith, Stanley, and Shores, in a section of "Theoretical Curriculum Issues," include chapters titled "The Source of Authority in Curriculum Building," "Educational Objectives: Individual or Social," "The Social Function of Education," "Criteria of Content." In a chapter on "The Validation of Educational Objectives," the topics dealt with are: "the criterion of social adequacy," "the criterion of basic human needs," "the criterion of democratic ideals," "the criterion of consistency and noncontradiction," "the criterion of behavioristic interpretation." (B. Othanel Smith, William O. Stanley, and J. Harlan Shores, *Fundamentals of Curriculum Development* Rev. ed. [New York: World Book Co., 1957], pp. xi, xv, xvi). Taba's section on foundations of curriculum development includes chapters on "Current Conceptions of the Functions of the School," "The Analysis of Society," "The Analysis of Culture," "Learning Theories as a Foundation of the Curriculum," "The Concept of Development, Intelligence and Mental Development," "Social and Cultural Learning," and "The Nature of Knowledge."

(Hilda Taba, *Curriculum Development: Theory and Practice* [New York: Harcourt, Brace & World, 1962], pp. ix-xi). The broad scope of curriculum foundations is illustrated by the entire content of *Curriculum Guidelines in an Era of Change* by Vernon E. Anderson (New York: Ronald Press, 1969).

3. Educational planners invariably attempt to find implications which hard data and established theories from the social and behavioral sciences offer for education. However, there is increasing caution about claiming validity for such extrapolations. For example, there is serious questioning of applying to classroom situations sophisticated learning theories developed on the basis of animal experimentation and experimentation with certain types of human learning in carefully controlled laboratory situations. While there is a need and desire to base practice on pertinent findings from various behavioral sciences, it must be recognized that serious questions can be raised about many such applications. For a discussion of the problems involved, see Samuel Messick, "Can You Do Real Research in the Real World?" in *Untangling the Tangled Web of Education* (Educational Testing Service: Princeton, N.J., 1969), pp. 21-26.

4. *A Central Objective for Educational Ministry in the Parish: ALC and LCA* (Philadelphia: Board of Parish Education of the Lutheran Church in America, 1969).

5. Here is a sampling of some interesting "definitions" of education. "Intelligence appears to be the thing that enables a man to get along without education. Education appears to be the thing that enables a man to get along without the use of his intelligence." (Albert E. Wiggam in *Familiar Quotations by John Bartlett*, 13th. rev. ed. [Boston: Little, Brown and Co., 1955], p. 857).

"Education is a thing of which only a few are capable; teach as you will only a small percentage will profit by your most zealous energy" (George Gissing, quoted in Bartlett, p. 774). "Education has for its object the formation of character" (Herbert Spencer, quoted in Bartlett, p. 614). "Nothing in education is so astonishing as the amount of ignorance it accumulates in the form of inert facts." (Henry B. Adams, quoted in Bartlett, p. 697) "Education is the instruction of the intellect in the laws of Nature . . . and the fashioning of the affections and of the will into an earnest and loving desire to move in harmony with those laws." (Thomas H. Huxley, quoted in Bartlett, p. 633) "Perhaps the most valuable result of all education is the ability to make yourself do the thing you have to do, when it ought to be done, whether you like it or not." (Thomas H. Huxley, quoted in Bartlett, p. 633)

6. Philip B. Gove, ed., *Webster's Third New International Dictionary of the English Language, Unabridged* (Springfield, Mass.: G. & C. Merriam Co., 1961), p. 723. *The Random House Dictionary* gives this

broad definition: "The act or process of imparting or acquiring general knowledge, developing the powers of reasoning and judgment, and generally preparing oneself or others intellectually for mature life." (Jess Stein, ed., *The Random House Dictionary of the English Language,* Unabridged edition [New York: Random House, 1969], p. 454.)

The great variety of dictionary and other definitions of education invariably causes confusion in discussions of the subject. One author maintains that one's definition of education ". . . . largely depends on some set of prior philosophic convictions about nature and human nature, man and society. The problem, of course, is that since there is a multiplicity of philosophic viewpoints there is no one clear, concise, agreed-upon definition of education. Some of the definitions most widely agreed upon have the greatest number of meanings, and possibly the least meaning as a consequence." (Charles J. Brauner and Hobert W. Burns, *Problems in Education and Philosophy* [Englewood Cliffs, N.J.: Prentice-Hall, 1965], p. 15.) Current unabridged dictionaries give a variety of definitions which are based on current usage of the term "education" and which are not entirely consistent with one another. The "Definitions" section of this chapter attempts to delineate the meaning of the term as it is used in this discussion, recognizing that other definitions are used in other contexts.

7. Surprisingly, many treatises on Christian education neglect to define their subject, apparently on the assumption that everyone interested in the subject agrees on what it is. Writers who make an effort to define it often present an objective disguised as a definition. To illustrate: "Christian education is the process through which the church seeks to enable persons to understand, accept, and exemplify the Christian faith and way of life" (Lawrence C. Little, *Foundations for a Philosophy of Christian Education* [New York: Abingdon, 1962], p. 103). "It is the systematic, critical examination and reconstruction of relations between persons, guided by Jesus' assumption that persons are of infinite worth, and by the hypothesis of God, the Great Valuer of Persons." (George A. Coe, *What is Christian Education?* [New York: Charles Scribner's Sons, 1929], p. 296.) "Christian education may be understood as the product of the creative interpenetration of a historical context, an active content, a personal process of growth, an educational science and art, and a working theology." (Wayne R. Hood, *Understanding Christian Education* [New York: Abingdon Press, 1970], p. 398.) "Christian education is the process by which persons are confronted with and controlled by the Christian gospel. It involves the efforts of the Christian community to guide both young and adult toward an ever richer possession of the Christian heritage and fuller participation in the life and work of the Christian fellowship." (Paul H. Vieth, *The Church and Christian Education* [St. Louis: Bethany Press, 1947], p. 52.)

8. It would be desirable to find a substitute for the term "instruction" because of emotional loading the word carries for many people. Since no satisfactory substitute appears to be available, the term will be used with the meaning indicated in the text. There are some descriptions that may help to elucidate the concept intended by the term. One source describes curriculum in a way similar to the way this chapter defines instruction. It guides experience ". . . toward fulfillment of the purpose of Christian education." "It is . . . not the entire social situation within which the person acts and with which he is interacting, but rather that part which is consciously planned. (Special Committee on the Curriculum Guide, *A Guide for Curriculum in Christian Education* [Chicago: Division of Christian Education, National Council of Churches of Christ in the U.S.A., 1955].) Chapter titles in one of the yearbooks of the Association for Supervision and Curriculum Development help to convey the scope of the concept of instruction: "The teacher selects, plans, and organizes." "The teacher introduces learning tasks." "The teacher helps the learner interpret his experiences." "The teacher utilizes group forces." (Association for Supervision and Curriculum Development, *Learning and the Teacher, 1959 Yearbook* [Washington, D.C.: The Association for Supervision and Curriculum Development, 1959], pp. v-vi.)

9. A more technical widely-quoted definition of learning is: "Learning is the process by which an activity originates or is changed through reacting to an encountered situation, provided that the characteristics of the change in activity cannot be explained on the basis of native response tendencies, maturation, or temporary states of the organism (e.g., fatigue, drugs, etc.)." (Ernest R. Hilgard, *Theories of Learning* 2nd ed. [New York: Appleton-Century-Crofts, Inc., 1956], p. 3.)

10. There are many ways of identifying levels of objectives. Burton identifies four levels: (1) "The broad social purposes or objectives of society . . . and hence the remote, general aims or purposes of education." (2) "The more specific social purposes or objectives of given social groups." This includes both overall objectives for the school and more specific objectives for segments of it. (3) "The teacher's purposes or objectives. These are . . . the results the teacher desires for his pupils." (4) "The pupils' objectives or purposes . . . the immediate things the learner wishes to accomplish." (William H. Burton, *The Guidance of Learning Activities* 3rd ed. [New York: Appleton-Century Crofts, Inc., 1962], pp. 125-127.) Burton warns against confusing the general objectives of education and the immediate objectives of units of study (see pp. 128-129). A central objective for educational ministry is almost identical in kind to what Burton calls general objectives of education. Specific instructional objectives are illustrated by those developed in connection with the project on National Assessment of Educational Progress and the inventory of instructional objectives being

developed by the Instructional Objectives Exchange at the Center for the Study of Evaluation at the Graduate School of Education, University of California at Los Angeles.

11. The Project on Instruction of the National Education Association describes the function of an overall aim thus: "The aims of education should serve as a guide for making decisions about curriculum organization as well as about all other aspects of the instructional program . . . The objectives of the school, with a clear statement of priorities, should give direction to all curriculum planning." (National Education Association, *Planning and Organizing for Teaching* [Washington, D.C.: The Association, 1963], pp. 166, 168.) Taba discusses general aims in similar fashion: "The chief function of stating aims on such general levels is to provide an orientation to the main emphasis in educational programs. Aims on this level establish what might be described as a philosophy of education . . . The general aims can be satisfied only if individuals acquire certain knowledge, skills, techniques, and attitudes." (*Curriculum Development: Theory and Practice*, p. 196.) Herrick notes that objectives indicate direction, scope, and emphasis in an educational program. (James B. Macdonald, Dan W. Anderson, and Frank B. May, eds., *Strategies of Curriculum Development. Selected Writings of the Late Virgil E. Herrick* [Columbus: Charles E. Merrill Books, 1965], pp. 91-96 *passim.*)

Wyckoff applies this concept of the function of a central objective to Christian education. "The solution proposed here . . . is that a basic objective be established as the fundamental guide to policy, and that all other types of objectives be subordinated to it as they perform their proper functions or basic function, the focus providing perspective for the entire educational process . . . One objective, in a comprehensive and meaningful setting, may be used in the broadest way to guide and evaluate curriculum plans and procedures . . . The basic objective is thus a policy statement intended as a guide for the whole Christian education process . . . [Its strength is in] its ability to give unity, direction, and selectivity to the entire educational plan." (D. Campbell Wyckoff, *Theory and Design of Christian Education* [Philadelphia: Westminster Press, 1961], pp. 61, 62.)

Three functions are assigned to the overall objectives developed in the Cooperative Curriculum Project of the National Council of Churches: (1) "To chart the direction in which the educational experiences should be planned." (2) "To serve as a standard or measure by which the short-term goals, the ways and means employed in the curriculum, and the resources which implement the curriculum may be planned." (3) "To serve as a means of evaluation of the curriculum." That objective is viewed as possessing two major characteristics in that it emphasizes the life-long nature of Christian education while recognizing "differences in awareness and response at various

143

stages . . . in terms of maturity and appropriateness of expression" and in that it is "firmly in the Christian perspective and formulated in terms of the Christian vocabulary." It is stated that "The value of the objective is that it provides direction and perspective for the entire educational ministry. It gives unity, direction, and selectivity to the curriculum." (Cooperative Curriculum Project, National Council of Churches of Christ in the U.S.A., *A Design for Teaching-Learning* [St. Louis: Bethany Press, 1967], pp. 8, 9, 11.)

12. A number of denominations are attempting to design and implement this type of educational program. A single book, *A Dynamic Church*, is to be used as the foundation for all new program suggestions and materials prepared for Southern Baptist congregations for the period 1969-1973. Development of this program was preceded by studies of tasks and relationships of various units within the Southern Baptist Convention. (See *Facts and Trends*, vol. 14, no. 5, p. 4 [May, 1970], published by The Sunday School Board of the Southern Baptist Convention.)

There is practical and theoretical justification for such an approach. ". . . although each educational experience is related to an ultimate objective, it takes place within a limited period of time and has a separate existence of its own. Some means must be found to relate these [various] educational experiences . . . There is in effect a weaving of educational experiences into a fabric or organization which will have a dual effect. The organization will give added meaning and significance to each educational experience, and each educational experience will in turn help build and give significance to the organization [of educational experiences]." Benjamin S. Bloom, "Ideas, Problems, and Methods of Inquiry," in *The Integration of Educational Experiences*, Fifty-Seventh Yearbook of The National Society for the Study of Education, ed. Nelson B. Henry (Chicago: University of Chicago Press, 1958), pp. 90-91.

13. Investigations in the field of social psychology and organizational development increasingly support the common sense observation that the convictions and values which pervade the life of an organization exert a more powerful influence than its overt teaching. Ellis Nelson's recent analysis of Christian education *Where Faith Begins*, (Richmond: John Knox Press, 1967), makes extensive use of these concepts. Some of his key ideas are expressed in the following excerpts:

"My thesis is that faith is communicated by a community of believers and that the meaning of faith is developed by its members out of their history, by their interaction with each other, and in relation to the events that take place in their lives . . . The clue that we obtain from these social scientists is the power of the human group, tribe, or subculture to form the basic personality structure of children and the way the social-interactional process among adults formulates questions about, and supplies answers to, the meaning of the past (history), the present (morals, customs, beliefs), and the future (end of history and life after death) . . . All societies . . . are made up of small organized and semiorganized groups of people. These primary societies are most effective in transmitting the cultural patterns of thought and action, in forming the selfhood of individuals, and in providing a place where the individual can establish and maintain a style of life different from that of surrounding culture . . . The first thing we have to do in this approach is to remove from our minds the notion that the communication of the Christian faith is directly dependent upon any instructional agencies or methods and fix in our minds the idea that faith is fostered by a community of believers, usually a congregation. Instruction is a necessary part of the life of the congregation, but instruction must be related to the life of the congregation." (pp. 10, 18, 38, 183.)

A statement developed by a study group of St. Stephen's Episcopal parish, Washington, D.C. suggests that in at least some congregations members are aware of the influence of the total educating community: "It is assumed that the education process of the church is not a special job or program within the life of the church, but that it *is* the life of church. The church is a process of redemption which is constantly both forming and expressing her own newness of life. The 'becoming' of the church *is* Christian education.

"We must assume, also, that this process has more to do with what the church does than with what it says. No amount of 'preaching' or 'teaching' can impart Christian formation if this formation is not, at the same time, what we are. This is why Christian education programs in the past have oftentimes paid the next generation out in false coin, because we were trying to impart something we did not live. And the new generation learned from the inauthenticity of our lives and discounted our words accordingly. Consequently, we must first overcome the pretension that we have already 'achieved' Christianity and are, from this vantage point, going to teach it to others. We must realize that Christian education includes us all. We are all involved in becoming Christians." (Rosemary R. Reuther, "Education in the Sociological Situation, U.S.A.," in *Does the Church Know How To Teach?* Kendig B. Cully, ed. [New York: Macmillan Co., 1970], p. 89.)

John W. Westerhoff III writes in the same vein: "Those who wish to limit church education to instruction in a school classroom have ignored their responsibility . . . Christian education is . . . a way of approaching or dealing with everything a church does . . . for every occasion or event is potentially educational.

"What I am suggesting is a radical shift in the way we think about education and the role of those responsible for it. Once we have freed ourselves from identifying church education with church schooling we are on the way toward discovering that new way to look at Christian education." (*Values for Tomorrow's Children. An Alternative Future for Education in the Church* [Philadelphia and Boston: Pilgrim Press, 1970], pp. 64-65.)

The influence of the climate of an educational institution on learning in the instance of public education is explored in *The Unstudied Curriculum: Its Impact on Childen,* Norman V. Overly, ed. (Washington, D.C.: Association for Supervision and Curriculum Development, 1970).

14. It is important to observe the distinction between educational objectives and goals for a group. It may be said that the goal of the church as a corporate body is to fulfill its mission in the world (leaving "mission" undefined for the moment). Certainly the church's educational efforts will then be related to the fulfillment of mission, but they can hardly be identical with the fulfillment of mission. Educational activities can help individuals, in the context of the congregation, to acquire understandings, skills, and attitudes which can be used to further the mission of the church. Education thus becomes an aide or an enabler in the service of a larger cause. Another way to say it is that education cannot cure all the ills of society, but it can help to equip persons with knowledge, skills, and attitudes that can be used to improve society. (See also footnote 9 for the definition of learning.)

15. Along with the current emphasis on stating educational objectives in terms of observable behaviors there is an emphasis on thinking of objectives in developmental, process terms. "Objectives are developmental, representing roads to travel rather than terminal points. Objectives need to be conceived in terms of a continuity of growth over a long period of time and through different contexts, each more exacting than the previous one, rather than as terminal points . . . This principle means also that the achievement of educational objectives needs to be planned for continuity and with a full appreciation of the developmental steps within that continuity." (*Curriculum Development: Theory and Practice,* p. 203.) "The immediate objectives are . . . the directional-process goals toward which the pupil grows by achieving increasing levels of maturity, insight, skill, and understanding. . . . The pupil progresses along the line of development as his capacity and maturity permit." (*The Guidance of Learning Activities,* pp. 130-131.)

There are two ways of thinking about process objectives. One way is to think of them as directional objectives that point to broad areas of personal growth and development. Very often, however, the term "process" is used to designate the development of specified skills. J. Cecil Parker and Louis J. Rubin present models for teaching process as content. The processes are such things as accumulating data, performing deductive and inductive analysis, consolidating and integrating the

146

material (*Process as Content: Curriculum Design and the Application of Knowledge* [Chicago: Rand McNally, 1966], pp. 50-66). Jerome Bruner's concept of process involves development of identifiable (and measurable) skills related to the basic structure of the subject being studied. See *The Process of Education*. [New York: Vintage Books, 1960].)

16. The theological content of the central objective is discussed at length in the yearbook chapters on the doctrine of the church, God's activity, and man and his community. Minimal attention is given to these concerns in the present chapter.

17. The history of modern educational theory and practice, from John Amos Comenius to Jerome Bruner, reveals a persistent search for ways to help pupils grasp the meaning of what they learn and understand and how it affects their lives. One of the causes of unrest among high school and college students is that their education does not do this. It is a truism that only low level learning can take place if students are not able to find personal meaning in the subject under consideration. In writing an educational prescription for the future, John Goodlad suggests: "Get into the curriculum problems likely to be facing young adults in 1980. These persons are currently in the primary years of schooling. If we were to begin now, we could plan for them a junior high curriculum organized around problems of population, poverty, pollution, and many more. Such a counter-cyclical program would not be organized around subjects at all but might well reach these young people in ways that present school fare seem not to do." "The Educational Program to 1980 and Beyond," in *Prospective Changes in Society by 1980*, Designing Education for the Future, vol. 1, eds. E. L. Morphet and C. O. Ryan (New York: Citation Press, 1966), pp. 57-58.

18. The concept of continual life involvements is a psycho-social concept with resemblances to some well-known analyses of human life in society. It is similar to the "Persistent Life Situation" curriculum concept developed by Florence Stratemeyer and associates at Teachers College, Columbia University. Robert Havighurst's concept of developmental tasks and their implications for education relate to the continual life involvement outline in that the shape and content of the life involvements change at different periods in the life span. Erik Erikson's "seven stages of man," a psychoanalytic approach to the developmental task concept, also can be related to the continual life involvement outline (with primary reference to the personal identity section). The continual life involvement concept provides a curriculum design base which recognizes the validity of both the individual needs and societal needs approaches to curriculum development and which provides a way of relating subject matter content to them significantly.

147

(For explication of these approaches to curriculum, see *Fundamentals of Curriculum Development*, chs. 5, 6, 22, 23.)

The continual life involvement concept also provides a way of meeting the need for an educational program to facilitate integration of learning within the person. (See the quotation from Bloom in note 11.) Bloom further suggests that a many-faceted program needs "integrative threads" to enable such integration to take place within the learner. As criteria for such integrative threads, he suggests the following: (1) They ". . . must have continuing usefulness in relation to a great variety of problems and questions." (2) They ". . . should be so chosen and organized that they can be altered, improved, and extended in meaning with time and future experience." (3) They should ". . . add meaning to experiences, to permit one to compare and contrast experiences which would otherwise be unrelated, and to permit one to relate past experiences to those that are taking place at the present." (4) They ". . . should be sufficiently comprehensive to extend over the entire range of subject matter or experience in some area of human endeavor." (5) They must be related to learners' lives, for ". . . only as the integrative threads are meaningful to the student and are used by him are they like to have any value for him." (*Ibid*, pp. 95-97.)

To deal with the problem in public education, John Goodlad has suggested the use of a two-dimensional grid. One dimension is the substantive, or content, area. The second is the behavioral. Theoretically an analysis of content and of behavior and of their interrelationships will yield "organized centers" for instruction that insure relevance. ("The Curriculum," in *Rational Planning in Curriculum and Instruction* [Washington, D.C.: National Education Association, 1967], pp. 27-28.)

The use of continual life involvements may make it possible for subject matter content to tap the emotive power of life's most significant situations and thereby enhance both cognitive and affective learning. See Richard M. Jones, *Fantasy and Feeling in Education* (New York: New York University Press, 1968).

19. See *The Functional Objectives for Christian Education, Volume I* (Philadelphia: Lutheran Boards of Parish Education, 1959).

20. The general educational problem of providing for relevance is perhaps more acute in religious education than in education outside the church. The problem is made more acute by contemporary questioning of the meaning of religion in a secularized world. The central objective for educational ministry attempts to deal with the problem by relating Christian faith to continual life involvements and by viewing continual life involvements in a Christian perspective. The approach is described in *A Central Objective for Educational Ministry in the Parish: ALC*

and LCA and is utilized in the age-level objectives which have been developed on the basis of that document.

21. Lawrence C. Little, *Foundations for a Philosophy of Christian Education* (New York: Abingdon Press, 1962), pp. 197-198 suggests seven "criteria for the formulation and evaluation of the general objectives of Christian education." (1) "Are the objectives *Christian?*" (2) "Are they *psychologically valid?*" (3) "Are they *relevant to all levels of development?*" (4) "Are they *dynamic* enough to inspire and motivate definite action *in real life situations?*" (5) "Are they such that progress toward their achievement is *measurable and subject to evaluation?*" (6) "Are the objectives *comprehensive* in scope?" (7) "Are the statements *clear and understandable* to those who will use them?" This list of criteria suffers from weaknesses commonly encountered in discussions of validation of objectives: it fails to recognize that somewhat different criteria are appropriate for a general objective and for more specific objectives based on the general objective.

Smith, Stanley and Shores (*Fundamentals of Curriculum Development,* ch. 5) discuss five criteria to be used in the evaluation of educational objectives: social adequacy, basic human needs, democratic ideals, consistency and noncontradiction, behavioristic interpretation. Robert L. Brackenbury suggests criteria of appropriateness, worth, and feasibility. ("Guidelines to Help Schools Formulate and Validate Objectives," in *Rational Planning in Curriculum and Instruction: Eight Essays* [Washington, D.C.: National Education Association—Center for the Study of Instruction, 1967], ch. 5.)

Virgil Herrick states five functions for objectives and implies that they can be used to validate objectives. (1) "Objectives define the direction of educational development." (2) "Objectives help select desirable learning experiences." (3) "Objectives help define the scope of an educational program." (4) "Objectives help to define the emphasis to be made in an educational program." (5) "Objectives provide one of the major bases for evaluation." (*Strategies of Curriculum Development,* pp. 91-96.)

In a recent article, D. Campell Wyckoff discusses the functions of and organizing principle for curriculum and the criteria it should meet. Since the central objective for educational ministry includes an organizing principle, Wyckoff's criteria may be applied to it. He writes, "When we seek an organizing principle, we are seeking an answer to the question, 'What is the soundest possible basis on which the educational plan of the church may be put together?' At least the following complexities arise immediately: First, the principle must be sound; that is, it must 'test out' in every possible way: theologically, biblically, scientifically, educationally, and under every conceivable circumstance. Second, the principle must be educational; that is, it must both reflect and reveal the very nature and process by which the most

149

profound changes in human being and becoming take place. Third, it must be genuinely in and of the church; that is, it must grow out of and express the life and mission of God's faithful people as they engage in the worship, witness, and work that is theirs to do. Thus, in raising the question of an organizing principle, we are asking the questions, vast and prior, of theology, biblical studies, the 'man sciences,' education, and the life and mission of the church as Christ's community." ("Understanding Your Church Curriculum," *The Princeton Seminary Bulletin*, vol. 63, no. 1 [Fall, 1970], p. 78.)

22. One analytic philosopher points out that questions of valuing are inherent in the very effort to define what education is. ". . . a search for the definition of education is most probably a quest for a statement of the *right* or the *best* program for education, and as such is a prescription for certain valued means or ends to be sought in educating . . . in a most important sense the very idea of educating implies that something of value is being passed on or learned . . . even though we might all agree that something of value must be passed on to the younger generation, the crucial question over which disagreements arise is, 'Just *what* of value should be passed on?' " (Jonas F. Soltis, *An Introduction to the Analysis of Educational Concepts* [Reading, Mass: Addison-Wesley Publishing Co., 1968], pp. 6-7, 70). For a more lengthy discussion of axiology and education, see chapters 39-43 in Young Pai and Joseph T. Myers, eds., *Philosophic Problems and Education* (Philadelphia: J. B. Lippincott Co., 1967). See also note 6.

Value as intrinsic to thinking about education is as old as thinking about education. The Greek philosophers were explicit about the inseparability of education from questions of values or virtue. ". . . true education is not concerned merely with training in methods of thinking and learning. Education presupposes a quest for awareness of ends to which man is to be led. It also presupposes certainty of the good which it seeks to attain. Plato uses the ideas of Socrates to express his own pedagogical effort, the attempt to show that the line of development which begins with the practical questions of education and virtue leads eventually to a confrontation with the divine principle of reality . . . . True *paideia*, whether it concerns education or legislation, is based on God as the highest norm." Aarne Siirala, *Divine Humanness* (Philadelphia: Fortress Press, 1970), p. 119.

Among modern philosophers, Alfred North Whitehead is explicit on the value-orientation of the aims and process of education: "The essence of education is that it be religious. . . . A religious education is an education which inculcates duty and reverence. Duty arises from our potential control over the course of events. Where attainable knowledge could have changed the issue, ignorance has the guilt of vice. And the foundation of reverence is this perception, that the present holds within itself the complete sum of existence, backwards and forwards, that whole amplitude of time, which is eternity." *The Aims of Education,* Mentor edition, (New York: New American Library, 1949), p. 26.

R. S. Peters may be the single contemporary philosopher with the greatest influence on educational theory. His definition of education is quite explicit in including a value orientation: "Education involves essentially processes which intentionally transmit what is valuable in an intelligible and voluntary manner and which create in the learner a desire to achieve it, this being seen as having its place along with other things in life." ("Education as Initiation," in *Philosophical Analysis and Education,* R. D. Archambault, ed. [London: Routledge and Kegan Paul, 1965], p. 102.)

In Christian education, the axiological question must be dealt with in reference to theological assertions. What is "the right or the best" program for Christian education hinges on fundamental beliefs about God and his relationship to man. Thus, validation of a central objective for educational ministry requires identification of its theological premises and their validity.

23. Robert Ulich demonstrates the impact of a society's values on its educational program in his historical survey of *Education in Western Culture* (New York: Harcourt, Brace, & World, Inc., 1965). The table of contents (pp. vii-viii) identifies broad eras of western civilization and education as follows:

The Greeks: Education for Reason
The Romans: Education for Order
The Jews: Education for the Covenant
The Christians: Education for Saintliness
The Middle Ages: Education for Hierarchy
Humanism and the Renaissance: Education for Individuality
The Seventeenth Century: Education for Communion
The Age of Reason: Education for Independent Thinking
Education for Information
Education for the State
Education for the Future

The Greek philosophers were quite clear on the matter of the relationship of education to society. "In consonance with Plato, Aristotle beheld education as a branch of politics. It is, he contended, a state function, and its nature, in essence, is a reflection of the society which it serves to protect and preserve—a view which, though under heavy assault by various posses of contemporaneous philosophers, is still after more than two thousand years, full of plain sense." Adolphe E. Meyer, *An Educational History of the Western World* (New York: McGraw-Hill Book Co., 1965), pp. 35-36.

Examination of the history of education in the United States reveals the strong influence which values dominant in various periods have had on educational practices. (See V. T. Thayer, *Formative Ideas in American Education* [New York: Dodd, Mead and Co., 1965] and R. Freeman Butts and Lawrence A. Freeman, *A History of Education in American Culture,* [New York: Holt, Rinehart, & Winston, Inc. 1953].) Similarly, shifting emphases in Christian education have reflected changes in dominant values in the churches conducting Christian education. (See William B. Kennedy, "Christian Education through History," in *An Introduction to Christian Education* Marvin J. Taylor, ed. [New York: Abingdon Press, 1965]).

With regard to the societal value basis for educational objectives, Brackenbury writes (*Rational Planning in Curriculum and Instruction,* p. 102): "Whether the educator is aware of it or not, value judgments underlie each objective that is employed in directing the educational program . . . Indeed, the basic values which the schools seek to perpetuate come, not from the professionals who run the schools, but from the social order itself in which the schools exist . . ."

24. Structural analysis uses the tools of philosophy, such as logic and linguistic analysis. It attends to topics such as epistemology, ethics, metaphysics, and, in the case of Christian education, to theology. For examples of how philosophy is applied to education, see the works by Soltis, by Brauner and Burns, and by Pai and Myers referred to in notes 6 and 22. (See also Van Cleve Morris, *Philosophy and The American School: An Introduction to the Philosophy of Education* [Boston: Houghton Mifflin Co., 1961].) For the application to the process to Christian education, see the work by Lawrence C. Little referred to in note 21. (See also J. Gordon Chamberlain, *Freedom and Faith, New Approaches to Christian Education* [Philadelphia: Westminster Press, 1965), ch. 6; and Nels F. S. Ferre, *A Theology for Christian Education* [Philadelphia: Westminster Press, 1967].)

25. See the volumes produced by the Lutheran Church in America Task Group for Long-Range Planning under the direction of Edward W. Uthe. *Social Change: An Assessment of Current Trends* (Philadelphia: Fortress Press, 1968), *Theology: An Assessment of Current Trends* (Philadelphia: Fortress Press, 1968) *Significant Issues for the 1970's* (Philadelphia: Fortress Press, 1968). (See also Edward W. Uthe, "The Challenge of a Changing Culture," in *Religious Education,* vol. 63, no. 3 [May-June, 1968], pp. 219-223.)

26. The sequence of program development activities stems from the reasons underlying program development. "The first function for which a curriculum policy must make provision is that of planning. Curriculum planning is in turn an essential part of educational planning, which sets out, explicitly or otherwise, the general objectives of an educational system and the means through which these objectives are

achieved." (Organization for Economic Cooperation and Development, *Modernizing Our Schools: Curriculum Improvement and Educational Development* [Paris: Organization for Economic Cooperation and Development, 1966], p. 60.)

In describing the functions of curriculum design Herrick points out that it should (1) account for all factors involved in the curriculum, (2) define "the coherency of these factors both to themselves and to their action points," (3) predict and control "the educational behavior of the learner," (4) define "the elements of curriculum and their pattern of relationships in curriculum development." (5) state the "means used for selecting and organizing learning experiences," and (6) indicate "the role of teachers and children in curriculum planning and development." (*Strategies of Curriculum Development*, pp. 18-19.) Herrick (*ibid.*, pp. 19-20) points out that "One way of examining . . . curriculum designs is to relate them to the important curriculum decisions teachers must make . . . any curriculum design must account for, and resolve in some consistent way, the following questions every teacher must ask himself.

"1. How can I know the child and prepare and manage a classroom environment which will promote his optimum learning?

"2. How can I identify, define, and use my instructional objectives to determine the scope, direction, and emphasis of the child's learning experience?

"3. How can I select and organize these experiences so as to aid the child to achieve worthwhile educational ends?

"4. How can I teach or manage the educational process so that these experiences are most effectively utilized by the child to achieve these ends?

"5. How can I evaluate so as to determine the extent and quality of the child's educational development toward these ends?"

Functions of a curriculum design or program design include achieving continuity and coordination in the program, providing a balanced and integrated program, and selecting and organizing materials and resources. (See Vernon Anderson, *Principles and Procedures of Curriculum Improvement* [New York: Ronald Press, 1965].)

The publication of the Organization for Economic Cooperation and Development previously referred to suggests that the following steps must be included in planning an educational program: selection of subject matter, coordination of levels of learning, provision of integration and balance, development of teaching resources, development of school organization, development of teaching strategies, preparation of teachers, evaluation.

An article in *Educational Leadership* identified the following eight basic curriculum design problems.

"1. Curriculum dissonance: contradictions, incompatibilities in teach-

153

ing methods and subject matter . . . experiences which produce conflict at a level to cause students to reject curriculum.

"2. Coordination, concern for commonalities as well as duplications with emphasis on wholeness in curricular experiences . . .

"3. Balance: concern for relationships of general education to special education, vicarious and firsthand experiences, product and process learnings.

"4. Hypertrophy of areas of experience, overexpansion of curricular offerings, excessive commitment of students' time . . .

"5. Continuity: preserving and expanding threads of experiences from grade level to grade level . . . observing principles of learning in concept presentation . . .

"6. Application of analagous developments in separate subject fields: . . .

"7. Evaluation of total curriculum design: gathering data on the total influence of the school experience . . .

"8. Assessment of internal and external pressures to effect change in parts of the curriculum and the impact on the total curriculum design." (Maurice J. Eash, "Supervisors: A Vanishing Breed?" in *Educational Leadership,* vol. 26, no. 1 (October, 1968), p. 79.)

For models of procedures and processes involved in an overall curriculum development program, see the following references. Edward W. Uthe, "Development Curriculum Design for Christian Education," in *Religious Education,* vol. 61, no. 3 (May-June, 1966), pp. 163-168. J. Galen Saylor and William M. Alexander, *Curriculum Planning for Modern Schools* (New York: Holt, Rinehart and Winston, 1966), pp. 7-18. John I. Goodlad, "Toward Improved Curriculum Organization," in *Planning and Organizing for Teaching* (Washington, D.C.: National Education Association, 1963), pp. 25-50. Robert Emans, "A Proposed Conceptual Framework for Curriculum Development," in *Journal of Educational Research,* vol. 59 (March, 1966), pp. 327-332.

27. A broad spectrum of empirical studies demonstrate that there is an orderly, sequential development of personal abilities, interests, and characteristics. Among the most well-known are those by Piaget and his associates, who have included some studies of moral development even though their major attention has been given to cognitive growth. Lawrence Kohlberg has studied the stages of conscience development in children, and Peck and Havighurst have done the same for adolescents. Jerome Bruner's most recent empirical studies of infants' skill learning support the view that certain behavioral patterns cannot be acquired prior to a given level of maturation, and that maturation levels are chronological. Ronald Goldman has conducted rigorous empirical studies of the religious development of children and adolescents and has found that levels or stages of religious development

correspond quite closely to the Piagetian stages of mental development.

The importance of calibrating objectives in terms of learners is emphasized by Maxine Dunfee's review of research on children's social studies concepts, skills, and attitudes. Contemporary studies continue to demonstrate the existence of sequences and stages of concept and skill development related to maturation, general social experience, and specific educational experience. More surprisingly, analysis of educational media shows that much of the media being prepared is inappropriate for and ineffective with its intended audience because it fails to utilize available knowledge about levels of development. (*Elementary School Social Studies: A Guide to Current Research* [Washington, D.C.: Association for Supervision and Curriculum Development, 1970], pp. 33-40, 53-55).

Results of the National Assessment of Educational Progress demonstrate the existence of different levels of development from age nine through adulthood. A calibration of citizenship objectives is given in *National Assessment of Educational Progress: Citizenship Objectives* (Ann Arbor, Mich.: Committee on Assessing the Program of Education, 1969.)

A recent summary of available research on learning in the area of religion reached the following conclusions.

"By far the most general and important [psychological] principle is that of *readiness*. That is, there must be an intellectual and emotional fit between the child's capacities at a given age level and the material to be presented. Much work needs to be done in this area, inasmuch as many of the assumptions that have guided religious education in the past were wholly untested against data.

". . . A child is given an allowance; he may be indulged or strictly controlled, but he is not expected to understand economic theory until college.

". . . Children are assumed to be able to comprehend the brotherhood of man when research demonstrates the inability of a ten-year-old to grasp the concept of society or of the continuity of the community beyond the life of the individual. . . .

". . . Religious learning obeys the same laws as other kinds of learning, or we may dignify by the name 'laws' the psychological processes discovered as the way the human mind works. What differences there are arise from the nature of religion, not from the learning processes, for it involves the various functions of the mind in different degrees of intensity and completeness than the learning of something else, say mathematics. But the same processes are present in both, in spite of the variation of degree to which they are involved.

". . . each individual passes through a number of stages in approaching what may tentatively be called maturity. The various stages are fairly clearly marked off from each other by the characteristics they display. We can classify the stages according to different criteria, such as intellectual development, physical attainments, emotional attitudes, social attitudes, adjustment to the real world, dependence or independence of personality, and so on . . . ." (Robert P. O'Neill and Roy S. Lee, "Understanding the Psychology of Religious Learning," in *Does the Church Know How to Teach?* Kendig B. Cully, ed. [New York: Macmillan Co., 1970], pp. 51, 53, 54, 56, 57, 61).

A related issue is the prestructuring of curriculum on bases such as are suggested above versus curriculum constructed entirely by pupils and teachers working together. The "structure of the disciplines" emphasis, stemming from the work of Jerome Bruner, would seem to suggest that some prestructuring of curriculum is desirable, if not necessary. The point of view receives additional support from David P. Ausuble, who maintains that the use of "advance organizers" facilitates learning. Empirical evidence related to this topic is presented in two articles by Canadian researchers in *Interchange: A Journal of Educational Studies,* vol. 1, no. 2 (1970). See "The Creation of Information Systems for Children," by Bruce R. Joyce and Elizabeth A. Joyce (pp. 1-12))and "The Place of Structural Experience in Early Cognitive Development," by Joachim F. Wohlwill (pp. 13-27).

28. The need to provide resources and services to congregations is clearly implied by the following description of the situation with regard to public schools.

". . . the insignificant portion of public school expenditures directed into meaningful research provides evidence of the inability of public schools adequately to research and develop their own materials. . . . Thus it is apparent that a greater number of schools will find it increasingly desirable to purchase all or most of their curricular materials from commercial sources.

"Curriculum committees composed of classroom teachers, principals, supervisors, and other representatives from the central office staff no longer can be expected to develop courses of study or curriculum guides for implementation within school systems. The costs of researching, planning, developing, and producing curricula for individual school systems, the larger ones included, are clearly prohibitive. . . .

". . . it is imperative that a school district have readily available curricula that (a) will meet the needs of boys and girls who, because of familial mobility, attend many different schools which are in and of themselves quite different, and (2) will be broad enough to encompass the tremendous diversity which exists within the walls of each school and within each classroom in that school.

"We must also be highly cognizant of the nature of other individual differences that exist within the schools. Just as boys and girls bring individual strengths and weaknesses to their school experiences, so do individual teachers. Some teachers work best with standardized materials and use them with varying degrees of success in the classroom. Others prefer to utilize commercially prepared materials as a basis for some of the decisions made in their classrooms, but also desire the freedom and the opportunity to vary the programs to meet the perceived needs of children. Still other teachers move far afield from established programs in their attempts to individualize educational opportunities for boys and girls." (Harvey Goldman and Luther W. Pfluger, "Multiple Curricula: A Strategy for Selection," in *Educational Leadership*, vol. 26, no. 7 [April, 1969], pp. 688-689))

"Materials aid the diffusion of educational innovations very considerably. The reasons for this are suggested to be the relative ease with which they can be designed and altered to fit the demands of teaching situations, their ease of reproduction and distribution, and their retention of substantial integrity when used by a wide variety of teachers in different situations. The existence of a very wide range of competence makes routinized procedures—including supporting materials—an inevitable part of the educational system. If the materials are comprehensive, and designed as complete units, as in the case of those distributed by the Physical Science Study Committee, teacher adoption becomes more likely.

". . . innovations with built-in innovation supports should diffuse more rapidly than those not so supported. For example, in the case of certain curricula prepared by national groups, training in the use of the innovation *is part of the innovation,* and is available at no dollar cost. If the support is via materials, the more 'self-teaching' they are, the more likely are adoption and continued use." (Matthew B. Miles, "Innovation in Education: Some Generalizations," in *Innovation in Education,* Matthew B. Miles, ed. [New York: Columbia University Teachers College Bureau of Publications, 1964], pp. 636-637.

29. For discussions of the problem of curriculum evaluation, including the evaluation of objectives, see the following publications. *Curriculum Innovations and Evaluation.* (Princeton, N.J.: Educational Testing Service, 1969); *Review of Educational Research,* vol. 39, no. 3 (June, 1969), chapters on "Curriculum Evaluation," by Robert L. Baker and "Methodological Issues in Curriculum Research," by Richard E. Schutz; *Perspectives on Curriculum Evaluation,* edited by Robert E. Stake (Chicago: Rand McNally, 1967).

John Jarolimek proposes twelve questions which can be used to evaluate an educational program in *Guidelines for Elementary Social Studies* (Washington, D.C.: Association for Supervision and Curriculum Development, 1967), pp. 11-27. Comprehensive criteria for evaluating an educational program are given by J. Galen Saylor and William M. Alexander in *Curriculum Planning for Modern Schools*

(New York: Holt, Rinehart, & Winston, Inc. 1966), pp. 254-256. See also the criteria listed at the end of the chapter by Vernon Anderson in this yearbook.

Educational Foundations—A Response

CHARLES R. BRUNING

This chapter will concentrate on teaching and will suggest that the church needs to study the teaching process if it is to accomplish the central objective. Much has been done recently in the area of theories of learning, and these findings have been used by people in parish education to develop curricular materials. In the seventies the church needs to invest more in people (the teachers) than in paper (the curriculum materials). What has been done in the past is good, but now we must face new demands.

A Conceptual Framework for Educational Ministry

Before looking at the teaching process as it relates to the educational ministry, it is necessary to identify a framework for that ministry. The beginnings for the conceptualization of an educational ministry are stated succinctly in the central objective:

> to assist persons
> to perceive, respond to and participate in
> God's continuing activity and revelation,
> particularly in Jesus Christ,
> in the human and Christian communities
> as they deal with their continual life involvements of
> being a person,
> relating to persons and groups, and
> living in society, culture and the physical universe.[1]

The author of the chapter "Educational Foundations" has delineated what needs to be accomplished from an educational perspective to attain the central objective. In other chapters, authors discuss their disciplines' role in achieving this objective. As one reads through these presentations, the similarities to public education can be noted. One added dimension, however, is the *theological*. Careful rethinking of the role of theology in the church's educational ministry suggests that a paralleling of education within the church and education in the public sector is no longer appropriate nor valid. The central objective document declares that "members of the Christian community must be helped to accept responsibility for becoming change agents in the world."[2] This seems to suggest that the Christian is to be an activist in this revolutionary age. This activism originates from the context of a community of believers in God. It is crucial to exist within this believing community for the support necessary to become a change agent in society. The central objective document suggests how this will occur: "The structures and processes of the community can be so planned that learning will occur as persons participate in the total life of the community."[3] To start with an assumption that members of the Christian community are to become change agents necessitates a peculiar stance in terms of educational ministry.

Conceptual Framework for Teacher Education

To implement an educational ministry it will be necessary to recruit and train those who will teach. The teachers within the church are any persons who assume responsibility for the teaching-learning environments within the church. The church depends upon many people to function as teachers; some have backgrounds in working in teaching-learning situations, some do not. However, everyone can and does and must play a part in teaching-learning if the central objective is to be met.

In order to accomplish the programs and processes that are designed to meet the central objective, it will be necessary to develop a conceptual framework for preparing the people who are to be teachers in the church (anyone who is responsible for a teaching-learning environment within the church's program). Even if one could parallel teacher education programs that exist in the public and private colleges, something more would be needed. Teachers in the church will be creating "structures and processes" that will sustain the community of believers. Nevertheless, the preparation of teachers for public schools can be a departure point for the development of a conceptual framework for preparing teachers for the church.

In a recent book by Haugh and Duncan, it is suggested that teaching has four phases:

1. a curriculum planning phase
2. an instructing phase
3. a measuring phase
4. an evaluation phase[4]

The churches have been known to be prolific in curriculum development. Many of these curricula have had predetermined objectives for the teachers of children. They have not been designed so that as the teacher moves into the teaching-learning situation, he has some guidelines for curriculum development. Much of the curriculum that is developed, whether in the church or outside of it, is cognitively based. It is not enough for the teacher to have children involved in rote-memorization of the content. The learner must be involved in a process that will continue outside of the situation that he is in at the present. Taba[5] has suggested that the teacher, as she researches the material that is to be taught, must (1) know the processes of thinking, (2) possess a good knowledge of the students, and (3) know the content to be taught. These become heavy demands on a prospective teacher within the church.

As we consider the teacher to be in charge of the teaching-learning situation, we must consider what it means to instruct. In the introduction to the booklet, *The Study of Teaching*, Dean Corrigan summarizes the contents as:

1. teaching implies action as behavior
2. because teaching depends on one or more human beings functioning in an interaction process, it requires the continuous adjustment of behavior
3. once teaching is viewed as an interaction process, the content, methods, materials, media, and evaluation aspects of teaching gain a new vitality
4. a fundamental premise of education is that behavior can be changed and improved
5. the study of teaching requires specialized skills.[6]

To date there have been workshops for teachers within the church for methodology and for the curriculum to be used. If one agrees that there is need for new emphasis on the instructional phase of the teaching-learning duo, then Corrigan's statement has added significance. It will make new demands upon the time, energy and resources of many people at many levels of the church.

In doing measurement and evaluation of both teaching and learning new demands are placed upon the church. But, if an objective is stated there must also be a means of assessing whether that objective is being reached. As the church gets involved in developing its own framework for teacher education, it must consider both evaluation and measurement.

It will be necessary for the church to generate from the central objective its conceptual framework for teacher education if any modicum of success is to occur. A summarization of N. L. Gage's research on teaching suggests that "theoretical analyses of teaching are as important as theories of learning and should be developed alongside of learning theories rather than inferred from them."[7] Learning theory is constantly being generated; the public schools and colleges are now beginning to develop conceptual frameworks for teacher education. The church can do no less.

Dimensions That Need to Be Considered

It is appropriate to look at two dimensions that must be inherent in a conceptual framework for education and a conceptual framework for teacher education. Ask several questions that might become guidelines as these frameworks are studied.

THE CHANGE PROCESS

1. How does a teacher become *free* enough internally to become a change agent?
2. How can a teacher become a *risk taker* within the church and maintain some semblance of his credibility as a participant of the community of believers?
3. How do you facilitate the process of *decision making* in the teaching-learning situation?
4. How does the church adjust itself to accept that "*process*" is essential in a change agent's role and that this is difficult to evaluate?
5. How can we teach those who teach in the church that *teaching-learning* is continuous for all in a community of believers and that this demands a new stance for those who teach?

161

HUMAN INTERACTION

1. Since the teacher is in power in a classroom, how does he *demonstrate interest and involvement in the life* of the student in the teaching-learning environment?
2. How does a teacher in the church classroom divorce himself from the stereotyped perception of the role of a teacher so that real *dialogue* occurs?
3. How does a teacher assist another *"to be a person"* in the context of a Christian community?
4. How does a teacher assist another to accept that *human diversity* does and needs to exist in a community of believers?
5. How does the church assist the teacher to become a person who *models behavior* in the community of believers?

These questions are not all inclusive, but do raise significant issues in the development of conceptual frameworks. Such questions are intended to extend our thinking about the educational ministry within the church and raise some question about continuing to parallel education in the public sector.

NOTES AND REFERENCES

1. *A Central Objective for Educational Ministry in the Parish: ALC and LCA* (Philadelphia: Board of Parish Education of the Lutheran Church in America, 1969), p. 31.
2. *Ibid.,* p. 7.
3. *Ibid.,* p. 7.
4. John Haugh and James Duncan, *Teaching: Description and Analysis* (Reading, Mass.: Addison-Wesley Publishing Co., Inc., 1970).
5. Hilda Taba and James Hill, *Teacher Handbook for Contra-Costa Social Studies: Grades 1-6* (Haywood, Calif.: Rapid Printers and Lithographers, 1965).
6. Dean Corrigan, ed., *The Study of Teaching* (Washington, D.C.: Association for Student Teaching, 1967).
7. John Verduin, *Conceptual Models in Teacher Education* (Washington, D.C.: The American Association of Colleges for Teacher Education, 1967).

Chapter VI

Sociological/Psychological Foundations

W. KENT GILBERT

Several years ago I spent a day climbing among the ruins of Delphi, wondering at the remnants of a civilization which had left so many imprints upon our own. Here were clearly discernible foundations of ancient buildings, and archaeologists had succeeded in modeling the kinds of structures which they once supported. That is one use of foundations, the recreation of the past in present form.

More recently I stood beneath Eero Saarinen's soaring gateway arch in St. Louis. Here was no repristination of the past, but a probing of the possible and a unique utilization of the known. The arch would have been impossible if it had not been consistent with the facts about foundations, but the foundations could be selected within the limits of those known facts. The arch was not strictly determined, therefore, by preconceived foundations. Instead the foundations were integral to and, in a sense, controlled by the creative concept which they supported.

It seems to me that the task before us in discussing the sociological and psychological foundations for educational ministry is more akin to the second illustration than the first. The task force which stated the central objective had at least the beginnings of an educational design in view. Later documents have developed this design further. In selecting the foundations one must have that concept in mind. We

163

will not attempt, therefore, to survey the fields of sociology and psychology *in toto* in order to construct an educational theory on this basis. Instead we shall examine those elements which would be crucial presuppositions for the educational design implicit in the task force's documents. In this way, we shall seek to test whether sound psychological and educational foundations would be possible for the envisioned educational structure. We shall approach the problem by dealing with four questions:

1. What are the key concepts in the central objective from a sociopsychological point of view?

2. To what extent are people controlled by the social context within which they live?

3. Are societal situations sufficiently similar to make life involvements a viable organizing principle for education?

4. Are persons sufficiently similar to make life involvements a viable organizing principle for education?

1. *What are the key concepts in the central objective from a sociopsychological point of view?* While almost every word of the central objective could be subjected to analysis, certain phrases have particular significance for our purposes in this chapter. The first of these is the phrase "to assist persons." This means that the locus of the learning process is in the person himself. No one else can learn for him or guarantee a predetermined outcome for a particular educative process. What actually happens when learning occurs is that the person's behavior, in the broad sense, somehow changes. He understands or feels or acts differently than he did before the learning experience. Since these changes are within the learner, all that the educator should or can hope to do is assist the process in a way that honors the integrity of the person he seeks to help.

Second is the group of action words, "to perceive, respond to, and participate in." They indicate that the learner must be actively engaged in a process of becoming. He is not viewed as a passive recipient of the activity of others.

Third, these actions of the learner are with reference to God's activity and revelation "in the human and Christian communities." This phrase provides the context for learning. "Persons are always located within a contextual situation which has social, cultural, and physical aspects. Within this context, the Christian seeks to identify, call into question, and interpret important forces and systems."[1] Learning, therefore, is not seen as taking place in isolation but within both the Christian community and the wider community of all persons.

Finally, and possibly most important for us here, is the statement that learning is to occur as persons "deal with their continual life involvements." These life involvements, which are detailed in the central objective document and the four-volume statement of age-level objectives, are the key oragnizing principles of the educational ministry program. It is here that people learn as they seek to cope with the unavoidable tasks of being human in contemporary society.

The idea of "life involvements" in itself is not new. The term was coined in 1958 by the designers of the present Lutheran Church in America Parish Education Curriculum. Those persons acknowledged an indebtedness to Robert Havighurst, who conceived the pattern of "developmental tasks,"[2] which are characteristic of persons growing up in our society, and to Florence Stratemeyer and her associates who employed the concept of "persistent life situations" as a means of curriculum evaluation.[3] There are emphases, however, which are different in the educational ministry approach. One is the strong emphasis upon the societal and cultural setting of these involvements. Man is seen much less individualistically and much more as a being in community. The other is a more open-ended approach to the outcome of the process of dealing with life involvements. The 1958 design spoke of "continual Christian learnings" which somehow matched "continual life involvements" and were regarded as desired outcomes.[4] The educational ministry document speaks of CLI's in "Christian perspective" without specifying fixed results. It emphasizes that the organizing principle "must indicate a direction for continuing growth and development rather than attempting to describe the complete Christian as the end product of the educational process."[5] While the predecessor program certainly could not be regarded as a "closed system," the difference in objectives in terms of open-endedness is marked and clear. The new educational ministry approach tends to be future oriented and expects that future to be markedly different from the past so that new solutions will be required for problems which have never occurred before.

The term "involvement" is one which is fraught with meaning for education. A social situation may be thought of as existing apart from

165

and independent of a particular person. Indeed some sociologists suggest studying situations in an objective way and preliminary to studying the behavior of persons in these situations.[6] Involvement, however, implies that a dynamic interaction is occurring between the learner and the situations which confront him. He cannot disengage himself with impuity. He must deal with them in some way, and in this process, genuine learning is likely to happen.

When the word "continual" is added, we begin to see life involvements as more than a series of discrete transactions. They tend to persist and to be a recurring part of the learner's experience. In this sense, they take on the characteristic of Havighurst's "developmental tasks."[7] The significance of the continual nature of life involvements is twofold: it makes a meaningful sequence of learning experiences possible; and it recognizes that the integration of new experiences is a function of the person who is dealing with these experiences. This latter point has great significance for the way in which one attempts to organize an educational program. All too frequently, the organizing principle of curriculum has been viewed as some logical thread of subject matter or the inherent structure of a discipline. Both of these assume that the job of integrating curriculum is performed *by* the educator for *the* pupil. It is a process that goes on largely outside the learner. What is implicit in the CLI approach, however, is that the educational goal is to assist the individual to become an integrative person, one who continually relates new experiences to what he himself now is and is now becoming.[8] It would be easy to assume, of course, that putting the learner's reaction in such a key position means that the teacher ought not to have clear educational objectives in mind. This is certainly not the case. In fact, it becomes essential for the educator to have his objectives sharply in focus. Otherwise he may not be a facilitator but an inhibitor of learning.

2. *To what extent are people controlled by the social context within which they live?* The central objective document acknowledges the tension between individual goals and societal pressures:

> Being a person in the fullest sense means having a sense of personal identity, with personal goals and purposes, in the midst of society and in the face of conflicting demands which threaten one's identity . . . In every age there are forces and events which are in conflict with Christian perspective. As the person lives in the midst of these con-

flicting forces, his efforts to be a person are often thwarted. In our own time, there are strong forces which the individual must face in his efforts to find and maintain a sense of personal Christian identity.[9]

The key question, however, from a sociological point of view is whether man actually is free to establish his own goals for learning and values for life or whether he is pushed and pressured by "an inexorability, relentlessness of social causation and social process as determinate as physical causation."[10] This has much to say about the openness or even the neutrality of the future and the extent to which it is plastic and menable to the conscious efforts of "free" men. If what man is and does is determined by the culture and his social location, is there any reality to the process of planning an educational ministry? It would seem to be an empty and meaningless fiction except to make more efficient the very process of socialization which is designed to make people conform to a shape set by society.

In considering the foregoing questions, three key terms ought to be borne in mind. These are "values," "culture," and "society." According to Kluckhohn, "A value is a conception, explicit or implicit, distinctive of an individual or characteristic of a group, of the desirable which influences the selection from available modes, means, and ends of action."[11] Haas, referring to Mercer, says, "Culture may be defined as 'that part of man's environment which he has himself created.' It is composed of all the attainments of all the people who ever lived, insofar as these attainments are remembered, stored, and communicable to persons now alive."[12] Nelson draws a distinction between these two terms and society when he says, "A society is the organized part of life. It is different from culture and from the individual in that it is a system in which roles must be played, work assigned, responsibilities fixed, and laws or regulations made, interpreted, and enforced . . . The phrase 'culture is the way of life of a society' can be turned around to state that 'a society is the way people are oriented to express the values of their culture.' "[13]

In the Lutheran World Federation Commission on Education's study of "Christian Education in a Secular Society," three scholars, Charles Glock[14], Harold Haas[15], and Solomon Inquai[16], all addressed the question of the extent to which man undergoes a process of enculturation as a result of the influence of the structures of the society in which he lives. All are agreed that this influence is tremendous and that man cannot be understood apart from his social context. But none of these writers was prepared to go the route of "cultural determinism." Haas puts it quite clearly:

> Cultural determinism, however, while it may be the operating context of the social scientist as scientist, needs closer examination before it is accepted in such fashion as to cut the nerve of all individual effort and theological concern. Not only is man too complex a phenomenon for that but so also is culture. A complicated acting and reacting process is involved between individual men and culture. While culture influences men, sometimes in determinative ways, men are constantly creating and changing the culture in which they live.[17]

Viewing the problem from a different perspective, the psychologist arrives at much the same conclusion: persons are not mechanisms which are manipulated by external circumstances. Although his actions are always circumscribed by events, a person is also a "self-starter." He makes his own unique contributions to the situations in which he finds himself. Maslow, for example, says:

> Man demonstrates in his own nature a pressure toward fuller and fuller Being, more and more perfect actualization of his humanness in exactly the same naturalistic, scientific sense that an acorn may be said to be "pressing forward" being an oak tree, or that a tiger can be observed to "push toward" being tigerish, or a horse toward being equine. Man is ultimately not molded or shaped into humanness, or taught to be human. The role of the environment is ultimately to permit him or help him to actualize his own potentialities, not its potentialities. The environment does not give him potentialities and capacities; he has them in inchoate or embryonic form, just exactly as he has embryonic arms and legs. And creativeness, spontaneity, selfhood, authenticity, caring for others, being able to love, yearning for truth are embryonic potentialities belonging to his species-membership just as much as are his arms and legs and brain and eyes.
>
> This is not in contradiction to the data already amassed which show clearly that living in a family and in a culture are absolutely necessary to actualize these psychological potentials that define humanness. Let us avoid this confusion. A teacher or a culture doesn't create a human being. It doesn't implant within him the ability to love, or to be curious, or to philosophize, or to symbolize, or to be creative. Rather it permits, or fosters, or encourages or helps what exists in embryo to become real and actual. The same mother or the same culture, treating a kitten or a puppy in exactly the same way, cannot make it into a human being. The culture is sun and food and water: it is not the seed.[18]

It would be presumptuous, however, for the church to assume that its educational program is normally the major force in this process of interaction between most persons and their culture. In fact, much research seems to indicate that even men's religious views and activities tend to be shaped more by their social location than by the church's educational efforts.[19]

A much more potent force for the recreation of culture today is likely to be government and the changes it seeks to effect in society. A new factor which must be reckoned with in this situation is the level of sophistication which has been achieved in planning social change and the way in which the state-controlled educational system is used as a tool in the process.[20] King and Brownell point out that national states tend to control much of behavior through such powers as taxation, legislation, and war.[21] In many cases the state actually creates a kind of secular religion through the promulgation of ideas, control of mass media, fostering of nationalistic patriotism, and management of the educational system. They go on to assert that when the state's claim on the content of education gains priority, the pedagogical characteristics which follow include: ethnocentricity, regulation of those who may teach, conceiving of schools as "manpower pools," elevation of "citizenship" to a higher value than the person, and favoring of certain disciplines, such as science, in the name of national interests.[22] All of this has a potent influence on the shape of the culture which in turn has its impact upon persons who share in that culture.

Although it would be overly optimistic to assume under such circumstances that any future educational ministry of the Lutheran Church in America will reshape the whole of society and world culture, the central objective does hold out hope that a reoriented Christian community can become a potent force in the lives of those related to it. As a sociologist, Haas affirms this possibility that the church can assume a new role as a group which provides a meaningful climate and contest for persons grappling with powerful social influences.

> It seems unlikely that the church can bring much influence to bear on persons merely by working with individuals. It cannot rely on tradition, authority, or the support of the general culture. Its major task, therefore, seems to lie in the direction of creating strong subcultures and, at the same time, seeking to comprehend the general culture and seek ways to provide it with a broad and relevant universe of meaning and values.[23]

As an educator, Nelson supports the idea that there is a great power in human groups which serve as subcultures, allowing their members a degree of freedom and providing support in coping with the whole of society. The church must, therefore, express in its structures and life the communal nature of the people of God. It is in this way that persons are provided with an environment in which their faith can grow. As people interact with people, powerful forces are generated which influence values and a characteristic life style.[24] As Nelson puts it, "We must see the congregation as a field of forces—individuals and groups—in lively interaction with each other; the grist of this interactional process *is* the content of their faith."[25] What can happen when persons' spirits are ignited by the strong convictions of such a community is a matter of history. The power then resides in highly-motivated people supported by communal relationships rather than in the form of a particular social structure.

3. *Are societal situations sufficiently similar to make life involvements a viable organizing principle for education?* The framework which the central objective provides for educational ministry in the concept of continual life involvements is clearly situational:

> Continual life involvements include three basic dimensions of: (1) being a person, (2) relating to persons and groups, and (3) living in society, culture and the physical universe. Recognition must be given to the interrelationships of these three dimensions as they occur in the actual life experiences of persons . . . The three dimensions pervade one another. All three probably are present to some degree in every human experience, but in many experiences one or another of the three dimensions is central.
>
> Using these three dimensions, it is possible to examine the range of human experience and to identify areas of experience which are virtually inescapable for any member of North American society. Even though specific content of the experiences varies from one person to another, the areas of experience are common to all.[26]

The assumption is that it is possible to identify those areas of experience which are virtually inescapable for any member of North American society. But this assumption immediately raises two questions: (a) Is the social situation sufficiently stable that it is possible to identify common experiences which will have some predictable continuity? (b) Is there sufficient similarity in the social locations of persons so that it is possible to make generalizations which will be useful in educational planning.

(a) *Is the social situation sufficiently stable that it is possible to identify common experiences which will have some predictable continuity?*

It is almost axiomatic today that changes will occur rapidly and frequently unexpectedly in our world. As Heilbroner puts it, frequently the events which come at us daily are:

> . . . charged with surprise and shock. When we think back over the past few years what strikes us is the suddenness of its blows, the unannounced descent of its thunderbolts. Wars, revolutions, uprisings have burst upon us with terrible rapidity. Advances in science and technology have rewritten the very terms and conditions of the human contract with no more warning than the morning's headlines. Encompassing social and economic changes have not only unalterably rearranged our lives, but seem to have done so behind our backs, while we were not looking.
>
> These recurring shocks of contemporary history throw a pall of chronic apprehensiveness over our times. Reading the morning newspaper has become an act no longer anticipated with mild pleasure but with uneasy suspense. The bewildering turnabouts of fortune, the abrupt shifts of expectations, the awareness of the innumerable microscopic factors by which our destiny may be affected, all conspire to make of our encounter with history a frightening and disorienting ordeal.[27]

What makes this so critical for educational planning is that it may readily be concluded the children and youth of today will need to live in a world which is so unlike the world of the past that it is difficult to capitalize upon the wisdom and knowledge of the past which has been the traditional source of educational content.[28] The changes which have occurred as a result of the rapid increment in human knowledge will serve as a case in point. Where once new insights came plodding century by century, knowledge is now expanding so rapidly that the sum of things known in many fields is doubling every ten to fifteen years. In addition, the introduction of computer technology has created a totally new phenomenon, the actual breeding of knowledge outside the human mind. As Walter J. Ong puts it, "The computer is a special milieu in which knowledge can be cultivated outside its normal habitat."[29] As more and more is learned about how knowledge comes into being and can be stored and retrieved, new knowledge can be engineered in advance.[30]

As these growth processes go on, several things are beginning to happen. First, man is inundated and overwhelmed by the vast scope of knowledge with which he cannot individually come to grips. Second, he finds a subtle change occurring in ways of thinking where the electronic era requires thought to be reduced more and more to quantified forms of data and mathematical modelings of reality. Third, he is involved in a change from older linear and mechanical forms of knowing to a new kind of simultaneous field awareness as a result of the electronic revolution which affect him and his ways of learning profoundly. As McLuhan puts it, "It is the simultaneous 'field' of multitudinous events in equipoise or interplay that constitutes the awareness of casuality that is present in ecological and nuclear models of perception today. Our electric mode of shaping the new patterns of culture and information movement is not mechanical but biological."[31] Fourth, there is a rapidly growing fragmentation of knowledge as a consequence of specialization with a resultant increase in the difficulty of interdisciplinary communication. "The world of knowledge has today become radically plural. It is a world of many different knowledges, pursued in varied ways to diverse ends. These many inquiries are normally carried on with little thought for their relation to each other."[32] Fifth, man faces a new kind of obsolescence in traditional thought forms and concepts which at best wrench at the structure of his thinking and at the worst render him "incompetent to deal with the shifting problems and dilemmas of a rapidly changing culture."[33] Sixth, and closely related, is the tendency to substitute probabilities for certitudes as a way of thinking. The scientist in particular is less dogmatic about his findings as he learns to deal with a universe which is never "surprise free."[34] Finally, there is a growing distrust of man's accumulated wisdom and the authority drawn from experience. As a result, people are less and less inclined to look to what was accepted as valued by their elders as a source of guidance for the future. The mode seems to carry over into the fields of philosophic and religious thought as well.

If what has just been said were all there is to the story, we would have good reason to doubt that societal situations have sufficient continuity to permit planning educational programs on the CLI principle.

But there is another side to the picture. Many substantial studies have been made which do indicate trends which may be anticipated for the future.[35] What is necessary is to be realistic about the nature of forecasting. The Lutheran Task Force on Long-Range Planning had this to say about the problem:

> There seems to be a consensus that fairly reliable forecasts may be made for a five-year period, but that even these must be subject to constant review and revision . . . . The assumptions are: (1) Future developments will be strongly influenced by crescive social trends and by stable characteristics of human nature. (2) The direction of future developments is likely to be indicated by frontier scientific discoveries, technological applications, and political-social-economic proposals. (3) While the direction and character of change can be anticipated with some degree of reliability, the exact degree and pace of change cannot be anticipated precisely. (4) Any forecast made on the basis of the best evidence available at a given time may be nullified by the introduction of truly novel elements and/or random effects on various geographical areas, population subgroups, and facets of an individual's life. (6) Change will be more rapid in the economic-technological areas than in functional social structures, with consequent social problems and stresses for society and individuals.[36]

From the standpoint of educational planning, it is important to underline the fact that although some kinds of changes, such as those in the technological field, are becoming more rapid, not all aspects of our world change at the same speed. People still have to deal with many of the same problems which have been present in varying forms for generations. People still are born, grow up, become sick, relate to other persons, cope with disaster, marry, have children, eat, buy, sell, experience wars, face suffering, provide for basic needs, learn, teach, deal with laws, pay taxes, and eventually die. The fundamental task of being a human goes on, and the process of helping persons to be human in the midst of impersonal social forces remains education's greatest challenge. More will be said about how the educator can plan for this responsibility in a moment.

(b) *Is there sufficient similarity in social locations of persons so that it is possible to make generalizations which will be useful in educational planning?*

Numerous studies have underscored a common-sense observation that there is really no homogeneity within the American population or the social location of its members. There are vast differences in economic levels, cultural deprivation and geographical characteristics. These conditions have become a source of great tension and concern particularly among those in the educative community. As Chase puts it:

> Inequities in access to knowledge and, consequently, in the distribution of opportunity, power, and other benefits outrage the human sense of fair play and lead to smoldering or explosive resentments, as well as depriving society of talents it needs.
>
> Those reared in city slums or the rural poverty of Appalachia are denied the early experiences which predispose to education. Most non-whites and members of non-English-speaking cultures face formidable barriers to the acquisition of knowledge and additional obstacles to fruitful use of knowledge acquired. These inequities, built on deep-rooted social attitudes and buttressed by institutional biases in education as well as elsewhere, constitute a major obstacle to the development of human capabilities. In the disadvantaged groups, such inequities shut off opportunities for the cultivation and use of qualities which enable individuals to plan well the roles that become mankind. In the favored groups, the inequities hinder the development of sensibilities that are essential to humanity.[37]

Government and educators alike have struggled to cope with the effects of these varities in social location with only indifferent success. Indeed there are those who feel that the inequities are so great as to make any comprehensive educational strategy virtually impossible.

In view of what has been said, it is natural to ask whether the continual life involvement concept provides the flexibility needed to cope with the variety of social locations. Perhaps the problem arises because we tend to overemphasize the particularities of societal conditions at the expense of understanding their commonalities.

Rorher and Sherif underline the importance of dealing educationally with certain tasks which are essential to all persons in their development:

> Learning is essentially a process which marks the maturation of the individual, and, in the final analysis, is employed best to designate the non-biological or modified biological responses he comes to control in effectively mastering the demands of his total setting. In the process of growing up, that is, the individual must, if he is to survive, adapt himself to his natural setting, and to the other individuals with whom he is to come into contact. But this is not all; he must also come to

control those resources of the ways of life of the particular group into which he is born that are essential to his survival as an individual. He must have a measure of awareness of his traditionally sanctioned conceptions of the universe, he will come to know its accepted modes of self-expression in musical and artistic and literary forms, he must order his life in terms of its value-systems and recognized goals. He must, in short, make a triple adaptation—to his natural setting, to the fellow-members of his society, and to the patterns of his culture.[38]

What the CLI system seeks to do is to identify generic human conditions. An examination of the lists in the age-level objectives documents reveals such categories as "relating to small groups, which involves membership in various small groups"; "relating to one's family, which involves empathy and compassion, tension and conflict"; "relating to other individuals as persons, which involves awareness of social forces which influence personal relationships"; "dealing with the givens and inevitables of life, which involves success and failure, health and illness, life and death, change and uncertainty"; "understanding and participating in political processes." All of these are inescapable human involvements which appear in various forms at different ages, in various social locations, and at different times in history. The difficult but not insurmountable problem for the educators, therefore, is to project as clearly as possible the shape which these situations will assume in the immediate future and, where necessary, in major types of societal locations. This is not a process of crystal gazing. Furthermore, to say that educational planning can occur within the scope of known life involvements, is not to ignore the importance of the unpredictable. Indeed this calls for a style of education which presumes flexibility and seeks to help persons to cope with unexpected changes. As Taba puts it:

> We need minds that can cope with the fragility of knowledge and concepts in a changing world. Young people need to face the possibility of living with continuous uncertainty and with a continual call for revising anything they believe to be true or count on as regularity. This requires a mental system totally different from what we have ever known.[39]

This is the only type of education which makes sense for persons living in our kind of society, and there seems to be no inconsistency between this need and the CLI approach. To educate for an openness to change, however, demands courage and imagination. It means that the Christian educator is concerned more with how the learner thinks and integrates new experiences from a Christian perspective in preserving specific formulations about the truth which may no longer be relevant to the learner. Whether the church can really accommodate to a style of thinking which sees meaning as emergent from the interplay of heritage and the contextual demands of living, however, is another matter.

4. *Are persons sufficiently similar to make life involvements a viable organizing principle for Education?*

Any educational program must face the question of whether each person is so unique that he bears no resemblance to other persons. If this is the case, an individual educational program must be prepared for each person. However, many significant aspects of a person's life stem from experiences which he has in common with others by virtue of being a human being living in society. Each person becomes involved in many situations, faces many demands, responsibilities, and opportunities which are essentially the same as those faced by others. These are the person's continual life involvements—areas of experience and relationships which persist throughout life with changing shapes and significance.[40]

Implicit within this statement is the assumption that persons have enough basic similarities that it is possible to capitalize on these commonalities in designing an educational program which will meet the needs of large numbers of people at any age level. In many ways this position presents in terms of personality development the same type of questions which were raised about social situations and life involvements. Are people really that much alike? Are their life involvements similar?

The evidence gathered by such students of human development as Piaget[41], Havighurst[42], Hurlock[43], Gesell[44], and Erickson[45], would argue that they are. This similarity is governed in part by the growth of the human organism itself and the way in which it develops various intellectual and physical capacities at certain ages which can be predicted with a fair degree of accuracy under normal circumstances. In addition, it is possible to relate these growth potentials to certain developmental tasks. As defined by Havighurst, a developmental task is "a task which arises at or about a certain period in the life of the individual, successful achievement of which leads to his happiness and to success with later tasks, while failure leads to unhappiness and difficulty with later tasks."[46]

Ronald Goldman's research in England has related the concepts of human development to the religious thinking of children and youth with similar results. Here, too, in the religious dimension he finds stages and patterns of development.[47] In North America, findings paralleling some of Goldman's insights are beginning to emerge from the Lutheran Longitudinal Study, the results of which are to be made public about 1972.

To say that such similarities exist in human development is not the same as saying that people are not unique. No developmental psychologist seeks to imply that people move through growth stages in a lock-step fashion. Indeed, they see the richness of human life emerging from individual differences.[48] As Allport puts it:

> Hence the individuality of man extends infinitely beyond the puny individuality of plants and animals, who are primarily or exclusively creatures of tropism or instinct. Immense horizons for individuality open when billions of cortical cells are added to the neural equipment of lower species. Man talks, laughs, feels bored, develops a culture, prays, has a foreknowledge of death, studies theology, and strives for the improvement of his own personality. The infinitude of resulting patterns is plainly not found in creatures of instinct. For this reason we should exercise great caution when we extrapolate the assumptions, methods and concepts of natural and biological science to our subject matter. In particular, we should refuse to carry over the indifference of other sciences to the problem of individuality.[49]

This interplay between similarity and uniqueness among persons provides a fascinating problem for educators. The challenge is to plan educational opportunities in a way that open up each person's potential instead of hammering him into an inflexible mold.

> Research findings in the areas of creativity, human development, and individual differences have emphasized the uniqueness of the individual. Children have not fitted neatly into categories of slow learners, gifted, academically talented, culturally deprived, under-achievers, and that most mystical of all categorizations—the over-achiever. Each one is an individual with a learning potential and rate of his own.
>
> Individuality and creativity have become more prized in a society in which the pressures are for conformity. Thus, the pioneers in secondary education today are speaking out for what Getzels and Jackson and others define as the creative individual, the person who is

177

inventive, imaginative, and flexible; the one who can produce new forms and ideas; the one who wants to explore the unknown and is unwilling to accept traditional answers without question; the nonconformist. You know, this can be a terribly unpopular fellow because he goads people into thinking.[50]

The intent of the continual life involvement approach is to provide for the balance between what is common to all and what is unique to each. This demands of any educational program built upon it both consistency and flexibility. When the planner's best is done, however, it is good to realize that in the final analysis, "a child literally grows himself up."[51] He is a remarkably resilient organism, "an energy system with high capacity for self repair and selectivity . . . a persistent personality with high capacity to resist deformation, stress, and trauma . . . a mechanism that meets life not as a storehouse or filing cabinet, but as an active system engaged in transforming input into outgo."[52] When the educator understands the full implications of such a statement, it becomes apparent that the program he plans does not control learning. Instead it must recognize and respect the dynamic quality of the learner's personality as he assimilates, reacts to, and shapes whatever comes to him in the process of making it his own.

A FINAL WORD

What I have attempted in this chapter is to test the assumptions of the Central Objective for Educational Ministry from the perspectives of sociology and psychology to determine whether they form adequate foundations for educational planning. On the whole it may be said that they do. At the same time, it must be recognized that the concept of viewing life involvements in Christian perspective is a relatively new idea and tests the limits of what is known about human personality, learning theory, and man's interaction with society. But this probing of the limits of the known is a necessary approach to the problem of educational development today. It involves risks, but the risks are no greater than those inherent in attempting to remain securely within the perimeters of past experience. While venturing forth in this way into uncharted territory must be done boldly, it must also be undertaken with some humility and an awareness that no new effort will result in a complete and final answer to the perplexing problem of education in a revolutionary age.

No matter what we do in education, it is at best an assist along the way to a fellow human whom we will never fully know and who is grappling with an infinitely complex society on a shrinking planet in an expanding universe. This is not to say all our efforts to understand him and to plan for him are of no worth. Indeed we can do no less. But in this whirling, buzzing confusion of human life, there is much we do not know and we grope forward as best we can. In that process, the direction taken by the Central Objectives for Educational Ministry is a promising one. It is an hypothesis that accords well with what we do know in the sociological and psychological fields. As with any hypothesis, its real test will come not from a series of essayists in a book but from the laboratory of life, the arena of action.

NOTES AND REFERENCES

1. *A Central Objective for Educational Ministry in the Parish: ALC and LCA* (Philadelphia: Board of Parish Education of the Lutheran Church in America, 1969), p. 28.
2. Robert Havighurst, *Human Development and Education* (New York: Longmans Green & Co., Inc., 1953).
3. Florence Stratemeyer *et al.*, *Developing a Curriculum for Modern Living* (New York: Teachers College, Bureau of Publ., Columbia University, 1957).
4. *The Functional Objectives for Christian Education* (Philadelphia: Lutheran Boards of Parish Education, 1959).
5. *Central Objective*, pp. 25-27.
6. James Bossard and Eleanor Boll, *The Sociology of Child Development* (New York: Harper & Brothers, 1954), p. 24.
7. *Human Development and Education*. See also Robert Havighurst and Robert Peck, *The Psychology of Character Development* (New York: John Wiley & Sons, Inc., 1960).
8. David R. Krathwohl, "The Psychological Basis for Integration" in *The Integration of Educational Experiences*, 57th Yearbook, National Society for the Study of Education, ed. Nelson B. Henry (Chicago: University of Chicago Press, 1958), pp. 45-46.
9. *Central Objective*, pp. 25-27.
10. Robert L. Heilbroner, *The Future as History* (New York: Harper & Brothers, 1960), p. 31.
11. Talcott Parsons and Edward Shils, eds., *Toward a General Theory of Action* (Cambridge, Mass.: Harvard University Press, 1954), p. 395.
12. Harold Haas, "What Influence Does the Secular Society Have Upon the Person Today Through Its Social Structures?" in *Christian Education*

in a Secular Society (Geneva: LWF Commission on Education, 1969), p. 5.

13. C. Ellis Nelson, *Where Faith Begins* (Richmond, Va.: John Knox Press, 1967), p. 37.

14. Charles Y. Glock, "The Controlling Factors in Our Society Which Influence the Development of the Individual," in *Christian Education in a Secular Society* (Carthage: Report of the North American Regional Conference, 1966).

15. Solomon Inquai, "What Influence Does the Secular Society Have on the Persons of Today Through Its Educational System?" in *Christian Education in a Secular Society* (Geneva: LWF Commission on Education, 1969).

16. "What Influence Does the Secular Society Have Upon the Person Today Through Its Social Structures?"

17. *Ibid.*, p. 16.

18. Abraham H. Maslow, *Toward a Psychology of Being* (Princeton: D. Van Nostrand Co., Inc., 1962), pp. 151-152.

19. Charles Glock and Rodney Stark, *Religion and Society in Tension* (Chicago: Rand McNally & Co., 1965), Chapters 10-11.

20. Jack Culbertson, "State Planning for Education," in *Effecting Needed Changes in Education,* Designing Education for the Future, vol. 3, eds. E. L. Morphet and C. O. Ryan (New York: Citation Press, 1967), pp. 266 ff.

21. Arthur A. King and John A. Brownell, *The Curriculum and the Disciplines of Knowledge* (New York: John Wiley & Sons, Inc., 1966), p. 12.

22. *Ibid.*, pp. 12 ff.

23. "What Influence Does the Secular Society Have Upon the Person Today Through Its Social Structures?" p. 84.

24. *Where Faith Begins,* p. 101.

25. *Ibid.*, p. 185.

26. *Central Objective,* pp. 21-22.

27. *The Future as History,* p. 101.

28. Gordon W. Allport, *The Person in Psychology* (Boston: Beacon Press, 1968), p. 155. See also Daniel A. Prescott, *The Child in the Educative Process* (New York: McGraw-Hill Book Co., Inc., 1957), pp. 362-3.

29. Walter J. Ong, "Knowledge in Time," in *Knowledge and the Future of Man,* ed. W. J. Ong (New York: Holt, Rinehart and Winston, Inc., 1968), p. 6.

30. *Ibid.*, p. 25.

31. Marshall McLuhan, "We Need a New Picture of Knowledge" in *New Insights and the Curriculum,* Association for Supervision and Curriculum Yearbook, 1963, ed. Alexander Frazier (Washington, D.C.: Association for Supervision and Curriculum Development, 1963), p. 63.

32. Hilda Taba, "Education for Independent Valuing," *Ibid.*, p. 237.

33. John H. Randall, Jr., "The World to be Unified," in *The Unity of Knowledge*, ed. L. G. Leary (New York: Doubleday & Co., Inc., 1955) p. 63.

34. Kenneth E. Boulding, "Expecting the Unexpected: The Uncertain Future of Knowledge and Technology" in *Prospective Changes in Society by 1980*, Designing Education for the Future, vol. 1, eds. E. L. Morphet and C. O. Ryan (New York: Citation Press, 1966), pp. 199-200.

35. Herman Kahn and Anthony J. Weiner, *The Year 2000* (New York: The Macmillan Co., 1967). See also Edgar L. Morphet and Charles O. Ryan, eds., *Prospective Changes in Society by 1980*, Designing Education for the Future, vol. 1 (New York: Citation Press, 1966); A. M. Greely, *Religion in the Year 2000* (New York: Sheed and Ward, 1969); Edward W. Uthe, *Social Change: An Assessment of Current Trends* (Philadelphia: Fortress Press, 1968).

36. *Social Change*, pp. 17-20.

37. Francis S. Chase, "Educational Implications of Changing Knowledge," in *To Nuture Humaneness: Commitment for the 70's.* (Washington, D.C.: Association for Supervision and Curriculum Development, 1970), p. 96.

38. John H. Rorher and Muzafer Sherif, *Social Psychology at the Crossroads* (New York: Harper & Brothers, 1951), p. 147.

39. "Education for Independent Valuing," pp. 236-7.

40. *Central Objective*, p. 20.

41. Jean Piaget, *The Moral Judgment of the Child* (New York: The Macmillan Co., 1965). Also by the same author, *Judgment and Reasoning in the Child* (London: Routledge & Kegan Paul, Ltd.) and *The Child's Conception of the World* (London: Routledge & Kegan Paul, Ltd., 1951).

42. *Human Development and Education.*

43. Elizabeth Hurlock, *Developmental Psychology* (New York: McGraw-Hill Book Co., Inc., 1959).

44. Arnold Gesell *et al., Youth: The Years from Ten to Sixteen* (New York: John Wiley & Sons, Inc., 1954).

45. Erik H. Erikson, *Childhood and Society* (New York: W. W. Norton & Co., Inc., 1964).

46. *Human Development and Education*, p. 124.

47. Ronald Goldman, *Religious Thinking from Childhood to Adolescence* (London: Routledge & Kegan Paul, Ltd., 1964).

48. *Developmental Psychology*, pp. 25-28. Cf. Bernard Berelson and Gary Steiner, *Human Behavior: An Inventory of Scientific Findings* (New York: Harcourt, Brace & World, Inc., 1964), pp. 52 ff.

49. Gordon W. Allport, *Becoming* (New Haven, Conn.: Yale University Press, 1955), p. 22.

50. Vernon E. Anderson, *Curriculum Guidelines in an Era of Change* (New York: The Ronald Press Co., 1969), p. 70.
51. William Koppe, "A Developmental Perspective," in *Confirmation and Education*, Yearbooks in Christian Education—I, ed. W. Kent Gilbert (Philadelphia: Fortress Press, 1969).
52. John E. Anderson, "Personality Organization in Children," in *Readings in Child Psychology*, ed. W. Dennis (New York: Prentice-Hall, Inc., 1951), p. 479.

Sociological/Psychological Foundations— A Response

VERNON E. ANDERSON

The purpose of these chapters, as I understand it, is to criticize, analyze, and comment on the failings or potentials of the central objective document, its delineation in the form of age-level objectives, and the staff writers' exposition of the major foundations of these objectives in an attempt to help the leaders in Christian education "learn what they did not know before." Quite an assignment! Several theological scholars and parish education specialists have written for this yearbook incisive statements regarding the foundations of education: historical, social, philosophical, psychological. What then, does one say that is new, different?

Yet, the assignment makes sense to me, especially in the light of helping someone learn something new. Although much of what is written in professional education—and I suspect it is true in theology as well—says what someone else has already said, each of us is an individual with different backgrounds, experiences, competencies, and ages. Each of us who has written a chapter of this yearbook, therefore, can bring something of himself to this task.

And that is what I believe planning for the educational ministry in the parish is all about. The program is for all age levels—early childhood through adulthood. It is for persons who have lived long, full, rich Christian lives with much interaction with people and for those who have lived lonely, isolated, drab existences; for those who are well educated in "book larnin" and those who have gained an education from the marketplace or the streets; for the young who rebel and for the old who reminisce; for the "sinner" as well as the "saint"; for the farm boy in Minnesota and the city girl in New York.

If there is any one firm thread that runs through all of the age-level objectives and comes out strong in the central objective, it is that the communities of people to be reached are all different, that any program which will reach them must of necessity be adapted and adaptable to the wide and fascinating individual differences among people. Thus, it is not only the community of believers that is to be sought, but, according to Christ's command, the "community of non-believers" as well. No educational program that points only toward those already in the fold will succeed in the world of tomorrow. That fact stands out strongly in Lindberg's chapter on the future. We must "go into the highways and the byways" where people are, not confine ourselves to within the church walls nor to the people we shake hands with in church every Sunday.

Is, then, the concept of the church as a "gathering together of the faithful in worship, communion, and as a means of sharing love and forgiveness with one another"[1] consistent with the idea that the church's mission is in relation to the world and that the present conditions are only temporary, so well expounded throughout the central objective statement and confirmed by historical and sociological perspective? Surely, a community of believers with a group identity is not for purposes of patting each other on the back nor for bridge or bowling with the same middle-class group, but is an outreach community that seeks continually to bring others into a group identity in such a mission of "assisting persons to perceive, respond to, and participate in God's continuing activity."[2] The coffeehouses, the meetings for worship in the old store fronts, the sky-pilot type of program of the Methodist church's home missions work do not conceive of the church as a place where one meets only with other believers of similar beliefs. What this means for the small rural parish is at this point difficult to conceive.

No, the objectives say to me that the challenge which educational ministry faces in an uncertain future for the church is one of reaching, really touching, the innermost lives of the kid in the ghetto, the Panther, the long-haired, the dirty, and the unkempt; the black, white,

183

or brown; the clean-washed and the well-loved; as well as the pampered suburban youngster. And it must pursue him through old age. The church can no longer feel comfortable in serving its parish in the traditional sense. The central objective clearly makes the distinction between education and acculturation. If as Lindberg and Johnston say in their chapter, "most institutional church-goers will be forty-five years old and older," then the new concept of the parish has to be the wider community, or we will have only a parish education program for older adults. The "church's perception of its mission changes as the changes occur in the world."[3]

Gilbert has so ably dealt with some of these issues in his chapter, which concentrates on the key concepts of the central objective and the validity of the assumptions made by the statement of objectives and design. I can only expand on these, for I agree with what he says. I shall, in addition, point out some of the implications which these concepts, imbedded in the central objective, have for the program and materials to be developed by the ALC and LCA for educational ministry in the parish.

Differences in Social and Cultural Settings

The social foundations of education deal with the setting in which learning experiences occur. Educators, sociologists and other behavioral scientists have studied the nature of the changing world, the rapidity of change, and what these mean for education.[4] The very magnitude and acceleration of change has amplified the need for education to deal with the social problems accompanying technological and related value changes: pollution, population explosion, racism, the sexual revolution, use of drugs, the increase of crime and violence, and the age-old problem of war. When education, with all its sophisticated means of predicting future needs is suddenly faced with an unpredicted excess of teachers, let us take heed. Let those of us in Christian education be alert to what theologians, sociologists, educators are telling us about the future of the church, much of which stern warning can be found in the chapters of this yearbook and in the central objective statement.

One can misread signs, to be sure, but one cannot misread the fact that young people—who are the church of tomorrow—are disillusioned, frightened, and angry. They are disgusted with hypocrisy, disenchanted with political chicanery in high places, dissatisfied with the emphasis on the material and the comfortable.

Youth can "cop out" of the church as an institution, whereas they need to stay in college to insure their future. Consequently, perhaps to the detriment of the church, they may work for change in the college, but stay away from the church. The meaning is clear: the church must be where the people are, where youth are. This does not infer fighting the establishment as a principle, using revolutional tactics, destroying that of which one is a part, nor—as some chaplains have chosen to do—leading youth to violence. But it does mean a leadership for a changing world on the part of the whole educational ministry, wherever it appears—on campus, in the church, or in the community.

The writers of the chapters for this yearbook say time and again that the church must move out into the community, use the "umbrella principle" with a great many places of worship, develop new models, be "where people are", risk the "revolutionary route", be seen as a segment of the world. Surely, this is part of the focus of the central objective.

It is not only the hippies who "cop out". There is more than one way to be out of touch. The celibate, the monk, the hermit, the recluse have much in common; only the exterior looks different. A modern educational ministry is alive in the modern world. The concept of an expanded educational ministry which includes as its agents the lay person means that many more of the community of believers must make their leadership felt in the community, not only in religious matters but in social concern, and in the tough political arena where social and economic policy is made.

This is what youth in colleges are asking, not to be led by a Hitler with raised arm to urge them on to destroy, but to be led by decent human beings who have a genuine concern for the ills of the world and who will exert personal or political influence to correct the situation.

What area of emphasis, then, is appropriate for the next decade in an uncertain future? What kinds of behaviors are fundamental to the Christian community which hopes to survive in a world of revolution and upheaval? One of the pertinent means is to teach children, youth, and adults how to cope with change through analysis, planning, dealing

185

with the catastrophic and the unexpected, and, most of all, through the experience of making changes in themselves.

This type of behavior change calls for an other-relatedness, for a genuine concern for human beings, not in the China-oriented missionary work, but in the kind that deals with the neighbor next door, at work, and in the nearby ghetto or rural poverty area. It calls for getting one's feet wet and one's hands dirty, not for marching or demonstrating as a means of securing action. Just as the possibilities for change in ourselves are best found in our classroom or congregation, in our everyday relations to people, so the most effective place for outreach in educational ministry is found in the community that surrounds us, and an ever-expanding community at that as the world shrinks in size.

Being future-oriented does not mean abandoning the traditions and heritage of the church. Instead, it means that those who prize their heritage, who believe that what we have is good, need to work with young people, talk with them, explain to them what it is that is important to them about the church, why it is that the church has affected their lives so keenly. Surely, there is a richness in one's church heritage as in other aspects of one's cultural background which others who face a different life can be led to understand and appreciate. This is a part of the layman's ministry in the church.

Nor does the church that pays attention to the individual differences of age, social background, sectional differences, and philosophical differences neglect programs that appeal to the more traditional folk. But they, too, live in a changing world. Are we to say that they should have no influence on what the future of that world will be like? In fact, they can be the stalwarts of influence on the church of the future, but not by leading a cloistered life which avoids the risks of association with the young, the black, the indigent, or the drug addict.

The writers of the educational materials to be used in parish education, therefore, should pay attention to a variety of content and programs—Biblical in orientation, but future oriented and focused on the life and problems of the community. Materials need to be prepared for different settings: churches, retreats, community-action programs, youth hostels and camps, the store-front gathering places, the home, colleges, the retirement home, the recreation spots of our country, even "bums row." We need to ask ourselves seriously, Will the weekday church school, the vacation church school, adult Bible classes, and Sunday church school be the answer? I doubt that the designers of the program can hold a future-orientated program to a past-oriented design for a locale or time of the week or year.

The main implication of social change may well be in the inter-relationships between the educational program and the community. As Gilbert points out, the context for learning is not in isolation but within the Christian community and the wider community. In the future, education—be it religious or secular—may not be found in the typical classrooms but in the meeting place of the teacher and pupil wherever it may occur. Jesus' way will be the most effective one. He sought out people, walked among Publicans and harlots, and taught wherever he went.

How does God reveal himself in the modern world? Through youth? Through Hiroshimas? Through Vietnams? Through the crying needs of the Black in the inner slums of the big cities (not too unlike the compounds we provided for the Japanese on the West Coast in World War II)? It undoubtedly takes participation in the human community to see God revealing himself today and tomorrow. He probably is revealed in my relationships to other persons with whom I come in contact, in my fulfilling myself as a person where the conflicting demands "threaten my identity."

To respond to the human community, as the central objective statement indicates, through "voluntary sharing of suffering and positive action to achieve social justice and fulfillment," (p. 17) is a noble goal, but even this objective could be misinterpreted through a modern Inquisition.

The fact that children, youth, and adults in the Lutheran church live in different kinds of socio-economic environments means that one book or course will not necessarily do for all. For too long, Black children, Indian children, Chicano children, have not been able to identify with the books used in their classrooms. Even the children's literature found in the library (if there were one) gave an unreal picture of the Indian. Only in recent years has this condition begun to be corrected. Different ways of adapting centrally-produced materials to local situations need to be explored.

The material used by all children should include illustrations, examples, and incidents realistically picturing the lives of youngsters

187

from minority groups. This has been rather well done in the LCA Board of Parish Education's recently-published materials. Some experimentation has taken place regarding local development of the course utilizing an experience-centered approach.[5]

Another implication is that perhaps the Boards of Parish Education in the ALC and LCA should search for and utilize more books and pamphlets already published rather than attempting to develop new course materials in each instance. The leadership program ought to assist teachers to use such a variety of resources. After all, even many who are experienced public school teachers were never effectively taught how to do so. It also means continued and expanded production of materials in various media, especially those within the means of the member churches: videotape, filmstrips, slides, pictures. Churches will need to combine their resources in regional instructional materials centers, promoted by the synods and cooperatively supported.

Differences in Abilities, Needs, and Interests of Individuals

The uniqueness of children in terms of their ability to learn is as important a concept for a curriculum program as is the variety of settings in which the children live. Curriculum developers and teachers need to recognize the facts that exist. In a sixth grade, for example, children may vary as much as eight grade levels in achievement, measured by standardized tests. The design of the curriculum has recognized this in the use of the age-level objectives rather than any mythical grade level. Grade levels do not exist in actuality, only in the minds of textbook writers and educators who want to categorize neatly and organize a school. One has but to note the growing interest in the non-graded type of school.[6]

The central objective statement recognizes that "persons should be central in the church's educational ministry" and that "each person stands as an equal within the community" (p. 3). It also points out that "the assumption that one curriculum can meet the needs of all situations needs to be reexamined" (p. 9).

Not only do a wide range of differences exist among children, both because of inherent abilities and as a result of the environment in which they have been reared, but also there are the extremes to be considered: the so-called "mentally retarded", "physically handicapped", "emotionally disturbed", "aged." Are they to be disregarded or recognized as important "minority groups' in the educational ministry of the church? I am sure that the answer is obvious. The solution is not.

If the relations between environment, man, and God are seen as a "tri-polar base" for the curriculum, then those who have an entirely different relation to their environment—the sightless, those confined to a wheel chair, or those so mentally deficient that they cannot manipulate their environment—need special kinds of materials and programs prepared for them. This situation calls for individuals in the field of special education on the central parish education staff.

Labels on abilities for instructional purposes are demeaning for the human being if all of us are equal in the sight of God. Rarely have we demeaned adults in this fashion; children are easier to manipulate. Such categories as "mentally retarded", "slow-learner", "emotionally disturbed", "disadvantaged", "gifted" tend to put children into convenient pigeonholes and imply to the teacher that the children within such a group are the same. They are not. Wide differences exist within each such category. A physically-handicapped youngster may be brilliant in academic ability; a "slow-learner' may be good at human relations, mechanical skills, or the creative skills. We simply do not have the know-how to classify people for instructional purposes with any great degree of validity. There are too many variables involved. Thus, any grouping scheme, even for the extremes in differences among children or adults, has to be a flexible one.

The uniqueness of individual development means that objectives for any program need to be open-ended. It is doubtful that we have ever discovered the limits of learning. Thus, objectives in any program are to be regarded as having unknown limits. It is generally the teacher (not the material) who places limits by the very nature of how he utilizes those materials.

Each person is unique. He will operate in his own way in any given situation, although there are similarities among people that make it possible to have commonalities in materials and experiences.

Regarding the Christian's responsibility in the political arena, the central objective says that "the Christian person will press for understanding, peace, justice, among all nations, especially taking into account the needs of developing and disadvantaged nations" (p. 29). But he will and should operate in his own way, according to his own life-style. Everyone does not have to be a politician, nor an activist, but each functions according to his own individual nature and ability to witness for Christ. To interpret the above-quoted statement literally would mean that the illiterate tobacco worker acts in the same way as the well-educated community leader. To say that "a Christian's means of expression and communication will be those that have the greatest relevance for the day" (p. 29) is indeed pertinent, but it is incomplete unless that means of expression is relevant for him as a person, as an individual.

No single type of experience outlined in a course, in the pupil's book or in the teacher's book, is meaningful in the same way to all persons. Thus, a wide variety of activities, from which the teacher who is alert to individual differences can select, is suggested in developing any course.

Much has been written about the psychological needs of children,[7] far less about adults. The need for love, affection, belonging, being an adequate self, security, and freedom from guilt is common to all ages. These needs are emphasized time and again in the statement of age level objectives for the early childhood years as the major concerns and objectives for a direction for learning, almost to the exclusion of cognitive learnings.[8] Research by Martin Deutsch, Bruner, and others has shown that children can learn more complex concepts at an early age.[9] Arvid Anderson's chapter in this yearbook indicates that only the physical universe in the cognitive field is given high priority in the materials dealing with the early childhood age level. I believe the task force needs to consider seriously the question of whether there are no important learnings about society, culture, political processes, economic processes, and religious and philosophical processes which could be imparted at the early age level. Are there not many concepts about and attitudes toward religion to be learned at that age level, at a time when many life-long attitudes are formed?

Individualized Learning

Although other authors of this yearbook have commented on a shift in the central objective from a psychological bent to a sociological one, I doubt that the task force meant this to be interpreted that the individual in the learning situation should be ignored. These statements in the document would belie such an interpretation: "Persons should be central in the church's educational ministry." "Each person stands as an equal within the community" (p. 3).

Uthe's statement in his chapter of this yearbook throws further light on what the program developers need to consider regarding individual differences in abilities and cultural background. He says, "If the population to be served contains groups that can be distinguished from one another on the basis of such factors as socioeconomic situation, mental or emotional limitations, theological and social viewpoints, strong and distinctive subcultural characteristics, then consideration should be given to expanding the central objective with specific reference to these various groups."

"Well and good," the parish education leader comments, "but what does this mean for the program in my congregation?" He may wonder whether it means the usual answer of public school people, dividing the children at various age levels into homogeneous groups. A homogeneous group in a classroom is a fiction. There is no such thing when it comes to learning what one needs to learn. Every group, no matter how pupils are classified—by age, ability, or interests—no matter what the criterion, is heterogenous in all other respects and is even not alike on the trait by which it is classified. It is only more alike on that one criterion than if no classification had occurred.

I think the answer lies in the shift from teaching-learning situations in which one teacher works with ten to twenty pupils in a group, to more person-to-person interaction, where more of the teacher's contact with the pupil is individual (like pastoral counseling), where the pupil learns by himself certain aspects in which the material can guide him, and where he learns with a group the values and clarification of concepts that comes from interaction with his fellows. Large groups for lectures (such as the sermon), small groups for discussion, personal interaction with community individuals and groups, individual study and reflection—all will need to be utilized if instruction is to be truly individualized.

Individualization of instruction is within our grasp because of the developments in instructional technology which can provide an individual tutor for the pupil. Newer media such as audiotape, videotape, overlays, slides, films, filmstrips, recordings, computers, and others yet to be invented, give us unlimited resources for information storage, processing, and retrieval. Packaged self-instructional materials can vary from simple mimeographed units to more highly sophisticated prorgammed instruction materials to multi-media packages and "systems" using different media, both visual and auditory.

Smaller congregations cannot support such technological devices, the "hardware" (machine) or the "software" (what is used by the machine, such as the film), but neither can small school systems. What public schools have done is to band together by counties or by geographical regions in order to support jointly an instructional materials center. If individualized instruction is ever to become a reality in the parish ministry, the materials center needs to be established as a resource bank for the congregations involved. Most congregations have a dearth of even printed materials, (and stuff the books and pamphlets that they do have into a closet or dusty bookcase). The regional service for instructional materials is just as much a possibility as the regional use of leadership resources.

Some of the needs in the ALC-LCA parish education program are publications helping to develop such an inter-congregational center, pre-packaged multi-media materials available to congregations, aids in both constructing and utilizing media, and a leadership program for individualization of instruction. The parish education staffs have shown the capability of developing creative materials and new media.

All visual media need not be expensive. Scrap materials, simple tools, materials for making slides and overlays can, in the hands of resourceful teachers, adults, and youth in the congregation, be turned into valuable teaching aids. It could be the best kind of project to bring the different age groups in the community of believers together!

Individualized learning is not the same as independent study. Instead, it is a learning program which provides sequential progress for the pupil at his own rate and in directions where interests and needs may take him.[10] If such a program is ever to be successful, we need to help teachers acquire the skills of writing behavioral objectives, that is, objectives in terms of the changes in behavior of the pupil (ways of thinking, feeling, acting) they wish to have occur. Thus far, we have failed miserably in the LCA parish education program in doing so because our examples of objectives, instead of picturing what the pupil will be able to do or say, how he will behave by word and deed, have often been a garble of general objectives and learning experience.

Granted that all objectives cannot be so specifically delineated, but many of them can and we can work at it. A start would be to use as a criterion that no objective is to be stated as a specific instructional objective unless one can evaluate whether or not the learning has occurred. If, for example, the objective is too general, such as "to help persons become a part of the community of believers", there is no possible way of evaluating such an objective unless it is broken down into more specific behaviors. How does a person act if he is a member of this community? What does he do? How is he different from the unbelievers? Statement of objectives that are truly behavioral ought to have a self-contained evaluation as a part of them.

There is nothing wrong with stating general objectives. That is the point from which to start in constructing a curriculum. But one does not stop there, or he has not provided a very usable guide for instruction. Often, it is the teacher's responsibility for constructing behavioral or specific objectives. He needs to develop the necessary skills to do so.[11]

But these ends cannot be achieved without skillful and knowledgeable leadership. I believe the central parish education program of the ALC and LCA will do better to put more of its energies into local leadership development, less into development of instructional materials to be put into the hands of the pupils.

This approach would place the focus upon learning experiences that children, youth, and adults will have in the parish education program. Workshops could be organized for vacation and weekend retreats on a regional basis for leaders in the various synods, ministers, religious education personnel, and lay persons. These, in turn, would organize workshops for groups of local congregations in the synod. In other words, the principle of preparing teachers of teachers would make the most effective use of the central church body's staff.

Such workshops could take different forms. Some could center around the development and use of print materials and audio-visual media for individualized instruction. Others could lead the group through actual experiences in selecting and using many kinds of books and pamphlets in group study. Some could feature giving participants a week's experience in a community where the leaders of a church are already deeply committed to being a part of that community and to solving its problems. Others could concentrate on writing behavioral objectives, planning with youth, or evaluating the outcomes of instruction. In a college community setting, the learning experience might illustrate how college students can become an on-going part of the church's parish education program. Now we tend to set college students aside with activities of their own, failing to see the potential that exists for their work with children in our church. We ought to consider how much more vital a church becomes to a young person away from home if he is given responsibility in its program, other than the reading of scripture, other than being regarded as a visitor.

This is a direction in which instructional "packages" can be used effectively. Leaders need to practice what they preach, using the procedures they teach to instruct teachers, who will best learn from seeing these procedures in action and having practice in their utilization.

Discovery and Inquiry: Christian Involvement

The "continual life involvement" is a rather new and strange design for a curriculum to many teachers. Yet, it makes a lot of sense as one studies the volumes prepared by the task force as working papers for the age-level objectives for early childhood, elementary school years, youth, and adults. The continual life involvements become translated into major concerns, objectives, and implications for process and program, the curriculum. They form the heart of the design or framework of the curriculum. They are the tasks which a person performs, the things he is involved with in becoming a person, in growing up and maturing and reaching old age. The process regards the person as someone whose development as a human being occurs from birth to death. "In Christian perspective, one finds personal fulfillment in wholeness, freedom, being for others, affirmation of life."[12] Of course, some of the fulfillment never occurs, or is arrested, largely because of a person's inability to cope successfully with his environment, relate to other persons, or to satisfactorily develop himself and his concept of himself as a person.

This design provides a way of relating Christian conviction and values to life rather than treating them as a separate entity or segment of life. It is a part of one's everyday living and becoming a person, a task which none of us ever stops working at from birth to death.

Therefore, it is natural to expect that a curriculum based on life involvements will emphasize interaction with life in one's surrounding community. Each pupil is to discover and interpret the meaning of life's events for himself. If the curriculum is successful in accomplishing its purposes, it leads to a life style of inquiry into religion, its forms, symbols, and values. To some persons, this is dangerous because such inquiry may lead to new forms and symbols, to a different type of Lutheran church. We had better awaken to the fact (if that is our thinking) that young people do inquire more, do question more the old values and ways, awaken to the fact that the church *is* changing. Unless we as adults give guidance in this inquiring and *work* with young people in doing so, the church has no future that could by any means be termed bright.

A part of the essence of the central objective is "to *perceive, respond* to, *participate* in God's continuing activity and revelation" (p. 31). Learning is an active process. These are action verbs that denote participation in relation to life's socio-economic problems, active involvement in relating to other persons. The definition given for "responding" educationally is an "atmosphere in which people are free to make decisions about the nature and meaning of God's anxiety and revelation, free to disagree, free to choose not to participate in any way" (p. 15).

Thus the educational process is one of active participation of the learner, not one of talking by the teacher who assumes that the pupil will learn only by listening. Freedom to disagree, freedom to be oneself, freedom to question—these concepts are foreboding threats to many who are used to making dogmatic assertions about life, religion or secular. These concepts call for an entirely new relation between teacher and pupil in many instances, but one in which the person becomes actively engaged under guidance in questioning from childhood to adulthood. A child and young person will question anyway, as a part of his developmental process. Only continued beating into him that he is worthless and of little value, and the "I'm a hundred per cent right" attitude that some teachers and preachers take will dull this inquisitiveness and interest in religion as related to his life.

195

The Educational Program and Total Church Life

In a real sense in the type of curriculum envisioned, the church is a part of the educational ministry in all of its facets and activities. If the young people's activities turn them off, they are no longer active participants. If women's groups follow boring "canned" programs that never utilize the creativity or imagination that exists in the congregation, the educational program for adults in that church is so much the poorer.

A main stress in the central objective statement is on Christians participating in the human community, on becoming a Christian community in a larger sense, on mutual service, on service to one's fellowman without asking anything in return, on valuing one's neighbor's well-being as much as one's own. These interactions with others are regarded as necessary to man's fulfillment of himself as a person, as a Christian person.

The implications for the program are that all that goes on in the church is educational, that everyone in the church takes some part in educational ministry. The idea that one teaches a Sunday school class to be involved in Christian education, then, is a misinterpretation. One can talk to young people, chat with them at the coffee hour. One can work with others in preparing dinners, offer his services in other ways large or small. But somehow, persons of all ages need to be involved in the life of the church and in the decision-making process. Not all can be members of the church council. Nor are non-functioning committees any useful basis for determining participation.

The campus church furnishes a good example. Such a congregation has rich, unequaled opportunities to affect young people's lives when they are at college, away from their home environment and home church, perhaps for the first time. Yet, what do we find? Too often, the campus congregation exhibits a "town-and-gown" division. Adults resent the time the pastor spends with the young people. The college counselor or education worker considers his job that of working with college students. He has little or no imagination on how to involve the "town" in the "gown", when that is actually his main responsibility. Yes, the parish education program has also a responsibility for a program for college youth. That is eminently clear, for parish education is a lifelong process. College Christian education is not to be left to another church body. The task forces and groups that looked at interrelationships among agencies within the Lutheran church have made that very plain.[13]

Criteria for Programs of Educational Ministry

As a summary for this chapter, questions which can serve as criteria for evaluating programs, objectives, learning experiences, and materials are presented. These criteria emphasize the meaning of the psychological and sociological foundations for the nature and direction of the parish education ministry. They may be utilized by a task force, an ALC-LCA staff committee, a synod or local church, or an individual writer or producer of materials.

Social Setting

1. Is the program appropriate for the next ten years?
2. Does it take into account that the educational ministry of the future will tend to be in different settings than in the past?
3. Is it open to new models, ideas, forms, and symbols?
4. Is the design of the program also open-ended, amenable to change as social changes occur?
5. Is it adaptable to many kinds of churches and communities in order that it can be used in different settings?
6. Does it consider and provide for the different values that exist among ALC-LCA churches in different cultural settings and different sections of the country?
7. Does it examine different existing values in society?
8. Does it assist the person to live in the midst of conflict and change?
9. Does it encourage interrelationships among church bodies at the national level?

The Congregation and Its Community

10. Does the program encourage interrelationships between the educational work of the local parish and its total congregational life?
11. Does it emphasize the function of the church in relation to its larger community?

12. Does it suggest means of utilizing both ongoing activities of the church and potentials for involvement in the community?
13. Does it relate life involvements to the Christian faith?
14. Does it make full use of its own resources for leadership within the congregation and its community?

Objectives and Evaluation

15. Are the goals of the program clearly understood by those participating in it?
16. In the program, in its resources and materials, are objectives stated in behavioral terms which can be evaluated?
17. Are suggestions given for evaluating these specific objectives?
18. Are the objectives of the course open-minded in order that the learner may go beyond the anticipated ends?
19. Is evaluation considered in planning and developing the program?

Active Participation in Learning

20. Does the program encourage and provide for active participation of the learner?
21. Do leadership activities clarify and demonstrate what it means to participate actively in the learning process?
22. Does it encourage decision-making by the individual?
23. Does it permit a person to discover and interpret the meaning of life's events for himself in order to arrive at a Christian perspective?
24. Does it suggest ways in which different groups in the church— adults, college students, youth, children—can become active agents for the educational ministry of the church?

Provision for Individual Differences

25. Does the program provide for all age levels?
26. Does the program consider the differences in abilities, interests, and needs among the age group for which it is intended?
27. Does it encourage each person to contribute of himself according to his own capacities and disposition in his own way?
28. Does it recognize that young children can understand the more complex concepts of religion if taught in simple form?
29. Does it provide for the interests of youth in the modern world?
30. Does it provide for individualized learning opportunities and person-to-person interaction?

31. Do leadership activities give practice in individualized learning?

Preparation and Nature of Materials

32. Does the program provide for a variety of materials, print and non-print?
33. Does it utilize a variety of the new media for the leadership preparation and for the educational ministry?
34. Are materials prepared for different cultural minority groups and for those who are handicapped in various ways?
35. Are they written so that they can be understood by persons with varying amounts of formal education?
36. Do they lend themselves to local initiative and adaptation?
37. Are they consistent with the concept of freedom to disagree with established practices?
38. Do the learning activities suggested have a clear relationship to the desired objectives to be learned?
39. Do the materials promote the overall goals of the program of educational ministry?

NOTES AND REFERENCES

1. *A Central Objective for Educational Ministry in the Parish: ALC and LCA* (Philadelphia: Board of Parish Education of the Lutheran Church in America, 1969)), p. 4.
2. *Ibid.*, p. 11. See also pp. 14, 18.
3. *Ibid.*, p. 1.
4. For example, Edgar L. Morphet and Charles O. Ryan, eds., *Prospective Changes in Society by 1980*, Designing Education for the Future, vol. 1 (New York: Citation Press, 1966), p. 268 and *Implications for Education of Prospective Changes in Society* (Denver: Project Office, Designing Education for the Future, 1967), p. 323.
5. For an explanation of this approach, see Vernon E. Anderson, *Principles and Procedures of Curriculum Improvement* (New York: Ronald Press Co., 1965), pp. 58-59.
6. Sidney P. Rollins, *Developing Non-Graded Schools* (Itasca, Ill.: F. E. Peacock Publishers, Inc., 1968), p. 198.
7. Louis E. Raths and Anna P. Burrell, *Understanding the Problem Child* (West Orange, N.J.: The Economics Press, 1963), pp. 7-20.
8. Task Force for Planning Educational Ministry in the Parish, The American Lutheran Church and the Lutheran Church in America, *Age-Level Objectives for Educational Ministry in the Parish: ALC and*

LCA, Volume I, Early Childhood (Philadelphia and Minneapolis: The American Lutheran Church and the Lutheran Church in America, 1970).

9. Jerome Bruner, ed. *Learning about Learning*, U. S. Office of Education Cooperative Research Monograph no. 15, Department of Health, Education, and Welfare (Washington, D.C.: U. S. Government Printing Office, 1966), chapter 2.

10. Helen McNamara et al., *Individual Progression* (New York: Bobbs Merrill Co., Inc., 1970), p. 94.

11. Useful paperback pamphlet materials for this purpose:
Robert J. Armstrong et al., *The Development and Evaluation of Behavioral Objectives* (Worthington, Ohio: Charles A. Jones Publishing Co., 1970).
H. H. McAshan, *Writing Behavioral Objectives: A New Approach* New York: Harper & Row, 1970).
Robert F. Mager, *Preparing Instructional Objectives* (Palo Alto, Calif.: Fearon Publishers, 1962).
Henry H. Walbesser, *Constructing Behavioral Objectives* (College Park, Md.: Bureau of Educational Research and Field Services, University of Maryland, 1970).

12. *Central Objective*, p. 26.

13. Edward W. Uthe, *Significant Issues for the 1970's: Report to the Lutheran Church in America Task Group for Long Range Planning* (Philadelphia: Fortress Press, 1968).

Chapter VII

Educational Ministry, Lay and Clergy

HERBERT BROKERING

The educational ministry of laity and clergy in the seventies will be mutual and supportive. The large debate distinguishing lay and clergy roles has given way to a common task, as they face the future as the Body of Christ. Together they will seek human potential in all life situations, calling upon the resources of the Christian community and society as a whole.

The responsibilities and roles of clergy and laity will be described as focusing primarily in the following areas: meaning for the gospel in the world; the congregation living out its history; the congregation in society; renewal in the congregation; and the creative climate for renewal.

In large measure this report orchestrates the expressed ideas of persons in various disciplines, who share a concern for life and learning in the seventies. The quotations are clues from reliable sources, whose concern and wisdom may provide an educational glimpse into the future.

If the selection and interpretation of these resources is correct, the seventies will be years of change, originality, revolution, imagination, and flexibility. Ministry will be interdependent and whole. It will consist increasingly of systems of events, interpretations, coalitions of persons, and media whereby the gospel will be relevant, gracious, and original.

THE MEANING OF THE GOSPEL IN THE WORLD

Laity and clergy, as one community, again raise the question, What is the Gospel in this day?

> In determining what the Gospel is in our time, one problem is the general acceptance of change as normal and as inevitable while the church has been accustomed to claim that what it offers is changeless. A new framework of understanding reality is prevailing, abandoning space as a primary category and using time instead. Even matter is understood more as a description of a sequence of events rather than a collection of substance. Other factors are increasing pressures, forcing churches to abandon their isolation and deal with the multiplicity of the system, and also to recognize the pressure of minority groups for recognition and justice. More and more the equation of middle-class values with Christianity is being exposed and questioned. Strategies for dealing with these problems should include informing church people of varying viewpoints, basing Christian education on the biblical message of radical grace, and studying Scripture in view of contemporary concerns.[1]

Education in the Christian and human community is a concern of each succeeding generation. The origin, value, and operation of theological perspectives are always in need of interpretation. This Christian perspective for the future of man in his world and the meaning of his historical situation is always a responsible and privileged matter.

Educational ministry is significantly related to interpretation, and may begin from the point of view of God, man, or environment and time.

> If one thinks theologically, the biblical word of the church assumes special importance. If one thinks anthropocentrically, then the pupil or the teacher is central, be they God related or autonomous. If one thinks in terms of the polis, education may take on a theocentric or democratic form. The question of whether world and reality are to be regarded idealistically, empirically, or materialistically determines the character of Christian education. If approached in terms of time, education may take on the form of being bound more to the past or to the experience of the historical present, or to being open to the future.[2]

The emphasis here will be on environment, which is sometimes called secular approach. This emphasis "expresses a profound concern for the other person, a non-Christian, and refuses to allow Christian education to detach itself from its context in a non-Christian world. It emphasizes a need for dealing with problems of social ethics and providing for political education."[3] Stress here is to educate the world, and if need be to educate people against the world, and to remain true to the faith. It expresses itself in decision and renewal, and is action oriented. Christianity has always been explosive.

At the same time Christianity struggles in culture and uses concepts which are derived from everyday, societal thinking. These concepts are shared by Christian and non-Christian. "Modern secular culture is directed almost exclusively to the present. With the shift in our whole cultural setting our picture of Jesus also has changed. It is the picture of man for others."[4] Culture, so understood, may be in conversation with the Christian faith. Educational ministry may be expressed in the common language of the world and the culture. Therefore, the problem of Christian education may be a linguistic problem. It will be necessary for Christian education thus to "clarify the relation between faith and life. Hence Christian educators must contribute to the formation of ethical thinking and action in society, influence concepts of law, politics and government, as well as economics, automation, and technology, along with affecting social, industrial, and racial groups, and also helping to shape understanding of the sexual with its implication for other aspects of life."[5]

The base from which this is to take place is the fundamentals of faith. "These include the conception of revelation, hermeneutical or interpretive necessity; the epistemology of faith, dialogue; the source of faith, knowledge and human imperatives; the contemporary forms of the Word, newness; the doctrine of creation, providences and the eschatological perspective and dimension, what is and what will be. In this perspective, characteristics of the life of the church in the world which have educational demands and implications, concluding that human potentiality 'must be seen in the context of the interrelationships of the gospel, man, and the world.' This means that the teaching ministry of the church belongs to the very nature of faith and its expression in the church . . ."[6]

So educational ministry has to do with the Scriptures. The process of secularization in America will cause educators to rethink the place of Scriptures in the educational life of the Christian community. With it comes the cry of some that the old and good is gone, that it will never be the same, that the new may be heresy, and that the meaning of the Bible has been eroded.

"Secularization opens up the possibilities of new freedom and of new enslavement for men. We have no doubt that it is creating a world in which it is easy to forget God, to give up all traditional religious practices, and at the same time lose all sense of meaning and purpose in life. . . . We believe that at this moment our churches need encouragement to get into the struggle far more than they need to be primed with warnings."[7]

It is a challenge for the Christian community to question the process of secularization over against the biblical understanding of history. The Bible for some "belongs to a religious world which is not admitted to belong to the world of secular events—the world in which we are when we read a daily newspaper. But this is to read the Bible wrongly. Whatever else it may be, the Bible is a secular book dealing with the sorts of events which a news editor accepts for publication in a daily newspaper; he is concerned with secular events, revolutions, enslavement and liberations, migrants and refugees, famines and epidemics, and all the rest. It deals with events which happen and tell a story which can be checked—and is being checked—by the work of archaeologists and historians. We miss this because we do not sufficiently treat the Bible as a whole."[8]

The Christian community in America has inherited the fact that for centuries the Bible provided a framework within which world history was taught in schools of Europe. Today the work of archaeologists and historians and biblical scholars and literary critics "have uncovered a thousand times more information about human history than the biblical writers knew, and that we have steeped ourselves in the histories of the great civilizations . . . and that we have far outgrown the narrow provincialism that thought of Judea as a center of the world."[9]

This is not to be seen as a threat to an educational ministry which has the Bible at its core. Rather, these are tools and clues for ways to use the Bible in an educational ministry of the future. At the center of this concern is the process and the meaning of interpretation and translation. The nature of translation is essential to educators, who ask what it means to translate. It obviously means to "take the old story and put it into the language of today. And this must be done repeatedly; even the best known translations of the Bible have many parts that are no longer understandable. But translating means more than a mere recasting in words. It means making 'relevant' too, so that the hearer remarks, 'why, that has to do with me!' "[10] It gives the Christian community the privilege and responsibility to see a story to its end, to wait and ask for the meaning, to raise the ultimate question, to inquire, to believe. It opens up the possibility for continual revelation, new forms of the old truth, new myths and stories and parables and miracles and incarnation on the loose. "No one can tell a story well unless he sees the point of the story. The hearer does not see it until the end. How then does one tell the story of the human race when we are still in the middle of it and do not know what the end will be? Can it be otherwise than on the basis of some belief, however provisional about the point of the story as a whole? And that means a belief which will precisely not be a demonstrable certainty."[11]

And so the educational ministers of the future go on telling the story by asking the ultimate questions. It is more than scrutinizing their own prejudices. It is rather lifting up the concerns of the people in raising the story of world history, of universal history, of contemporary man, of issues and events, and expecting and awaiting an answer that is of God.

This points the way for the church in its educational ministry to view God's place in the affairs of man, in all of life involvement. Every area of life is a legitimate context for educational planning. Life involvements are tested by the ultimate questions of meaning, in a community of faith. The believing community is part of biblical history.

This places action at the center of educational ministry. It is action of a believing and faith community in which there is room for forgiveness.

> I believe that God's will for me is that I should behave in the way which is a response to what he has done in Jesus Christ, and I believe that this is his will for all men. Because of this I know that I ought so to behave, and therefore in my best moments I do intend so to behave, though the intention is never perfect and is sometimes totally perverse. In fact I do not so behave. I constantly disobey what I know to be the will of God. Because it is a matter not merely of my intention of God's will, I will express to Jesus Christ, there is room and need for the whole relationship of repentance, forgiveness, and asking for fresh strength, so that even my perversities become the way by which I am cleaned

of self-love and enabled with a more consistent intention to love my neighbor.[12]

It is at this point that the entire Christian community are the actors, the change agents, the enablers, the lovers, the educators. In Christ the entire community of believers are offered up to the Father, with all of mankind, and with the whole created world. We are all in the same offering. "We are made sharers in Christ's royal priesthood for the whole life of the world. We are sent out to exercise that priesthood in the world . . . the church is (to quote Bonhoeffer) nothing but a section of humanity in which Christ forms . . . This the Christian community can only be because 'at its center there is a place where, in the word and sacraments of the gospel, he himself can lay hold upon us so that we may be not conformed to this world but transformed by the renewing of our mind.' "[13] And so educational ministry is to be caught up in his love and to love the world as Christ loved. Educational ministry then is the ministry of love and care and action. That is the mission of the educational ministry.

From it will necessarily flow a program that takes seriously problems, media, humanness, issues, discovery, motivation and stimulation, the learning process, creative methods, valuing processes, models and games, data selection, openness to participation, problem solving, and the process of theologizing. These processes find their root in the insights of such persons as Teilhard de Chardin, Buber, Bonhoeffer, McLuhan.

Modern man suffers the pain of fragmentation with the increase of knowledge and affluence, and the electric bombardment of events. There is a need for wholeness. There is a need to relate scientific knowledge, political and economic facts, social revolutions. Relationships are drawn between the meaning of inner space and outer space depths. Modern education is called on to communicate deep relationships and continuities of life. This is an education toward wholeness. The educating community will be called on to discern the living reality of Christ where man is struggling for integrity of meaning. God is revealed in Christ, the reality in whom man may find true wholeness.

The highest worship of God involves a celebration of life in its depths and potentialities of wholeness . . . education of wholeness is concerned not only with imparting facts about the Christian faith. It is education for participation in the life of faith, participation in the life of faith, participation in the community of faith, and participation in a redemptive witness in the world. Thus, education seeks to create settings in which growth in wholeness can take place. Such education is lifelong and involves re-education . . . continuing rebirth . . . focuses on living in issues, providing settings for education in decision making and Christian witness . . . in the world.[14]

THE CONGREGATION LIVING OUT ITS HISTORY

Educational ministry in the seventies takes place among a host of heralds. They are transmitting to the congregations intimations, hunches, and predictions which need interpreting.

In a day when many see the church under change, fire, and judgment, there is a tendency to doubt its durability and its longevity. Some remind us that the church cannot survive. They say it as those who have had enough institutionalization in their lifetime. There are, however, those who are piling up evidence that the church will rise again and who imagine that the church will conserve institutionally "what has been most precious and most human in American civilization."[15]

Still others speak of the new theological radical and refer to those who have sought to get out of the church's ghetto as persons who discovered that to be unchecked by the discipline of the community is to be open to the demonic. They recognize that "church, though a part of a system allows perhaps more room for phophetic witness than do many secular structures", and that "because of its pluralism the institutional church may serve as a launching pad for a small committed communities in mission."[16]

Those who are clairvoyant regarding the church, seem to be saying that the church, the congregation, the institution, still have an important part in human history. The new model may well be freeing, facilitating, enabling, and creative.

"The Church as an institution will develop the 'umbrella principle'. It must shelter us enough to enable us to move freely. That is comic. It must be aware that it exists for functional reasons, and that functions are not evil—except when human beings serve them rather than vice versa—the church as an institution must see control as facilitative rather than directive or prescriptive. It must be an efficient oragniza-

207

tion designed to permit movement and diversity within it. For beneath the 'umbrella' of the future institutional church the value, orientation, and 'civic religion' concerns of the society as well as the activities of the 'believers community' will find shelter. In cities, towns, and neighborhoods the 'umbrella principle' will lead to the founding of ecumenical religious centers that accommodate a great diversity of modes of worship, provide multi-media equipment and . . . have flexible inside walls that can readily be moved around to make rooms of any size desired. In other words, the institution will be the enabler, a pluralistic expression in tradition, confession, celebration, and modes of exploration, and its buildings and equipment will reflect its style.

> It could be that, in the syndrome of institution and technology, the church can become the one institution which is free enough of the motive of utility, manipulation and control to be able to perform a valuable role of reconciliation. For in the days ahead reconciliation will be accomplished, if at all, in the apparent no-man's-land lying between the inevitable advances of science-technology and the desire to protect the personal, the natural and experiential.[17]

If true, educational ministry under the umbrella principle will be involved in the role of facilitating, experimenting, enabling, supporting diversity and flexibility, equipping, all toward the mission of reconciliation. The ministry will be organized, have movement, provide diversity, permit a scale of values, and accommodate and communicate between cities, towns, and neighborhoods. Human and material resources will reflect this.

The church in the future may be a church in which a personality or celebrity ministry will become a creative and significant factor.

> We have been told that the success of the church is in its message and its sacramental nature; told that personalities are unimportant . . . Yet every major breakthrough, reliable reformation or new movement in Christian history has had its celebrities and every celebrity, because of his charisma and his popularity, has had his 'temptation in the wilderness'. No message can get across in our day without the use of television and other electronic media. Such media require the preparation and projection of certain personality images. They need and they create celebrities and stars.[18]

For educational ministry this would mean a new kind of leadership, and go beyond most present church school styles. It sees educational ministry as focusing on charismatic people, and persons raised up and trained to communicate various thoughts and attitudes.

Such education leadership will require a reappraisal of administration, professionalism.

> Many if not all of the clergy of the coming institution will be occupationally based elsewhere in society. Perhaps occupation isn't the term. At least many of those who will serve in the order leadership of various phases of the institution's life will not be dependent upon it for livelihood. Certainly the "believers communities" will have hardly to be led by a "clergyman", though their sacramental lives may well call for his services . . . As we move toward a leisured society with gradations of guaranteed food, clothing and shelter, the lines of professionalism will be less clearly drawn. The professionalism will be shared professing . . .
>
> Professionalism will operate not in the realm of the "believers community" but at the level of value orientation. There will have to be people who are schooled in guiding human emergence as well as in the content of the tradition of faith. Some of these people may well be clergy. The task or value orientation will be the more important as we go farther away from the organic source of morality. It still permits us to pretend that we can rely almost entirely on the situation for our ethics. We shall have to be trained to understand where values come from, what values we possess, and how we can acquire the methods of sound judgment that will carry us through life. The church will certainly want to share in this process.[19]

An educational ministry depending on all the skills of all the people is before us. It will rely on the observable, the evaluative, and the scientific. It will set out to seek that which is true, test goals, require methods of sound judgment, and rely on the empirical data. This will require increased uniqueness, trust, honesty, and openness.

Some predict that "the church as institution will be such that it once again attracts the skills and the interest of youth . . . seminary students . . . individuals searching for new developments in the experiential dimension of religion. . . . Churches may be the institutions that possess sufficient freedom and such ability to foster . . . new . . . human expression and service."[20] Many refer to God as under thirty. They refer to the concept of change and antiquation, insisting that those who stop looking forward to the next day, no matter how old, have left the source of youth, and will petrify.

This view toward the future sees the church as post-pluralistic. Experience with this dimension of religion is not exhausted by the institutional pluralism. It has to do with the ecclesiology of hope, the looking for the Christ who comes from the future.

A common theological image or metaphor of the wilderness pervades. Old institutions have shown increasing signs of disintegration and persons are more and more pilgrims in a strange land. Alienated from unsatisfactory structural solutions for the time, man moves gropingly toward a time when new structures can be discovered which free. In other words, the people of God are moving from Egypt into the wilderness and toward the Promised Land, from the events of these times into an unknown, emerging society.

THE CONGREGATION IN SOCIETY

After several world wars it is no longer possible to ignore the fact that civilization is in very deep trouble. The role of the congregation should know the changing society of which it is a part. Educational ministry in the seventies will need to understand the cultural revolution in which America finds itself.

There has been a radical shift from rural to urban. The rural concept of neighborhoodness was open, face-to-face. The movement is to a society in which to win is to lay down life for structures or justice and being interested in the well-being of all people. To know one's own neighbor is not crucial. More important is to offer him a new life, and to minister to him. It is the matter of facing the issues of life and death.

It is historical for the church to seek new forms in ministry and to formulate vision into images and models that communicate. This may call for new structures for coordinating. Ministry will attack social issues jointly, push into the political, economic, and cultural aspects of American life in order to be the people of God. It is traditional to operate significantly in the congregation. Educating will be done for the sake of the total congregation. The educational ministry will no longer be a splinter of concern. Education will be learning to meet the world and to live in it doing the will of the Father.

Basic society structures are stressing the area of relationships. "Throughout history, the family has been a vital unit for survival, starting as a defense system for survival, and gradually becoming a unit for economic survival. Now, of course, the family has too many physical and economic liabilities rather than assets . . . The bonds of marriage and family are no longer functional, but affectional. People used to come to love each other because they needed each other. Now it's just the other way around. They need each other because they love each other."[21] And so ministry has to do with communication of feelings, relationships of affection, understanding of shared goals and values, and with companionship. The same can perhaps be said of civil rights movements that was said of marriage.

Industry today accents the temporary. People have the need to develop a personal sense of security, stability, familiarity, and consistency. They find themselves in a world where things are continually changing. Everything in sight is temporary. The incidence of invention is accelerating, "The only people who live successfully in tomorrow's world are those who can accept and enjoy temporary systems . . . Moments, then, are the most we can expect from the things we create and produce. We are beginning to change their basis and evaluation from the permanent use of things to their ability to create moments of positive experience."[22]

Moments, expectation, creation, production, change, positive experience, temporary, these are the words that belong to the human community and society, in which the educational ministry of the church is. The phenomenon to participate, to join in, to be part of, is part of the contemporary life on campus, in the church, in mass media, in business, industry, on the streets of the ghetto, and in the family. It is noticeable that people are abandoning old concepts. The myths that creativity, competence, and wisdom are rare have given way to the thought that they are common. There is change.

Contemporary society has significant gaps. Experts indicate that

society may be experiencing a reverse transmission of culture. To put it simply, today's young people probably know more than their elders. Wisdom and culture have always been transmitted from the older generation to the younger. Now, perhaps the first time in history, there is a reversal of that process. Young people used to want to be like their elders; today it's the other way around. Now adults are learning from youth about the nature of society, about world affairs, about human relations, about life. The young have much to teach in matters of taste and judgment, in ethics and morals. They are attending school in greater numbers, staying longer, and learning more than the former generations did. All kinds of people—advertising executives, futurists, artists, designers, social scientists—now look at youth as the leading edge of the temporary culture.[23]

In this kind of society ministry is less gradual in its changes. Big changes are relatively easier to make and cannot easily be resisted. It is a ministry that believes in implementing environment instead of trying to improve people. "All too often the conclusion is reached that all problems boil down to such people problems as basic attitudes, differences, and personality clashes. And it is believed that work must first be done to change people. But that may not be the best strategy. People . . . change little in their personalities and attitudes. They can however, change markedly in their responses to different environment situations, and conditions."[24] Since it is possible to create conditions which will evoke the full range of human behavior from about anybody, it is essential that the ministry see as its mission in the context of the conditions in which man lives. Therefore situations, environments are part of the goal of educational ministry. It goes beyond the classroom and sees the persons both individually and collectively, less in class membership and more as part of society and the environment from which they come and in which they live. In that sense education does not take place in rooms or buildings but takes place in life situations. Learning in this kind of understanding has less to do with numbers of lessons and more to do with the amount of confrontation, energy, legislation, consideration, provocation, which bring about change in environment for that person.

Many circumstances have thrust people into subcultures, into roles of opponents of the status quo, and forced them into the conflict to produce social change. Persons who break iron fences and systems and customs are necessarily aggressive. "They are capable of pursuing their objectives of fervor and singleness of purpose. If they were not they would not succeed. And it is sad but true that in shaping themselves into bludgeons with which to assault the social structure they often develop a diamond hard rigidity of their own. The survivors have a familiar problem of what to do with the revolutionaries when the revolution is over."[25] The church must help persons deal with life directly, not with heads in clouds or in the sand. The church is action oriented.

Biblical history has always pictured God's way by his actions.

Man knows that God is around because things change. And it is the speed at which God is changing things, coming up against man's resistance to change, that makes violence inevitable . . . We are always being told to get back to God. But there is no way back to God: we can only fight our way forward to him . . . But it must be new, not just different; no reshuffling of old packs, no novelty for its own sake. Paul Tillich (*The Shaking of the Foundation*) in preaching on God's word to Isaiah, "Behold, I am doing a new thing," declares: "The new is created not out of the old, not out of the best of the old, but out of the death of the old."[26]

The societal and cultural insight which the church will face is the political and ideological effect on life style. It is style of life toward those in the Third World, and a deep concern for what it means to be human. Though the protest in society may die away, "it will leave behind it a volume of untapped social energy and unintegrated idealism which in the right proportions could become explosive."[27] As the explosion can be devastating, so also it can be creative, liberating and renewing.

Renewal in society depends on the individuals in society. This is difficult in a day when an individual in society is so dependent upon society for his survival. Too, it is a day in which the machine, which controls him and suppresses him, is the machine that also releases him to become leader, producer, and innovator in his society.

"If a society hopes to achieve renewal, it will have to be a hospitable environment for creative men and women. It will also have to produce men and women with a capacity for self-renewal. Thanks to recent research, we now know a good deal about the creative person and about the environment which fosters creativity. . . . But renewal— a society's or individual's—depends on some measure of motivation, commitment, conviction, values men live by, and things that give meaning to their lives."[28] The believing community is a motivating community.

"Unless we attend to requirements of renewal, aging institutions and organizations will eventually run our civilizations to moldering ruins. Unless we cope with the way in which modern society oppresses the individual, we shall lose the greatest spark that renews both societies and men. Unless we foster versatile, innovative and self-renewing men and women, all the ingenious social arrangements in the world will not help us."[29]

Persons develop their abilities in a dialogue between themselves and their environment. The church ought not educate by removing persons from their environment and then placing them into situations that are not authentic, critical, or meaningful. "Most abilities are not so readily evoked by the common circumstances of life. The 'mute, inglorious Miltons' are more numerous than one might suppose, particularly in an age when even an articulate Milton might go unnoticed, certainly unrewarded. Most of us have potentialities that have never been developed simply because the circumstances of our lives have never called them forth."[30]

This exploration of potentiality ought not to be left to chance, but to be pursued systematically. Some persons pursue it often unnoticed by the community. Potentialities are more than skills but are the full range of capacities "for sensing, wondering, learning, understanding, loving and aspiring."[31]

All this has much to say to the congregations' educational ministry in the seventies. Education is to take place where persons perceive and become involved, and wherever they respond. The shift is to the person in his peculiar environment and in terms of his uniqueness. "The ultimate goal of the educational system is to shift to the individual the burden of pursuing his own education. . . . Not only does education continue when schooling ends, but it is not confined to what is merely studied in adult education courses. A world is an incomparable classroom and life is a memorable teacher for those who aren't afraid of her."[32]

A renewing society is continually refreshed by new talent from all segments and strata of the society, many of them discovered, reinforced, supported, and refreshed by and within the believing community. In a time of mobility, the church will see its educational ministry as equipping persons who are on the move.

Change means risk. Of all communities, the church ought to support the lives of changing people. Christian communities ought to provide a trusting atmosphere for persons to live with their weaknesses as well as their strengths, to grow from strength to strength, and from lonesomeness to community, and in styles of life open to newness, failure, and to forgiveness.

One of the reasons why mature people are apt to learn less than young people is that they are willing to risk less. Learning is a risky business and they do not like failure. In infancy when a child is learning at a truly phenomenal rate—a rate he will never again achieve —he is also experiencing a shattering number of failures. Watch him. See the innumerable things he tries and fails. And see how little the failures discourage him. With each year that passes he will be less blythe about failure. By adolescence the willingness of young people to risk failure has diminished greatly. All too often parents push them further along that road by instilling fear, by punishing failure, or by making success seem too precious. But the adult can usually select the kinds of activities on which he allows to be tested, and takes full advantage of that field of choice. He tends increasingly to confine himself in things he does well and to avoid the things in which he has failed or has never tried . . . we pay a heavy price for our theater area.[33]

The ability to live with failure, to deal with life at its worst, as though it were required and not an option, is a style of life that the church ought to face in its educational ministry. It provides for an educational ministry of fumbling, chafing, failing, risking, receiving, lifting up, discovering. A church cannot achieve this if imprisoned. Joy and suffering are a part of the church's experience. It cannot join the isolated, the failing, the discouraged only vicariously or analytically. Its educational ministry ought to be direct, have new perspectives, and ultimately see education as a human affair with people. For this kind of renewal of self, reestablishing of direction and action, those in educational ministry need to know about motivation for change.

So educational ministry ought to bring persons into direct contact with nature, face-to-face with humans, and to help them fashion things creatively. Motivation is basic to creating. Thus people under severe deprivation, whether economic or social, need to be able to try out new ways of doing things. "In all creative achievement there is a certain recklessness or gambling quality that is often suppressed in a society close to the margin of survival."[34]

For this there is challenge in environment, human community, and in the world. Many have failed to understand the challenge there is bringing life into being, in making something new out of what is, and seeing creative relationships in society and culture.

The educating community ought to provide a system for renewal.

It ought to work with evaluation systems by which to judge the effectiveness of its educating. It ought to provide a changing and supporting climate. It ought to release. "All too often we are giving our young people cut flowers when we should be teaching them to grow their own plants. We are stuffing their hands with the products of early innovation rather than teaching them to innovate. We think of the mind as a storehouse to be filled when we should be thinking of it as an instrument to be used."[35]

The action of education is to the external as well as to inner life and experience. An educational community ought increasingly to celebrate diversity as essential to community. It will live with the continuities in its tradition. It is community in which the word of God still speaks as men interpret their daily lives.

Renewal has to do with timing. The church has theologically and educationally to deal with timing.

> There is a readily discernible difference between the society that is oriented to the future and the one that is oriented to the past. Some individuals in society look forward and have a future ever in mind, others are preoccupied with the past and now are antiquarian in their interests. The former have a vivid sense of what they are becoming, the latter a vivid sense of what they have been. The former are fascinated by the novelty of each day's experience, the latter have a sense of having seen everything. . . . No society is likely to renew itself unless its dominant orientation is to the future. This is not to say that a society can ignore its past. A people without historians would be as crippled as an individual with amnesia. They would not know who they were. In helping a society to achieve self-knowledge, the historian serves the cause of renewal. But in the renewing society the historian consults the past in the service of the present and the future.[36]

Each generation faces the crucial battles of its times and either brings new vitality to values and ideals or allows them to decay. This is no dull task for the church. "It goes on in the dusk and the clamor of the marketplace, the daily press, the classrooms and the playground, the urban apartment and the suburban ranchhouse, and it communicates itself more vividly through what men do than what they say. . . . It is an attribute of a functional social system. As such it is a living, changing thing, liable to decay and disintegration as well as revitalizing and reinforcement, and never any better than in a generation that holds it in trust."[37]

THE CREATIVE CLIMATE FOR RENEWAL

A congregation that is open to change in the midst of conflict and revolution, will learn from those who walk into troubled times to possess a sense of humor and hope. Its spirit will be open to amazement, laughter, and delight. Creativity is vital to an educational ministry that moves into a convulsive decade. Once considered primarily a gift of artists and scientists, creativity is now seen as the gift to many. It has become more than an art form. It has that quality which can excite and motivate in educational ministry.

Creative teaching is alive with the spirit and is action at its best. It has a credo against prejudice in any form, against false attitudes, and against that which would cripple the human spirit. It seeks to withhold judgment of others whether it be an impassioned cry or a statement of humor and satire. Those who live in creative groups grow in developing the gift for telling great truths. Authority rests largely in one's own experience. Educational experiences and assignments take on form depending upon the experience. Creative educators may move in an open-ended style, seeking originality.

Creative qualities will be important in an educational ministry that is to deal seriously with revolutionary cultures, from the point of view of the Christian perspective and reference. These qualities of leadership toward creativity include the following: "Considerate of others, independent in taking, determination, industrious, sense of humor, curiosity, sincere, courteous, doing work on time, healthy."[38] Perhaps education of special and gifted persons provides primary clues for dealing with the unusual educational ministry to come.

Those who deal with gifted children take seriously the environment in accordance with the person. They speak of environment as the frontier and of the possibility of creating responsive environment to which children "are propelled by their curiosity."[39] Gifted persons need help in developing themselves, for they may even despise an outstanding gift, if it makes them different from their peers. "This makes far too many gifted children willing to emasculate themselves and consciously and unconsciously hide or destroy their talents."[40] This being so, the church's ministry ought to deal with the person's uniqueness and to consider his talent a welcome frontier.

It may be that within the criteria of creativity the quality of leadership and facilitation at all age levels can be discovered. These may

217

include: rewarding varied talents, helping persons recognize the value of their talents, developing creative acceptance of limitations, not equating divergency with delinquency, changing emphasis on sexuality, supporting the divergent child, developing pride in achievements, reducing isolation, providing sponsors or patrons for persons, exploiting the opportunities of the moment, and developing a sense of mission. "Studies of outstanding men and women in various fields almost always reveal that such people seem to be impelled by some strong feeling of mission or purpose. They believe that what they are doing is tremendously important . . ."[41]

Christ urged mankind to possess the perspective of the child, "Children enjoy using magnifying glasses. The closer look that it gives them opens up new wonders. The child will be satisfied to watch from a distance at first. This look from a distance however, does not satisfy his curiosity. Thinking and learning are driven off course when the children have no opportunities for a closer look, when they are forbidden to touch, when there is no real chance to encounter all of the exciting things about them."[42] In the educational ministry ahead people ought to be looking up close. What was once considered waste may in the future be considered a resource. Imagination ought to be developed and encouraged.

> The fantasy of kindergarten children should be kept alive, developed, and guided. Many teachers and parents try hard to eliminate fantasy at the time children enter school in kindergarten or first grade. They do this because they believe fantasy is unhealthy and fail to recognize that fantasy can be useful even in adult experience. . . . We are of course interested in developing a sound type of creative problem solving in decision making. Fantasy must be kept alive until children achieve the kind of intellectual development that makes this kind of thinking possible. For some time it is through fantasy that children must do their experimenting and exploring period. In a somewhat different way it also has its uses for adults and should never be abandoned completely.[43]

Educational ministry ought to free the Spirit for the prophetic, the charismatic, and the visioner.

The radical nature of creativity should receive the trust and sensitivity of the redemptive community. By creativity is not only meant adaptation and extension of existing forms. It does not, for example, primarily ask, How can we change this bridge into a better bridge?

It would rather ask, Why have bridges? It is irrational, expectant, and open to the present and to newness. A person who is creative will not turn off split second opportunities. This kind of Christian serendipity may be described as "the faculty of making happy chance discoveries so your total life becomes a total yes, yes, yes. You are then free enough to be ready, not to slouch, but to crouch and to pounce, to grab some moment; to be ready to find that moment."[44] The creative person is tolerant of possibilities. He plays and lives off the moment.

Creativity also struggles and opposes. "Before a new idea is born, something old has to die, as the horse had to go for the car to come. There has to be some headknocking. A person may indeed have to oppose things that society contains, and through all opposition create this new thing. . . . If we enter the next decade slowly and sluggishly there must come those who knock through."[45]

With recent technology has come a simplistic, closer observation of nature itself. Creation is being taken seriously. Men watch birds fly, and fly planes. They strive to perfect the hidden mysteries and miracles in creation. The church cannot ignore this turn to nature, a return to the simple, and a look to the earth. With this observation has come exclamation.

Education has been named "ecstasy, joy, the ultimate delight." Past civilization has "tended to fear and shun it as a threat to reason and order. In a sense, they have been right. It is hard to imagine a more revolutionary statement for us than 'The natural condition of the human organism is joy.' For, if this is true we are being daily cheated, and perhaps the social system that so ruthlessly steals our birthright should be overthrown."[46] When blades of grass shatter concrete, and spring flowers bloom in Hiroshima, and roses bloom in rubble, it is obvious that life and joy cannot be subdued. "Those who would reduce, control, quell, lose in the end. The ecstatic forces of life, growth, and change are too numerous, too various, too tumultous."[47] Albert Einstein said, "It is in fact nothing short of a miracle that the modern methods of instruction have not yet entirely strangled the holy curiosity of inquiry . . . It is a very grave mistake to think that the enjoyment of seeing and searching can be promoted by means of coercion and a sense of duty."[48] Affirmation is in the air. Christ's yes to his Father's world is sensed. "Life has one ultimate message, 'yes!' repeated in infinite number and variety. Human life, channeled for millennia by civilization . . . is beginning to express the diversity and range of which it is so easily capable. To deny is to swim against the current of existence. To affirm, to follow ecstasy in learning, in spite of injustice, suffering, confusion, and disappointment—is to move more easily toward an education, in a society that would free the enormous potential of man."[49] Radical grace in Christ opens this potential.

The total environment, the interrelatedness of everything within an educational setting, are seriously considered by large corporations. Educational communities are now free marketplaces for new ideas, and rely on the behavioral sciences. Words like matrix, response, communal, visionary are part of the vocabulary of the educating world. There are new horizons for education. "Education's new domain is not bound in by the conceptual, the factual, the symbolic. It includes every aspect of human existence that is relevant to the new age. To move into it we don't have to wait for the twenty-first century. Experimenters all around the United States and in some other nations as well already have established beachheads in a new domain."[50] For the church there are enormous possibilities which lie ahead. Of all who have vision, the believing community can lead in having eyes to see.

For the Christian community the creativity rises out of a significant question.

> Only when we orient ourselves to God's question do we begin to think and act theologically. This question of God asks: How can I get my creature back again? Only this point of view is fundamental: How does God get at his world, his creation, his own? Bonhoeffer expressed it in his letters from prison in this way: How is the world that has come of age challenged through Jesus Christ? The Lordship of God, the kingdom of God, happens where the will of God enlists human beings in his service and leads the world beyond that which is inherent in itself.[51]

NOTES AND REFERENCES

1. Gustav K. Wiencke, ed., *Christian Education in a Secular Society*, Yearbooks in Christian Education—II (Philadelphia: Fortress Press, 1970), p. 51.
2. *Ibid.*, p. 51.
3. *Ibid.*, p. 55.
4. *Ibid.*, p. 54.
5. *Ibid.*, p. 55.

6. *Ibid.*, p. 217.
7. Leslie Newbigin, *Honest Religion for Secular Man* (London: SCM Press, Ltd., 1966), p. 19.
8. *Ibid.*, pp. 19-20.
9. *Ibid.*, p. 20.
10. Helmut Thielecke, *How Modern Should Theology Be* (Philadelphia: Fortress Press, 1969), p. 9.
11. *Honest Religion for Secular Man*, p. 21.
12. *Ibid.*, p. 67.
13. *Ibid.*, p. 151.
14. Harvey Potthoff, "In One Spirit," Christian Education Emphasis, 1969.
15. Peter Berger, "Between Tyranny and Chaos," *The Christian Century,* October 30, 1968, pp. 1365-70.
16. Dale Brown, "The New Theological Radical," *The Christian Century,* November 13, 1968, pp. 1431-34.
17. Richard E. Wentz, "Save Your Clerical Collars, Boys!" *The Christian Century,* September 3, 1969, pp. 1133 ff.
18. *Ibid.*
19. *Ibid.*
20. *Ibid.*
21. Richard E. Farson, "How Could Anything That Feels So Bad Be So Good?" *Saturday Review,* September 6, 1969, p. 20.
22. *Ibid.*, p. 20.
23. *Ibid.*, pp. 20-21.
24. *Ibid.*, p. 21.
25. John W. Gardner, *Self-Renewal: The Individual and the Innovative Society.* (New York: Harper Colophon Books, 1965).
26. Colin Morris, *Unyoung, Uncolored, Unpoor* (New York: Abingdon Press, 1969).
27. *Ibid.*, p. 47.
28. John M. Larson, *The Learning Community*, p. 4.
29. *Self-Renewal.*
30. *Ibid.*, p. 11.
31. *Ibid.*, p. 12.
32. *Ibid*, p. 12.
33. *Ibid.*, pp. 14-15.
34. *Ibid.*, p. 19.
35. *Ibid.*, pp. 21-22.
36. *Ibid.*, pp. 105-106.
37. *Ibid.*, p. 121.
38. E. Paul Torrance, *Gifted Children in a Classroom* (New York: The Macmillan Co., 1965).
39. *Ibid.*, p. 44.
40. *Ibid.*, p. 45.
41. *Ibid.*, pp. 48-49.

42. *Ibid.*, pp. 55-56.
43. *Ibid.*, pp. 56-57.
44. Reinhold Marxhausen, Lecture, Holden Village, 1970.
45. *Ibid.*
46. George G. Leonard, *Education and Ecstasy* (New York: Delacorte Press, 1968), p. 230.
47. *Ibid.*, p. 233.
48. *Ibid.*, p. 233.
49. *Ibid.*, p. 234.
50. *Ibid.*, p. 193.
51. Dr. Heinz Edward Todt, "Creative Disciples in the Contemporary World Crisis" Heidelberg: Lecture, Lutheran World Federation, July, 1970.

Educational Ministry, Lay and Clergy— A Response

WALLACE J. ASPER

The focal point for potential illumination is in this statement from the central objective document: "The concept of the church's educational ministry includes several key elements. . . . It is a reciprocal ministry, in which leaders and learners minister to one another."[1] A new look at educational ministry calls for identifying key elements and exploring their potentialities for the seventies. One of these key elements is reciprocity in learning, particularly as this may find expression in the mutual, supportive ministry of believers to believers. Within the household of faith this includes lay and clergy ministering to each other; "leader and learner" likewise; and learner to learner, leader to leader; and agency, organization, school, committee, class mutually helping each other toward fulfillment of the central objective for educational ministry in the parish. Still there is more. This mutual ministry extends out from the household of faith into the "human communities" where families live, and vocations are carried out, where public institutions, political structures, and various generations with varying life styles are found. But how far shall one attempt to reach? For the most part, it appears to me that intent of this investigation is to deal primarily with the ways in which a mutual ministry might be realized more fully within the Christian community.

Finding Major Motifs

Whereas the headings used by the writer to mark the progression of sections in the preceding chapter are of significance to his stance and style, the most impressive characteristic to me is the presence of recurring thrusts. Functioning somewhat as a redactor, he orchestrates (his term) quotations to communicate certain motifs for educational ministry. If these motifs could be richly woven in and out of the mutual ministry of leaders and learners we would, I think, be hearing "a new song" in the Christian community—or a new symphony of supportive teaching–learning experiences more inclusive of life situations than in the past. It may be helpful to replay some of the dominant themes as I hear them:

—Educational ministry is interdependent and seeks wholeness in community, yet acknowledges pluralism and celebrates diversity.
—Educational ministry not only anticipates change but serves as an agent of change.
—Educational ministry continually rethinks the place of God and the Scriptures in all of life's involvements.
—Educational ministry will search for new forms and anticipate continued revelation from God to man in the nowness of life.
—Educational ministry seeks to be enabling; it is facilitative rather than directive or prescriptive as persons are freed to live authentically in their environment.
—Educational ministry may claim charismatic leadership, yet it needs all the skills of all the people.
—Educational ministry is to be caught up in the love of God and to love the world as Christ loved.
—Educational ministry involves a systematic pursuit of ways to free human potentialities.
—Educational ministry is oriented toward the future with a spirit of expectancy, but believes great gifts of God can be claimed in the present.
—Educational ministry needs a willingness to run the risks inherent in creative quest, for that type of quest must be tolerant of possibilities

(success or failure, discovery or discouragement, acceptance or rejection).

Thrusts of this nature are inspiring and exciting, are they not? Do you, with me, find them majestic and optimistic? Do they not elicit a sense of challenge to mutual ministry in the seventies?

Raising A Major Question

Is all this realistic? A challenge not only presents a desirable goal and a requirement of real effort, it presents a realistic demand or an achievable accomplishment. Despite the explicit intention to distinguish between educational ministry and other types of ministry, once Christian educators recharge their batteries for a great new effort, there is a tendency to slip into what Edward Farley calls the "Brahman complex of Christian education."[2] Somewhat as the Hindu "great One Thing of all things," the educational ministry is set forth as "doing everything to accomplish everything." Even this one aspect of working toward a reciprocal, mutual ministry stands in danger of attempting to incorporate everything into itself and reaching for "goals so heavenly they are no earthly good." The last part of the last sentence is in quotes since it was a common reminder to curriculum designers and writers of the sixties.

Perhaps it is an unnecessary jeremiad to interpose in this series of studies the reminder that in both the human community and Christian community we live in sick societies. Franklin Littell, however, suggests that neither universities nor churches have given adequate attention and support to the study of social pathology.[3] And in the preparation of this chapter it has repeatedly occurred to me that even the dialogical can be diabolical. This has been reinforced by Lewis Sherrill who writes:

> The possibility that interaction in the Christian community can be demonic has to be borne in mind always; else the church begins to make itself into an idol to be worshiped, begins to regard what it communicates as infallible, and withdraws itself from standing under judgment. In such a case the church begins to become a monster, the more terrifying because it claims the name of Christ and offers the grace of God to broken lives.[4]

He then proceeds to illustrate various types of interaction which can be called demonic. For example, ". . . when the changes it produces in persons are such as to weaken, damage, paralyze, or delude the self in whom the change takes place."[5]

Several times I have introduced the subject of "mutuality in educational ministry" for discussion in a class of college juniors and seniors. There was full agreement as to the desirability of the goal, but there was rather low expectancy for major change. They may feel open to change, but they doubt the older generation will change much. They may respect pastors, but they suspect pastors will tend more to be "tellers" and "proclaimers" and "administrators" than educators who enter into a mutual ministry of disciples. They are impressed by the wide spectrum from effective to ineffective work of volunteer teachers in the church schools, and they wonder if "mutual ministry" might mean chiefly "sharing of ignorance." If placed in contact with the more educated, experienced, talented person(s), some wonder "what would I have to contribute?" They also think many congregations are polarized in various ways, and they wonder if this really will be overcome. Many of these students think there is too much emphasis on bigness, large groups, beautiful sanctuaries, elaborate ceremonies, and denominational distinctions. They wonder if the church will be much different in the seventies than it was in the sixties or fifties. In general, their comments seemed to be saying: we'd like to go in the direction of a more mutual ministry of believers, and some of us will really be involved in this; but, on the basis of past experience and present knowledge, we don't know how far we will get.

When members of this class were examining central objectives, they noted that both the present LCA and the new ALC-LCA objectives use the expression, "to assist persons." They reacted negatively to the ALC's expressions of "confronting, nurturing, and guiding persons." They sounded too vulnerable to manipulation, coercion, and monolog. "To assist persons" seemed more loving and open to dialog as well as a more realistic and modest way of stating an aim. Roger L. Shinn has expressed himself along those lines, too:

> [This] . . . comment concerns an appropriate modesty and ambition in Christian education. A modesty is necessary because education cannot do everything that wistful people expect of it. No educational process can assure that persons will become Christians or that they will experience the riches of Christ . . . Freedom and sin are part of human

225

life, and any educator who thinks that he can always manipulate students or direct their lives is dealing in pretentious nonsense.[6]

In fairness to Herbert Brokering, I want to point out that he does deal with a linguistic problem, and he does not spare us or himself in noting human perversity and disobedience. He indicates that an educational ministry must take problems seriously, and that one of those problems is that "civilization is in very deep trouble." But it seemed appropriate to raise the question, Are we being realistic?, and to press it rather hard.

There are, of course, ways of finding some reassurance for setting high aims for our educational ministry. Christian educators reflect a rich variety of theological resources and commitments that motivate, sustain, and guide their efforts. In the following paragraph Lewis Sherrill not only summarizes much of what has been said above, but offers an encouraging base on which to stand and from which to function:

> The Christian community, as other communities, is a body of relationships which carry both constructive and destructive forces. But the Christian community is a self-transcending community; and in the Christian community, as in no other community, the fact of revelation faces us. This means that corrective, redemptive, and re-creative power is forthcoming into the Christian community, to reinforce the constructive forces which are at work, and to overcome other forces in the human self and in human relations which are contrary to it.[7]

Rather than being overly concerned as to whether or not we are in a period of time called "post-pluralistic" or some similar designation, it is essential to remember we are "Post-Pentecost." The Tower of Babel account in Genesis 11, describes the human situation remarkably well. But we live in an era that knows something about the reversal of Babel. The confusion of language, the lack of communication, is potentially healed by the outpouring of God's Spirit to each believer and to the whole fellowship of believers. There still are too many barriers to communication; but, with the abiding presence of the Holy Spirit, we know that members of the Christian community can more and more become agents of a common purpose. To use Pauline language, if we "walk by the Spirit" and are "led by the Spirit" and show "the fruit of the Spirit," surely we can grow in our educational ministry to one another.

Commenting on Conditions for Mutual Ministry

A few days ago I received a brochure on a new book that purports to offer answers to this question: Why don't people do the things they know how to do—and know they're supposed to do? The subtitle of this study on performance problems, *You Really Oughta Wanna,* keeps running through my mind.[8]

Having realistically faced the problem that there are many hazards and hindrances to an educational ministry that is mutual and supportive—including the fact that many "don't really wanna"—we know that there are enough persons with a high degree of motivation in this direction to make a huge difference in the seventies. And we know God has not withdrawn his Spirit from this planet. Therefore we continue to explore possibilities for renewal and growth in educational ministry.

Reciprocity Without Condescension

Neither the Christian community nor the American citizenry provides us with the most outstanding history of reciprocity in the human community. It appears to me that the influence of Confucianism on many centuries of Chinese civilization is the most noteworthy at this point. Pre-Communist Chinese culture placed primary emphasis on five reciprocal relationships in society: sovereign and subject; man and wife; father and child; elder and younger brother; senior and junior friend. There is a cluster of attitudes appropriate to each of these relationships, but all of them are marked by reciprocity; and each member recognizes the dignity, freedom, and integrity of the other. If one looks at this from the standpoint of Martin Buber's religious approach to "I-Thou" and "I-It," one gains additional appreciation of this outstanding element of Chinese culture in times past.[9] But even this enlightened approach to man-in-society has some features that one would not want to incorporate in the Christian community. One of these features is the constant consciousness of deference to those "higher in rank"; the other is the passive principle of receptiveness on the part of those "lower in rank." Some treat reciprocity as though it were linked etymologically more with *receptus* than with *reciprocus*; the elements of strong counteraction and interaction often are missing.

How does this get expressed? Let a few examples suffice. One of my colleagues sometimes comments in jest, "My idea of a discussion is me talking and them listening." We may joke about it, yet that is often the way we function. The college class mentioned some paragraphs back, was engaged one day in reflecting on a special event with religious significance. One young man had a vivid remembrance of lining up with his class following the confirmation service so that they could be greeted by the congregation. I asked, "What did they say? What did they do?" Beyond shaking hands he couldn't remember anything specific, but he recalled this general impression: "They seemed to be saying, 'Isn't it nice of all us people to come by and pat you little lambs on the head?'" I couldn't resist asking whether the fathers in the congregation communicated the same kind of message to the young fellow in the congregation who was the local high school's basketball center or football quarterback.

The gap between specialist and generalist, often unintentional and situational, is also of serious concern. Along with others, Martin Marty points out: "The theologians write manuals of arms for the believers, and by the time the lay people begin to get their marching orders, the theologians have gone off in a different direction."[10] Early in *The Report of the Joint Commission on the Theology and Practice of Confirmation*, is expressed an awareness that the confirmation instructional program has been independent and separated from other educational ministries.[11] One wonders if pastors really want a shared ministry, or if they are too insecure educationally to become interdependently related to the wider program, or if they fear their "higher ranking" efforts might get contaminated by "lower ranking" personnel and endeavors.

It is encouraging to note an example of reciprocity in the report referred to immediately above. The Joint Commission concluded studies of 175 congregations through which replies were received from nearly 1,500 individuals in both 1966 and in 1969. The report states: "It is clear that the opinions of many people were changed by the churchwide study of confirmation and first Communion. The Commission also found that some of its own viewpoints were changed and its thinking clarified as a result of the reports from study groups."[12] It does point in the direction Hendrik Kraemer was pressing when he wrote about a mutual cooperation of theologians and lay people in which both are teachers and taught.[13]

A good leader is eager to communicate and is convinced about the urgency or significance of what he wants to communicate. But these very qualities may become barriers to communication. Reuel Howe mentions, for example, "agenda anxieties" in one of his writings.[14] The leader can become so preoccupied with the content and purpose of his message that he becomes so blind and deaf to the needs of students and their search for meaning that only monological communication occurs. Agenda anxiety is part of a monological illusion that communication is accomplished by telling people what they ought to know and do. Many teachers get "agenda anxiety" over curriculum leader's guides or student workbooks, and despite excellent intentions of teachers or curriculum producers, reciprocal relationships become minimal. Leaders of workshops, conferences, retreats, institutes, and seminars may be able to look back on a long, long trail of agenda anxieties. They may recall some positive results. But can we get even more positive results through reciprocity? The potential is present in the Christian community to experience reciprocity at the highest level yet known in civilization. We can inform each other, encourage each other, and "cheer each other on," rather than engage in "little lamb head-patting."

Listening Without Prejudging

Members of the Christian community are continually confronted with the need to evaluate, establish priorities, weigh relative merits of alternative proposals, and the like. In other words, Christians are involved in an ongoing process that calls for various kinds of judging. But, if we are concerned about mutuality in educational ministry, there is little room for prejudging. The leader or learner who assumes the stance, "I know what you're going to say before you say it," shuts the door to communication. Other samples from the same cluster of attitudes and expressions: "I've heard it all before"; "There's nothing new for me here"; "I've already made up my mind once and for all"; "I know him, I know her. He (or she) couldn't possibly have anything worthwhile to offer"; "Who does she think she is? She just joined

229

the church last month!" "I'll have nothing to do with those who go around in beards, beads, blue jeans and bare feet!" "What does anyone over forty know about life?"

In this matter of listening, perhaps the most critical point for the seventies is the need for communication lines across the generations. A proposal heard some years ago while listening to Dr. Abraham J. Heschel lecture on our campus lingers with me. It was to the effect that education at its best requires the full participation of not only two but *three* generations. This ideal, going back to the ancient Hebrews, has many twentieth century handicaps. In his study on the dynamics of interaction, Lewis Sherrill uses a couple expressions that help illumine the generation gap as well as other gaps. One of them is "selective perception."[15] We perceive or recognize meaning in what is presented from the outer world in light of the meaning which life already has for our own individual inner worlds. If what comes to us from the outer world supports, fits, and gives strength to our inner world, we respond positively. If what comes to us from the outer world threatens us or bores us, we respond negatively. When we enter a group or otherwise make contact with the outer world, we exercise a selectivity of perception and respond in the light of our inner world.

The other expression is "armored perception."[16] We tend to protect ourselves from having our patterns of selective perception disturbed. We wall ourselves off from emotional or mental involvement by daydreaming, fidgeting, whispering, retreating, superficially nodding—anything but really listening. For listening involves running the risk of changing cherished ideas. The true listener runs the risk of letting someone "get inside"—even as a kind of intruder. We should be able to do this within the Christian community so that we do not feel unduly threatened or insecure or battered. Nevertheless, what is difficult even within peer groups, often is progressively more difficult along the lines of two to three generations. And when the generations include both those within and without the household of faith, communication problems multiply.

At the risk of flagrant superficiality even within the limits of this response, there are two ways in which I would like to illustrate the disturbing excitement of listening without prejudging in the seventies. It may be that both are part of a single phenomenon. One is the stunning case that Charles A. Reich makes for "Consciousness III" in *The*

Greening of America. As presented by Reich, Consciousness III is emerging with such emphases as these: freedom from automatic acceptance of the imperatives of society;[17] honesty, wholeness, and genuineness in all things;[18] rather than being judgmental one to another, value what is unique and different in each self;[19] be wholly honest with others, using no other person as a means;[20] genuine relationships with others, friendship, companionship, love and the human community are among the highest values in life;[21] being responsible participants in decision-making processes of our times;[22] live in the state of becoming by being open to any and all experience;[23] with enthusiasm attempt to restore, protect, and foster human consciousness or awareness.[24] If, as Reich proposes, that segment of society characterized by Consciousness III cultivates the feeling of being an outsider from the establishment; and if, as I propose, this segment of society tends to think of the church as part of the establishment, we have a real communication problem on our hands in educational ministry. If the establishment is thought of as dead, and the only way to stay "alive" is to remain an outsider, how do we get at a mutual ministry?

The other illustration, which I suggest may be part of the same phenomenon, relates to the dynamic presence of what is commonly called, "The Jesus Movement." Many of us in California have moved from a vague awareness of its beginnings a few years ago to a steady consciousness (and mixed feelings) of its force in the lives of youth, some of whom are converts from the drug culture and all of whom seem to have had various types of alienation experiences in relation to the older generations and the establishment. It is a movement that the church, and Christian educators in particular, may find one of the most challenging of the seventies. But it appears to be a movement that will not fit the institutional structures of the fifties and sixties. And it is perplexing to observe how it is possible to be "turned on to Jesus" (whether young or old) and still "tune out each other" (young or old, but maybe more the old). Frankly, their naive fundamentalism, simplistic evangelism, and biblical literalism tend to make me more uncomfortable than Peter probably was dreaming on the rooftop before meeting Cornelius (Acts 10). But, like Peter, I must admit that something authentic is happening, and that I have more listening and learning to do. So do the members of the "Jesus Movement" and of "Consciousness III."

Diversity Without Apathy

The problem of celebrating diversity in the Christian community has been around a long time. Paul's Corinthian correspondence, using the analogy of the church as the body of Christ, shows how ridiculous it is for one part of the body to say to another, "I have no need of you" (1 Corinthians 12:21). This may be said belligerently, but more often it is communicated by apathy. The more freedom is given, the more diversity is encouraged, the more each one is given elbow room "to do his own thing," the more room there is for apathy.

Franklin Littell's recent study on totalitarianism, *Wild Tongues*, approaches this concern in terms of the relationship of the Christian community to other segments of the human community. Much to the consternation of some church members, he asserts that the greatest scandal in America today is the lack of a practice of biblical separation of the church from the world.[25] "Well-meaning people often spend more time providing a forum for totalitarians than for those of reasonable views, and of listening to the extremists than to those who have something to contribute to the public opinion."[26] Whether we think of the threat of the Left or the thunder of the Right, something sorely needed for our times is a new and more vigorous style of Christian citizenship.[27] If the Christian community is going to be strengthened so as to meet apostates, false prophets, and lighthearted attitudes toward standards of church membership, the church must not only carry out its educative functions more diligently, it must also recover the principles and practice of Christian discipline.[28] Implicit here is the conviction that, if the Christian community lacks a clear identity distinct from the human community, they have little or nothing to say to each other. Dialog does not occur.

If there is a spirit of not caring within the Christian community the same lack of dialog occurs. The J. B. Phillips translation of Romans 15:1 says this rather well: "We who have strong faith ought to shoulder the burden of the doubts and qualms of others and not just to go our own sweet way. Our actions should mean the good of others . . ."* Perhaps for too long in our educational ministry we have stressed that the sin of Adam and Eve, Everyman and Everywoman, has been the prideful, heroic desire to wrest control of the world and our own destiny from God, the Rightful Ruler. As Harvey Cox proposes in *On Not Leaving It To The Snake,* the basic problem has not been wanting to be more than man, but slothfully and indolently allowing ourselves to be less than man. We tend to renounce the dignity of humanity by abdicating in part or in whole from sharing the full measure of life's pain and responsibility. We refuse to live in reciprocity with our fellow human beings and even turn away from our responsibility to take care of this planet as we should.[29] There are, however, more hopeful signs of diversity without apathy now than at any prior time in my life in the church. As one who comes and goes from many congregations in one part of the country, I find a heightened awareness that the opposite of *agape* is "not caring." And I find an amazing range of talents, skills, programs, types of worship services, and approaches to learning being used, both when Christians are gathered for study and worship and when they are scattered into society.

Solitude Without Detachment

Obviously it is much simpler to express a concern than to know exactly what to do about it, and that may be especially obvious in stating that an educational ministry should carry a concern for leaders and learners having opportunities for solitude. In this quest for interaction, mutuality, dialog, reciprocity, and interdependence, is there any way we can serve each other by sharing responsibility for the occasional privilege of privacy? Meditative moments are needed to assimilate learnings, to ponder possibilities, to dream dreams, to wonder, to marvel, to struggle inwardly.

Recently a radio speaker was toying with the possibility that part of the difficulty children and youth have in "growing up" today is that we live in the post-penicillin age. Children rarely are home sick more than a day or two and they are pushed out the door and back into the hubbub of life. They rarely are required to spend long days and nights in solitude thinking—perhaps—long thoughts. But who wants to return to an era without penicillin?

The desirability of solitude without detachment is expressed here chiefly for two reasons. First, there is a heightened interest in meditative, contemplative, mystical religion on college campuses today. This may well be a felt need and not merely a fad. Some, of course, are mainly interested in exploring alternatives to Christianity; and they become, for a time, at least, especially interested in the oriental religions. Some students are amazed to discover that Christianity also carries mystical emphases and possibilities. How intentional instruction and Christian mysticism are related, however, has its vagaries. Second, responding to Brokering's wilderness motif raises the question, Are there ways in which the educational ministry can provide for desert experiences?

Eduard Schweizer's *Christ In The Wilderness* offers illuminating references to the lonely struggle of working out a sense of mission and method. The Apostle Paul also had a desert experience after meeting Christ on the way to Damascus. We may assume this was an especially fruitful time for him as he struggled to reconstruct his inner world. One wonders, too, if Amos formulated his great pronouncements on social justice while he was in the marketplace. To be sure, he was not detached from the marketplace; but there were long periods of time out with the sheep in communion with God and nature that must have been his major learning sessions. Israel was schooled for years in the wilderness. What about the seventies? Without knowing how it can best be done, a mutual ministry in education should provide for some solitude without detachment for constructing our inner world in communion with God. Paul Holmer's chapter in *The Continuing Quest,* evidences a critical concern over the deadening possibilities of continually dealing with only the outside of holy things and teachings in theological seminaries.[30] The central church offices, the church-related college, the parish, and even the family are not exempt from the same possibilities. We do not chatter our way into a deep personal faith.

Structures Without Strictures

At the national level of both ALC and LCA, there seems to be emerging a new concern for team ministry. Perhaps in the early years following mergers it was essential to identify areas of responsibility with considerable precision, to circumscribe areas for particularized functions, and to staff offices with highly specialized personnel. No doubt many such needs still exist. But there is a new spirit for mutual ministry by exercising a greater teamwork among boards in extending services to geographic areas and congregations.

Fragments of information about exciting new avenues of service for congregations by national boards of parish education have also been picked up here and there. One is the possibility of helping congregations work out an educational ministry to fit their particular situations. If the central office can receive adequate data about a congregation (such as age, location, facilities, occupations, distribution of age groups, interests, special needs, type of community) this could be fed into a computer service that may prove to be of great help in providing analyses upon which to base recommendations for programs, materials, conference or district resources, budgets, and the like.

Here's hoping we also achieve a more wholistic approach to the educational ministry at the congregational level. We should be past the time when the several organizations of the church so jealously guard their respective libraries, projectors, and audio equipment that only a few chosen ones can benefit from them. Regardless of where the ministering is done, we will undoubtedly need structures. Libraries need to be housed and staffed; audio-visual materials need responsible "central service" supervision; the various schools and agencies must have "responsible groups" to head the work. But a greater sense of team ministry can free congregations from strictures that bind, fragment, and limit progress. One wonders what life in the church might be like if all these whirling wheels of activity were to gear together at the right places!

Hope For The Future Without Abandoning The Present

Mutuality in educational ministry in the seventies needs vital relationships to the past, present, and future. This may sound trite, but there is a tendency within the Christian community to think, "Nothing good is happening now, but at least I have some hope." In *The Greening of America*, Christianity is viewed as one of several forms of giving up the present for the promise of something better in another world.[31] Whether this comes from an overdose of "theology of hope" or an underexposure to Christianity, we must still admit there are Christians who demonstrate that type of consciousness. If nothing good can happen in the *now* of life, we will have chiefly an educational ministry of trying to sustain people who are tired of waiting.

One of my Tillichian colleagues talks of affirming being in the grip of non-being. Others speak of affirming creation's joyful cry, "I am!" I find myself more at home in the Johannine expressions of "life abundant" and "fulness of joy" as well as the declaration: "these are written that you may believe that Jesus is the Christ, the Son of God, and that believing you may have life in his name" (John 20:31). The awareness of "God ahead of us" has great implications for educational ministry, but I trust not at the expense of "God in us" and "God with us" in the midst of continual life involvements. Among the qualities of renewal in the life of a people there are "the warm immediacies of interpersonal relationships through which the daily good of life is secured."[32] This occurs in an atmosphere where God's gifts of grace flourish in the daily ministry of leaders and learners.

NOTES AND REFERENCES

1. *A Central Objective for Educational Ministry in the Parish: ALC and LCA* (Philadelphia: Board of Parish Education of the Lutheran Church in America, 1969), p. 2.
2. Edward Farley, "A Continuing Discussion: Where Is the Holy Spirit in Christian Education?" *Religious Education,* May-June, 1966, pp. 233 ff.
3. Franklin H. Littell, *Wild Tongues* (New York: Macmillan Co., 1969), p. 69.
4. Lewis J. Sherrill, *The Gift of Power* (New York: Macmillan Co., 1957), p. 172.
5. *Ibid,* p. 172.
6. Roger L. Shinn, "The Educational Ministry of the Church," in *An Introduction to Christian Education,* Marvin J. Taylor, ed. (New York and Nashville: Abingdon Press, 1966), p. 13.
7. *The Gift of Power,* p. 65.
8. Robert F. Mager and Peter Pipe, *Analyzing Performance Problems* (Belmont, Calif.: Fearon Publishers, 1971).
9. S. V. McCasland, G. E. Cairns, and D. C. Yu, *Religions of the World* (New York: Random House, 1969), pp. 7-8.
10. Martin E. Marty, *The Search for a Usable Future* (New York: Harper & Row, Inc., 1969), p. 52.
11. Joint Commission on the Theology and Practice of Confirmation, *A Report for Study* (Minneapolis: Augsburg Publishing House, St. Louis: Concordia Publishing House, Philadelphia: Board of Publication of the Lutheran Church in America, 1969), p. 1.
12. *Ibid,* p. 5.

13. Hendrik Kraemer, *A Theology of the Laity* (Philadelphia: Westminster Press, 1958), p. 115.
14. Reuel L. Howe, "The Dialogical Foundations for Christian Education," in *An Introduction to Christian Education, op. cit.*, p. 87.
15. *The Gift of Power*, p. 170.
16. *Ibid.*, p. 171.
17. Charles A. Reich, *The Greening of America* (New York: Random House, 1970), p. 225.
18. *Ibid.*, p. 226.
19. *Ibid.*, p. 226.
20. *Ibid.*, p. 228.
21. *Ibid.*, p. 229.
22. *Ibid.*, p. 232.
23. *Ibid.*, p. 233.
24. *Ibid.*, p. 254.
25. *Wild Tongues*, p. 16.
26. *Ibid.*, p. 112.
27. *Ibid.*, p. 114.
28. *Ibid.*, p. 21.
29. Harvey G. Cox, *On Not Leaving It to the Snake* (New York: First Macmillan Paperbacks Edition, 1969), p. xv.
30. Paul L. Holmer, "Theological Education and Personal Faith," in *The Continuing Quest*, James B. Hofrenning, ed. (Minneapolis: Augsburg Publishing House, 1970), pp. 43-66.
31. *The Greening of America*, p. 346.
32. Ross Snyder, "Group Theory and Christian Education," in *An Introduction to Christian Education, op. cit.*, p. 278.

Chapter VIII

A Look at the Future

LUTHER E. LINDBERG and
WENDELL JOHNSTON

The Objectives of This Article

1. To identify some of the recent significant attempts to look into the future of the church and to assess their implications for educational ministry.
2. To examine substantial forces or trends within education today that may influence the educational ministry of tomorrow.
3. To suggest several functions that must be involved in the planning of change if educational ministry is to have a significant role in supporting the mission of the Christian church of the future.

A new century is not far away. It is not easy for us to realize that even now we are involved in shaping a century which we can hardly image, much less understand. Our children will be dealing with information not yet uncovered by means of techniques yet to be developed. They will be solving problems we have not yet defined. They will be facing challenges beyond present conception. We do anticipate, however, that there will be a Christian church—in some form or other—in the twenty-first century.

But hold back for just a minute! Perhaps we will not be so overwhelmed by our forward look if we lower our eyes to those years between now and the end of the present century. Do we dare to call the years this side of that century demarcation line "the foreseeable future?"

How does one go about anticipating the styles of educational ministry in the foreseeable future? One way to do it would be to make a study of the trends that now are evident, to project these into the future, and to attempt to analyze some of the processes that may interrupt or accelerate them. Another way to go about the task would be to ask what kind of educational ministry we want to exist in the future and then to attempt to design an approach that will shape that ministry. In this latter instance we would be attempting to draw clues from the future through a probing process. This kind of approach would be idealistic and is based on the belief that man can indeed shape and determine his own future, at least in part, by the plans he makes today. It is based on the belief that change can be planned. In this article we will attempt to combine these two approaches under the aegis of planning.

There are evidences of a new emphasis on planning in the church today. Now that we have entered the decade of the seventies, we see planning being done at every significant level of the church. Congregations are planning becouse the boom of the sixties (members and buildings) is over. Districts and conferences are realizing more and more that they are paper entities, and their congregations are realigning themselves into planning clusters. Synods and districts are involved in self-studies and are planning new kinds of structures. Church agencies are planning and working together so that they will not be caught flat-footed when the unknown changes of the seventies materialize. But perhaps the most significant kind of planning is taking place in the teaching-learning experience itself where learners are being given the opportunity of planning or choosing the learning activities in which they will be involved. Planning is beginning to be seen as a legitimate part of the learning experience in the congregation, just as multi-disciplinary education is seen as a part of the new university. Admittedly it is still mainly in experimental situations where learners have a high degree of involvement in determining their learning problems.

Planning has now become a continuing necessity. During the early fifties, we believed that each generation should define anew the nature, direction, and aims of educational ministry. This is no longer true. Now we have learned that it is necessary to be involved in the process of planning *constantly* because of compounded and rapid change in society. *"Educatio semper Reformanda!"* Curriculum programs designed for eras of stability simply are not appropriate for eras of instability.

The content of this chapter lies somewhat beyond the normal scope of curriculum development and planning. Smith, Stanley, and Shores have standardized the task of curriculum development into four phases: (1) the determining of educational directions, (2) the choice of principles and procedures for selecting and ordering learning experiences, (3) the selection of a pattern of curriculum organization, and (4) the determining of procedures for change and evaluation.[1] Although educational styles of the future relate somewhat to both the directional and change phases, such futurism adds the dimension of probability.

The Feel of the Future

The rate of change is accelerating so rapidly in our society and its educational patterns that it is only with extreme tentativeness that anyone can talk about the educational ministry styles of the future. However, when one is bold enough to make such predictions, he usually has a responsive audience. Among the many current attempts to probe the future, three stand out as having special importance for this study.

Roland Tapp has made an exhaustive study of the changes he sees for Protestantism (especially his own Presbyterian church) in the near future.[2] His summary statement says that "part of the upheaval now going on in the churches is temporary, but much of it will have permanent effects. The long-range prospects are good for essential Judeo-Christianity, but not for the institutions." The following are Dr. Tapp's predictions of changes and trends:

1. There will be a reenactment of the fundamentalist-liberal fight of fifty years ago. There already has been a marked polarization of the church at all levels, and the split may become irreparable.

2. There will be a growing trend towards merger with Catholics at practical levels; but the cooperation will be between fundamentalists of both groups, and between liberals.

3. Most institutional churchgoers will be forty-five years old and

older. There will be a steady decrease in total membership and fewer youths will be involved with the church.

4. On the other hand, there will be increasing interest in religion and Christianity among college students and young adults, but they will continue to avoid the institutional church.

5. Total church membership will decrease, but those remaining will be more knowledgeable and committed.

6. More people—not all necessarily Christians—will believe that the Christian's primary concern is with social action.

7. Christian teachers will see themselves more as fellow-seekers than as transmitters of a heritage.

8. There will be a unification of major Protestant denominations amid "great wailing and gnashing of teeth," but the new connective church will be no more of a monolith than the denominations are now.

9. There will be no more denominational Christian education programs.

10. There will be no more projects for building huge church plants.

11. Integration of all minorities will become a fact in churches.

12. Church property, now valued at 80 billion dollars, will go on the tax rolls. "In a pluralistic society, with Christians rapidly becoming a minority, this kind of tax-exempt wealth cannot be tolerated, and it won't be."

13. Foreign missions will be less emphasized, probably replaced by Peace Corps types of actions.

14. "Lay Academies" will rise in number.

15. Denominational theological seminaries operating without reference to university level education will decline.

16. Theology will shift from transcendence to immanence to pantheism (which holds that God is in everything).

17. Along with mergers, boards within denominations will coalesce.

18. Sermons will disappear along with the Sunday morning worship services. "The death rattle will be long and loud and gruesome."

19. Fellowship devices will be less help in attracting new members to local congregations.

20. Some people will belong to more than one church. There will be less interest in separate men's and women's programs.

21. TV will be used in church school teaching by clusters of churches in an area.

22. Breakdown of authority, both personal and doctrinal, will be more evident.

23. The church stands in very great danger of losing the intellectual elite of the country.

24. Resurgent interest in formal worship is only momentary.

25. The church of A.D. 2000 will not be recognizable to anyone of today.

Lyle Schaller's book, *The Impact of the Future,* is organized around twenty trends he sees as determining the shape of the future. He suggests that a helpful antecedent to every projection would be: *"If* the trend that developed (during) these years continues, *and if* no new force comes into play to modify this trend, thus and so will happen."[3] Certain similarities can be seen between Dr. Tapp's predictions and Dr. Schaller's trends:

1. Decentralization has replaced urbanization as the dominant characteristic of the changes in the population of the United States.

2. There has been an increase in discretionary time available to Americans, but this has not resulted in an increase in leisure time.

3. The nature and characteristics of the American family are changing.

4. The age mix of the American population will change as the number and proportion of younger and of older persons increases while the number of those in the thirty-five to forty-five age bracket decreases in both absolute and comparative terms.

5. The population of the United States will increase by 67 to 70 million persons between 1965 and 1985, a larger increase than occurred between 1945 and 1965.

6. Between 1950 and 1985 the Negro population will more than double with the greatest increases being in the under age thirty-five groups, and in several Northern and Western states.

7. The rate of migration and mobility is not expected to change significantly during the next twenty years, but the cumulative effect of continued migration will cause important changes.

8. The next housing boom will be substantially different from the housing boom of the 1948-59 era.

9. The size of the middle class in the United States is growing at an unparalleled pace.

10. The level of income of American families is rising rapidly, but relatively few individuals or families have large quantities of accumulated wealth.

11. The agriculturely oriented rural community of yesterday is being supplanted by a new community that is rural in terms of appearance, population density, and scale, but that has a strong urban orientation in terms of employment, culture, values, and communication.

12. The population of the United States increasingly is being divided among geographically separated homogeneous compartments.

13. The alienation of the individual from the structures and institutions of society will continue to become more pronounced, more visible, and more widespread.

14. The worldwide surge for power to control one's own destiny is being expressed in all segments of society and will continue to expand.

15. Knowledge is emerging as the most important source of power.

16. Power in the United States is being divided among an ever-increasing number of groups and organizations.

17. Change and social progress will continue to produce a demand for additional changes, a reordering of priorities, and a redefinition of goals.

18. In recent years the churches in the United States have been developing a closer relationship to government, especially to the federal government, and this trend will continue.

19. The sects and denominations outside the mainstream of cooperative Protestantism have become the fastest growing religious bodies in the United States.

20. Connectionalism will continue to replace congregationalism in the polity of American religion, and this will continue to enhance the role of the denomination.

Our feel for the future, however, cannot be adequate without more of a reference to what is happening in the society within which the church exists, especially in the area of general education. What we call educational ministry must be seen as the product of acculturation. It is shaped by the entire life and work of the community in which the congregation is set. Vernon Anderson focuses on education and sees the following concerns in the future:[4]

1. There will be a premium on looking at problems.
2. More provisions will be made for individuality.
3. Education will involve more experience in experimentation and discovery.
4. Educational experiences will be more issue oriented.
5. There will be increasing learner independence from the teacher.
6. Interdisciplinary concerns will be on the rise.
7. More laboratory experiences (e.g., simulation) will be involved in education.

Although these three perspectives of the future have been necessarily brief, one draws from them the distinct impression that change will be coming "fast and furious," instead of gradually, as in the past. This will, of course, draw reactions of a conservative nature from many quarters—"a retreat to the orthodox," as Clyde Kluckhohn has noted.[5] The LCA Task Group for Long-Range Planning shared the same feelings and suggested that one of the first tasks educational ministry must face is the issue that "the church as a whole is pulled in two contrary directions: toward a closer identification with the world on the one hand and toward a reaffirmation of traditional styles and values on the other."[6] The question of reconciling the "revolutionaries and the gradualists,"[7] of coming to grips with change, is therefore another of the initial functions of educational ministry.

Expecting the Unexpected

One safe assumption that we can make is that we cannot predict the future of educational ministry with much accuracy. Kenneth Boulding has suggested that "one thing we can say about man's future with a good deal of confidence is that it will be more or less surprising."[8] Vernon Anderson says much the same thing: ". . . we can be certain only of the uncertainty of the future."[9] Does this mean, therefore, that prognostication is nothing but complete foolishness?

If, by prognostication, we mean a confident foretelling or prediction of the future from the signs and symptoms of today, our answer has to be positive. We have ample evidence that straight-line prediction is most often inaccurate.[10] When Thomas Edison, for example, saw the movie machine for the first time in an educational setting, he predicted that the classroom teacher would disappear. When Skinner invented the teaching machine, many people again thought that the direction of education would take a drastic, non-personal turn. Further, the fact that men do unpredictable things makes prediction questionable from a common sense point of view.

One reason we can predict only up to a certain point has to do with the shrinkage of the world due to communications and travel breakthroughs. What this means, basically, is that a force moving predictably can be touched and nudged and made to alter its progress (both direction and speed) by another, perhaps heretofore unrelated, force that could not possibly have been taken into consideration.

Prediction might not be so difficult if all changes were for the better. But they aren't! Educational ministry takes the position that not all change is to be desired. Educational ministry has a value system to apply to change and works against those changes that are not for the good of man.

244

On the other hand, educational ministry also sees the necessity of prognostication. The famous quotation from Lord Byron is appropriate: "The best of prophets of the future is the past."[11] The prognosis of the future of any social institution begins with an analysis of its past, but especially of its present. In dealing with the church and with the process of educational ministry, we must take into account the settings, influences, attitudes, and mores of society.

It is at this point that we can be helped by examining the concept of prophecy in the Old Testament. The prophetic movement was one of the most creative movements in all of history. The Hebrew word for prophet is *nabi*. This was translated into the Greek *prophetais*, which may mean "before" or "in behalf of." The prophet is one who speaks on behalf of someone else, one who operates out of "insight" more than "foresight" (this element in prophecy is incidental). It is on the basis of insight into the now that we can draw conclusions about tomorrow. Intelligent planning must take current forces and trends into consideration. Therefore we can add another dimension to our attempt to visualize the educational ministry styles of the future by examining some of the significant present realities in general education.

New Educational Technologies

The question as to whether or not educational ministry should attempt to follow or otherwise relate to general education is exceedingly perplexing. On the one hand, educational ministry wants to take advantage of the effective methodologies that are being developed and tested by general education. On the other hand, the kind of education in which the church is involved is admittedly unique in that it rests on the person of Jesus Christ, on God's continuing action in the world and in the lives of men, and on the process of ministering (it is important to understand that educational ministry does *not* consider these to be solely content-oriented terms).

The observation has been made that one of the greatest advances in general curriculum development in recent years has involved a reselection of content within given subject areas and an emphasis on basic concepts. No doubt one of the strengths of the Christian education of the past has been its concentration on essential Christian concepts. Educational ministry seeks to sustain this thrust while also picking up clues relating to methodology from general education.

The greatest leaps in educational technology in the past ten years have involved multi-media, individualized instruction, and the learning environment. All three of these are already being felt to some degree in educational ministry, mainly because the concept, educational ministry, heightens the church's realization of its responsibility to deal with learners within the influence of the church in ways that approach the quality and nature of general education. Not only is the church taking advantage of the latest thinking regarding curriculum development, she is also examining carefully the technological aspects of general education for their appropriateness to educational ministry. We will use these three general categories in our all-too-brief examination of some of the more significant forces operating currently in general education.

1. *Multi-media.* Technological advancements in this decade have provided beginning answers to the question of reaching the learner through more than a single sense at a given moment. While it is still difficult to come to a completely satisfactory answer as to the specific components of "multi-media," the genus would include: screen education items (including cinema, instructional TV, cassette videocorders (ERV), overhead and opaque projectors, and perhaps even the computer with the printout screen. The types of films that belong in this category are increasing in number but presently include motion pictures, slides, transpanencies, filmstrips, and film loops), audio items (the cassette recorder is fast taking over the education market because of its usability, simplicity, and low cost), and printed resources (books, articles, pamphlets, leaflets, posters, mimeoed or dittoed throwaway items, and paperback booklets which are keeping book costs within reach of the learner). This is obviously not an exhaustive listing of the items that fall under the genus multi-media but merely a suggestion of the material resources that will probably be utilized in the educational ministry of the future. The *Second Report of the Project* Designing Education for the Future concludes that: "The most promising materials are those which are designed to be responsive to the exploration of the student; enable the student to be self-propelling; extend the range of stimuli to several senses; provide

alternative means to common ends; and free the teacher from burdens of routine correcting and testing."[12]

While some of the new multi-media approaches are group oriented (designed to relate to an entire class or group of persons), others are oriented toward individualized learners. This fact raises the distinct possibility that advances in these two types of approaches may work against each other, depending on the disposition of the educational theoretician. Of course the media have valid use in both areas.

Although most of the media mentioned here have already been used in educational ministry for a number of years, the new "Leader-in-the-Box" leadership series of the LCA is one of our first attempts to combine a large number of media into a single program.

But to provide only new curriculum resources or new technologies for educational ministry would be like developing safer automobiles as quickly as possible without continuing the slow process of driver education.[13] It would be a gross mistake for educational ministry to concentrate solely on the development of educational hardware without also developing the process of teaching (the facilitatig of learning).

2. *Personalized education.* The movement toward individualized instruction (I prefer the term personalized instruction) is currently being strongly felt in general education and is beginning to be used in educational ministry.[14] Individualized instruction is a highly flexible system of multiple materials and procedures

". . . in which the student is given substantial responsibility for planning (*sic*, author) and carrying out his own original program of studies, with the assistance of his teachers, and in which his progress is determined solely in terms of those plans."[15]

The concept of individualized instruction involves a number of related or subconcepts, not all of which are accepted by even its advocates. Instruction is individualized when the learner is allowed to proceed through content materials at a self-determined pace that is comfortable to him (self-paced instruction). The learner should be able to work with these methods appropriate to his needs (relevant methodology), at times convenient to him (convenient timing), and should begin instruction in a given subject area at a point appropriate to his past achievement (readiness).[16] Individualization can be achieved by furnishing the learner with a wealth of instructional media from which to choose (selection).[17]

It is important to note the difference between "individual" and "individualized" instructions:

> "Individual instruction," where one studies in isolation from other learners, should probably be distinguished from "individualized instruction," where the scope, sequence, and time for instruction are tailored (to the needs of the learner). . . . "Individualized instruction" can still be in a group setting and in fact, was commonly practiced in rural one-room schools . . .[18]

Harold E. Mitzel prefers the term "adaptive education" to "individualized" or "personalized instruction": "By adaptive education we mean the tailoring of subject matter presentations to fit the special requirements and capabilities of each learner."[19] This adaptation is based on the idea that no system should make the learner fall short of his potential in any given area of content. It means using new knowledge about the differences between learners and could well be based on the learner's immediate past history of responding. Interestingly, Mitzel believes that such adaptive education can be either deductive or inductive in nature: ". . . for some students, learning will be facilitated by the deductive approach: others will learn more rapidly and with better retention if an inductive mode is adopted."[20]

One important aspect of this personalized education is that it involves a high degree of learner self-evaluation. In past Christian education, the test has been simplistic: regular attendance and cooperation with the teacher were the primary modes of evaluation. Some church schools have given low grades or held students back if they failed these two primary tests (some schools have added a third type of test built on teacher expectations). Educational ministry realizes that evaluation is rendered possible by the clear statement of objectives. Progress can be measured only when the question, Progress toward what? has a distinct answer.

What has come to be known as "programmed instruction" might well be considered at this point. Such instruction has existed for many years and has developed apart from the rather recent machine approach. Programmed instruction does not require the use of a mechanical device. However, interest in personalized instruction had a surge about fifteen years ago when B. F. Skinner of Harvard advocated an educational technology built around the use of what he called a "teaching machine."[21] The machine approach codifies learning into learning paths and the learner follows an appropriate track to a given learning depending on his personal deficiencies or needs. This machine approach enjoyed some initial success with highly motivated learners, but the programmed learning idea has not caught on in the lower schools, or in higher education, or in Christian education as a major educational device. The reason is probably that it removes, to a large degree, the person-to-person facilitation aspect of learning.

Related to this machine approach, yet quite different in its purpose, is the increasing use of computers in the educational process. Computers are being used to store information, to assist the learner in building learning paths, and to analyze learning systems. General education is making use of this approach especially at the junior and senior high school levels where schools share resource banks via individual keyboards. General education is finding such an approach more and more necessary because of the knowledge explosion. Robert Woodruff reminds us that "current estimates are that man will increase his fund of information by over sixteen times in the next thirty-five years."[22] Ralph W. Tyler adds: "Probably three-fourth of the knowledge now available to man was not known at the close of World War II."[23] While computer resource banks to store burgeoning knowledge may be helpful, it is important that we see that an educational system which encourages nothing but the assimilation of facts (some theories of Christian education fall into this content-fact category) is no longer tenable. (As we have already noted, a computer can also deal with ideas and the interrelationship of ideas as well as with factual knowledge). If Christian education concentrates chiefly on giving learners specific knowledge, then we must recognize that each student's supply of knowledge ". . . will be largely obsolete by the time he is 35."[24] Again, (cf. the Weinberg illustration) it would be a gross mistake for education to concentrate solely on one type of technology in learning. Robert Woodroof expands our horizons when he says that "there are no 'only' methods; the knowledge explosion (must) be built around many imaginative projects aimed at teaching students to 'think' and 'experience'."[25] While educational ministry must constantly be aware of the latest information, it must also keep sharp its affective (those

249

dealing with feelings, values, attitudes, and beliefs) and executive (those dealing with action) tools.

Our concern with multi-media and personalized learning appears to coalesce in the current resurgence of interest on the part of general education in what are called "learning packages." Such packages can be designed to relate to individual learners or to groups of learners. The possibility of personalizing learning is resident, however, in both types of packages. *Educational Leadership* magazine has recently reported several instances of public school systems contracting with outside firms to teach reading, arithmetic, and other skills by means of instructional technology (packaged programs and projects) under a money-back guarantee to produce results.[26] While educational ministry does not deal chiefly with cognitive learnings and skills or with guaranteed results, the concept of learning packages is intriguing for educational ministry because it is a way of putting a handle on the best in multi-media and some of the promising aspects of personalized education.

A learning package can be either a boxed assortment of learning materials or a complicated learning system made up of subsystems. It combines teaching and learning and emphasizes personalization. It is based on broad concepts organized into manageable modules or units of instruction and uses multi-media, diversified learning activities. Perhaps its most distinguished characteristic (from the point of view of educational ministry) is that entrance into its process is through an objective that must be clearly stated and understood at the very beginning. *Educational Leadership* suggests that "without doubt, the package seems likely to be a feature of education life for some time to come."[27]

A typical learning package might contain: (a) pamphlets, (b) cassettes, (c) films, (d) apparatus, (e) ditto or mimeo masters, (f) paperback booklets, (g) notebooks, (h) transparencies, and (i) a resource list. It is interesting to note that packages are considered to be programs and not materials because they contain within them a plan for their own use. One obvious failure of current systems of Christian education is their inability to deal with the differing abilities and needs of learners. Application of such personalized learning emphases as the package may help Christian educators to see the uniqueness of each student.

Along with the growing emphasis on personalized instruction in general education there has been an increasing use of the tutorial type of facilitation in which a limited number of students (usually one, two, or three) work with a given teacher. There is, as we have noted, an increasing emphasis on learner involvement in the planning of learning programs. At lower levels, this carefully guided involvement in planning may mean such things as choosing between several learning activities, setting modest learning goals, selecting resources, and determining ways to evaluate learning activities. At higher levels, it may mean learner involvement, not only in designing programs or learning experiences, but also in developing and discovering objectives and goals. The point here is that there ought to be much more involvement in the total learning process on the part of the learner.

Our present dealing with learning and the facilitating of learning would not be complete without reference to the trend toward the differentiated teaching staff.[28] Voices are being heard today saying that the job of the teacher has become completely unmanageable and that the "self-contained teacher" and the "self-contained classroom" are obsolete. No longer, it is said, does a single individual have the competence, energy, or time to deal effectively with all the responsibilities assigned to one teacher. No teacher can afford to operate in isolation from the other teachers in the school and from the other classrooms and concerns. The stimulation of colleagues and interdisciplinary contact is needed now more than ever before. The outstanding strength of this new approach is that it includes more than the teacher and the student in the learning process. It also involves the parents of students, short-term experts and helpers, and one-shot visitors.

The concept of the differentiated teaching staff has implications for educational ministry in that it is a concept of organization that seeks to make better use of widespread talents and resources in the human and Christian communities. It is a way of making optimum use of human interests, abilities, commitments, and time. In the context of educational ministry the differentiated teaching staff might include: the teacher or the team of teachers, a variety of special service persons (perhaps parents), subject matter specialists, administrators, student teachers, persons from various professions (public school teachers, professional people, craftsmen, laborers), volunteers and

251

diagnosticians. The concept is an extension of the role of the teacher or team of teachers—a spreading out of involvement in and responsibility for educational ministry. Although the concept is still experimental, the model referred to has been developed by Dwight Allen of the University of Massachusetts School of Education in connection with a public school system. It is my feeling that this concept ought to be carefully examined by the church because it appears to run parallel to the expanding concerns of educational ministry in which the responsibility for ministering rests on the shoulders of many persons and many agencies of the church.

3. *The learning environment.* Many efforts have been made recently both in general education and in educational ministry to break out of the restriction of the formal classroom. A fascinating paper entitled *The Learning Community* based on the educational ministry program of the First Congregational Church of Everett, Washington is but one example of an educational program that felt the need to experiment in order to make the Christian faith more relevant to learners.[29] In short, instead of dividing learners into age groups, the procedure allows for learners to make choices as to which one of three or four learning groups they will attend on a given occasion. Children (perhaps in gross divisions according to their public school system) are encouraged to engage in whichever of the activities or projects attracts them. This non-graded approach, although it entails problems relating to such things as sequence, content and objectives, is opening up the educational ministry program of a congregation in such a way that learners are stimulated by a new environmental factor—the presence of persons of other ages. This approach places a good deal of trust in the learner and believes that decision making is in itself a valuable part of the learning process. Even such a non-graded approach, however, must have clearly stated goals in order to be effective.

Closely associated with this idea is the open classroom approach which is based on the strong belief that environment is one of the key factors in learning. The open classroom or "school without walls" is perhaps best seen in the experimental Philadelphia Parkway Program.[30] The "program" is not a "school" in the commonly accepted sense because it does not have a single-building orientation. The concept is based on the belief that school is not a place but a process.[31]

The city, or the park—wherever the student is—becomes his classroom. Students travel to hospitals, theaters, offices, banks, businesses, industries, and homes according to a planned schedule. Such innovative programs are helping us to see that educational ministry can also break out of the classroom and gather learners wherever significant things are happening in the human and Christian communities. Perhaps more experimental centers are needed in educational ministry in which innovative programs (involving modular scheduling, informal learning, ecumenical approaches, cluster approaches, etc.) can be tested in relation to environment. We can no longer afford to attach such innovation to the end of educational ministry.

> Learning through the environment and learning about the environment proceed simultaneously. To the individual, the environment must not be something to overcome, but to be altered for the task; not something mute and inexplicable, but something that reveals itself to one who knows how to ask. A person thus trained to control, to perfect, to question and find answers, gains many ways to amplify and extend the power of his thought and consciousness.[32]

A learning environment which sparks the minds of learners to an understanding of the startling relationships between subject areas and persons provides an expanded atmosphere for educational ministry that is at the same time exciting and satisfying. Mark Hopkins saw the importance of environment in learning when he said, "Education includes everything that exerts a formative influence and causes a young person to be, at a given point, what he is."[33]

The foundational documents in this curriculum project have demonstrated the belief that educational ministry is based on interactive environments, persons, concepts and objectives. The proposed curriculum cannot be adequately described by using the normal categories (subject curriculum, activity curriculum, core curriculum, or experimental curriculum) because it contains elements of each.[34] Evidences that what is happening in educational ministry is part of what Gail Inlow calls "newer curriculum directions"[35] are: (a) an emphasis on healthy interpersonal relationships (cf. section II of the Continual Life Involvements outline), (b) an emphasis on creativity (cf. especially the innovative—innovative for Christian education—emphasis on ideas sparked by the environment of the human community), and (c) an emphasis on problem solving, especially its action dimension (cf. especially the Youth Section of the Age Level Objectives document and the Youth Section of the Program Design).

Although predictions deal with the future, they provide a significant part of the background for the development of educational ministry. The central objective has a future orientation in that it is based on a theology of hope, both in reference to God's continuing activity and man's continuing response. It is open-ended (cf. the process objectives) in its attempt to be relevant to the life styles of the present and of the future and in its recognition of the reality of change. In fact, the foundations being laid appear already to have at least one foot in the future because they recognize the reality of change.

The Reality of Change

It would be possible to summarize the first two major sections of this paper by referring to their underlying change orientation. Both the perspectives of the future and the emphasis on new educational technologies bring us to the conclusion that, if education and educational ministry in the future are to survive in any meaningful way, they must somehow be able to cope with change. In the second education yearbook, Dr. Gustav Wiencke notes that "Christian education everywhere in the world is challenged by changes in society and even greater changes must be anticipated in the future."[36] The 1964 yearbook of the Association for Supervision and Curriculum Development describes our time as an era of "unclarity, complexity, and flux."[37] It continues, ". . . change is all about us, and as a consequence, the presence of change often seems the most credible fact of man's experience."[38] The implication would seem to be that change itself must be consciously dealt with as we face the future. It may well be that the most significant thing that the educational ministry of the future can do is to equip Christian people to cope with, influence, and plan the changes that will surely come. Rather than looking at change as an enemy, we need to see it as a friend and bringer of new and exciting opportunities.

We face the future, then, by making certain assumptions about change. Throughout the remainder of this paper we shall assume that: (1) change is real, (2) change is inevitable, (3) change will continue at a more rapid—in fact compounded—pace, (4) some changes will be beneficial and some harmful, (5) men can plan and guide change to a significant degree, (6) education is an extremely important factor in the change process, and (7) education *itself* (educational ministry included) must change if it is going to be a significant factor in shaping our future. One of the reasons we do not feel uncomfortable about all these assumptions regarding change is that we are also making another assumption, this one about man. The person is ". . . the human constant in the midst of rapid change."[39] Because we are primarily concerned with this person in the midst of change, our eyes have been especially sensitive to the plight of the learner and the leader. Where evidences of change can be seen in the areas of media and teaching methodologies, perhaps the greatest change in educational ministry needs to involve the role of the learner. In an article in *Saturday Review* entitled "The Rise of the Free School," Bonnie Barrett Stretch talks about what she considers to be the most significant change in recent years in the realm of education:

> The revolt is no longer against outdated curriculums or ineffective teaching methods—the concerns of the late fifties and early sixties. The revolt today is against the institution itself, against the implicit assumption that learning must be imposed on children by adults, that learning is not something one does by and for oneself, but something designated by a teacher.[40]

It is in this area that we need to press for further change in educational ministry. Present styles depend, in a word, on what is designed by and satisfying for the adult leaders involved in Christian education and not primarily on what is needed by or stimulating for the learner. What has happened is that we have set the goals of present Christian education to meet the needs of adults rather than students.

Attempting to keep the learner in mind, we suggest that a number of principles ought to be considered when educational ministry faces the question of change or movement toward desired goals:[41] (1) The unique nature of the particular change under consideration must be clarified. Changes are of many kinds. We need to give priority to and support to change that results in the improvement of personal experiences. (2) The most significant changes are those that happen to persons. (3) If change is to take place, the need for change must be seen clearly. If persons are not personally convinced of the need for change they will resist change in any way they can. (4) The nature and implications of the change must be dealt with openly and honestly. Causing change is not a matter of hoodwinking people into doing what they really don't want to do. Change decreed by authority is seldom accepted. (5) The forces that present barriers to change must be located and dealt with squarely. We cannot proceed as though objections to change don't exist or as though change is equally easy for all persons. (6) Persons must be free to get the "feel" of a proposed change before the change is actually made operational. (7) Change will come about only as fast as the persons involved are willing to change. (8) Change is a group concern as well as an individual concern.

What we are suggesting, then, is that, although we can gain a certain feeling for the future, we cannot predict accurately the shape of the educational ministry of the future. Neither can we make straight-line projections into the future of current trends in either general or Christian education. We can be sure, however, that the word "change" can be used in relation to the styles of the future when they are laid alongside what we now call educational ministry. For this reason our attention is now focused on change. We hope that, if we understand the nature of change more adequately, we can better plan for the things we want to be a part of the educational ministry of the future.

Three Essential Functions in Planning Change

Increasing sophistication in curriculum design and in developing educational methodologies make it mandatory that we gain increasing competence in educational ministry. This factor has already been noted by Wiencke in the second education yearbook: ". . . competence in Christian education is needed. This means learning from the great ferment in secular education today and applying secular methods in the development of Christian education."[42] It is significant that all three education yearbooks focus on elements of change in educational ministry and push for increased competence on the part of educational ministers. We have gone beyond the truism that the Christian church cannot survive without Christian education. We say now that the church cannot survive without the most competent kind of educational ministry.[43]

But what is the nature of the competence that we need in educational ministry? Surely we need increased competence in curriculum development, in relating "Christian" to "education," and "education" to "ministry," in designing learning activities, and in taking advantage of varying environments. I am pleading here, however, for increased competence in the area of change agentry. Unless educators can see themselves as agents active in the process of planning and implementing change, education will continue to be satisfied with being locked in the classroom and dealing with "the way things were.'

The essential functions involved in the planning of change, I suggest, are: consulting, facilitating, and researching. I do not mean to suggest that a neat separation can be made between these three aspects of the change process; the division is only for heuristic purposes. Likewise, no sequential order is intended. It must also be recognized that there are many types of consulting, facilitating, and researching. What I intend to convey is the fact that at least these three functions must be carried out with increasing competence in the planning of change:

1. *Consulting.* If desired change is to take place on the local level, there must be adequate diagnosis of "the way things are right now." The well known 1962 ASCD Yearbook, *Perceiving, Behaving, Becoming,* is a statement of the thesis that the individual (perhaps the individual congregation?) perceives, interprets, and integrates uniquely in terms of his previous experiences and *present needs and purposes* (italics mine). Increasing competence is needed at the local level if, as present trends indicate, program planning in the future is to be done and more and more at that level.

Consulting is the process of attaching an outside (usually) person to an existing social system for the purpose of diagnosis. The process is temporary but needs to be repeated at intervals. It is based on the authority of ideas or analysis rather than on the authority of administrative relationship.

The need for such a function is underscored by the possibility that our educational ministry system will actually be developed around the principle that learning is a lifelong process[44] with: (a) alternative routes (traditional/innovative, formal/informal, peer group/transgenerational)[45] and (b) many entrance and exit points, depending on the changing needs and interests of the participants. When we view the church as a "total learning community" then we must look to the process of educational ministry to meet a wide variety of purposes including basic understandings, conflict resolution, meeting life crises (social, vocational), the interpersonal, and acting. The consultant is one who enables the local group to see just where it is so that it can set goals and proceed toward where it wants to be.

It is not by accident that the present church agencies charged with "feeling the pulse" of congregations have taken a decided trend toward providing consultative services for congregations.[46] This function must not only continue but must grow in the future. It is a part of educational ministry.

2. *Facilitating.* As the end for educational ministry becomes more crucial, the quality of local leadership must be improved. Someone must be on hand to pay special attention to the persons who are changing. Facilitating (usually called training in the context of change planning) leads to the internalization of skills and their ultimate transfer into action. The goal of such facilitation is not to tell learners *what* to think but to help them know *how* to learn and *where* to find resources for learning. As such, facilitating leads to the releasing of potential which is personal, individual, frequently unpredictable (another reason for our hesitation to predict the future style of educational ministry), ". . . and it is literally almost limitless."[47] "Potential is also multi-dimensional, appearing in multiple forms in the individual learner and spreading widely into areas of human accomplishment which have been examined but little."[48] Carl Rogers likes to talk about "freeing up the learner"[49] so that he will be able to act in his own unique ways.

In normal change agent terminology, this process consists of balancing task (goal attainment) and maintenance (interpersonal relationships) requirements, usually through the intervention skills, awareness, and action abilities of the facilitator. Kenneth D. Benne believes that traditional teaching has failed because it has emphasized either diagnosis or action without considering the necessary connection between the two.[50] Understressing diagnosis leads to "how to" exercises and overstressing diagnosis results in abstractions. The kind of facilitation needed in educational ministry for the future is that which provides a social (group) base while recognizing the uniqueness of the individual. "Change processes need to be concerned with altering both the forces within the individual and the forces in the organizational situation surrounding the individual."[51] If educational ministry is going to be actively involved in the planning of change, it must train and support the facilitator in every conceivable way. The kinds of changes educational ministry envisions for the future cannot take place without insightful, emphathetic facilitators.

3. *Researching.* Another function that must be carried on is research. We are using the term here in its broadest possible sense to include the examination of all the elements that have gone into the learning process (the consulting, the facilitating, feedback, the resources used, and evaluation processes). The kind of change agentry we envision is a cyclical process in which consulting, facilitating, and researching are continually involved. It is the research, however, that kicks the process into gear and keeps it going. Research both begins the process and comes at its end in that it is constantly questioning the relevance of what's happening. Without this function, its continuation and improvement, educational ministry in the future will become irrelevant.

Conclusion

The purpose of this article has been not so much to try to predict the shape of the educational ministry of the future as it has been to focus thinking on some of the forces and functions that must be taken into consideration as we proceed into the future. It is not so much our hope that these brief glances into the future will be accurate, but rather that they will stimulate and challenge the educational planning of today. We have, in essence, answered the question concerning future styles of educational ministry by saying that the Christian church needs to develop continuing ways to stay on top of the needs and changes that influence both learners and leaders now, whatever the educational ministry styles of the future may be. If educational ministry does not speak meaningfully to the present needs of her constituents she will die by her own hand.

At base, educational ministry is not a matter of the mix of leaders, learners, resources, programs, and evaluations but—as the Joint Commission on the Theology and Practice of Confirmation has said[52]—a matter of concern and identification between Christian persons, usually between the wise and experienced (and we are learning that these are not always the adults) and the becoming-wise and the becoming-experienced. Educational ministry today is caring, accepting, and listening to persons, where they are, where they have been and where they are going. Educational ministry tomorrow will involve the same things.

NOTES AND REFERENCES

1. B. Othanel Smith, William O. Stanley, and J. Harlan Shores, *Fundamentals of Curriculum Development* (Yonkers-on-Hudson, N.Y.: World Book Company, 1957), p. vii.
2. Roland Tapp, "Church Trends, Product Analysis and Planning Report" Philadelphia: The Westminster Press, 1969, pp. 32-36.
3. Lyle E. Schaller, *The Impact of the Future* (Nashville: Abingdon Press, 1969), p. 12.
4. Vernon E. Anderson, *Curriculum Guidelines in an Era of Change* (New York: The Roland Press Company, 1969), pp. 86-91.
5. Clyde Kluckhohn, Foreword to *Cultural Foundations of Education* by Theodore Brameld (New York: Harper & Brothers, 1957), pp. xii-xiii.
6. Edward W. Uthe, *Significant Issues for the 1970's: Report to the Lutheran Church in America Task Group for Long Range Planning* (Philadelphia: Fortress Press, 1968), p. 140. Note the attempt of the new central objective to speak to both arenas.
7. *Ibid.,* p. 109. Cf. Jeffrey K. Hadden, *The Gathering Storm in the Churches* (Garden City, N.Y.: Doubleday & Co., Inc., 1969).
8. Kenneth Boulding, "Expecting the Unexpected: The Uncertain Future of Knowledge and Technology" in *Prospective Changes in Society by 1980*, Designing Education for the Future, vol. 1, eds. E. L. Morphet and C. O. Ryan (New York: Citation Press, 1966), p. 199.
9. *Curriculum Guidelines in an Era of Change*, p. 56.
10. *The Impact of the Future*, Introduction.
11. Quoted in E. L. Morphet and C. O. Ryan, eds., *Implications for Education of Prospective Changes in Society*, Designing Education for the Future, vol. 2 (New York: Citation Press, 1967), p. 116.
12. *Ibid*, pp. 54-55.
13. The illustration is from Alvin M. Weinberg, "Can Technology Replace Social Engineering?" *University of Chicago Magazine* October, 1966, pp. 6-10.
14. Cf. the learning lab section of the new revised LCA Confirmation education courses to come out in 1971.
15. *Educational Leadership* 28:775, May, 1970.
16. Note the implication here that progress in learning is linear and that locating the present position of the learner is important.
17. This assumes that the learner will instinctively select the media or

resources that will enable him to do his best work. The evidence that this assumption is correct is not strong.

18. Harold E. Mitzel, "The Impending Instructional Revolution," *Phi Delta Kappan* April 1970, pp. 434-439.
19. *Ibid.*, p. 436.
20. *Ibid.*, p. 437.
21. B. F. Skinner, "Teaching Machines," *Science* 128 (Spring 1954).
22. Robert Woodroof, "The Changing Concepts of Education," *Minutes,* the magazine of Nationwide Insurance. Quoted in the LCA Minister's Information Service, February 1970, p. 8.
23. Ralph W. Tyler, "Purposes, Scope, and Organization of Education" in *Implications of Education for Prospective Changes in Society,* Designing Education for the Future, vol. 2, eds. E. L. Morphet and C. O. Ryan (New York: Citation Press, 1967), p. 36.
24. *Ibid.* The implication is that Educational Ministry must start the child on a lifelong career of continuing learning and support him in the entire process.
25. "The Changing Concepts of Education," p. 10.
26. *Educational Leadership,* p. 763.
27. *Ibid.*, p. 767.
28. For a complete description of the concept see *NCSPS News* (Washington, D.C.: National Committee for Support of Public Schools, January 1970).
29. John M. Larsen and Albert A. Hieb, "The Learning Community" Everett, Washington: First Congregational Church, 1969.
30. Cf. *Phi Delta Kappan,* vol. 51, no. 9 (May 1970).
31. How reminiscent of the Christian's contention that the church is not a place but a "fellowship of believers." The current trend downward in Sunday church school attendance and enrollment may not be as alarming as some would have us think. To ask, Why aren't the children in Sunday school? is to reflect a belief that educational ministry happens in a place called the church classroom. Actually, only a very small part of educational ministry takes place here.
32. W. E. Schroeder, Jr., *Grade Teacher* January 1970, p. 109.
33. Quoted by Chris A. DeYoung, *American Education* (New York: McGraw-Hill Book Co., Inc., 1960), p. 289.
34. Cf. the types enumerated by Smith, Stanley, and Shores.
35. Gail M. Inlow, *The Emergent in Curriculum* (New York: John Wiley and Sons, Inc., 1966), pp. 47-68.
36. Gustav K. Wiencke, ed., "Impact of Secularism on Christian Education," *Christian Education in a Secular Society,* Yearbooks in Christian Education—II. (Philadelphia: Fortress Press, 1970), p. 19.
37. *Individualized Instruction,* 1964 ASCD Yearbook (Washington, D.C.: Association for Supervision and Curriculum Development, NEA, 1964), p. 3.

38. *Ibid.*, p. 3.
39. *Implications for Education of Prospective Changes in Society*, p. 2.
40. Bonnie Barret Stretch, "The Rise of the 'Free School'", *Saturday Review*, June 20, 1970, p. 76.
41. The principles suggested here are based on two sources: *Curriculum Guidelines in an Era of Change*, pp. 19 ff. and Kenneth D. Benne and Max Birnbaum, "Change Does Not Have to Be Haphazard," *The School Review*, vol. 68, no. 3(1960), pp. 292-293.
42. *Christian Education in a Secular Society*, p. 128.
43. Marshall C. Dendy, *Changing Patterns in Christian Education* (Richmond, Va.: John Knox Press, 1964), Introduction.
44. Cf. the strong Joint Commission on the Theology and Practice of Confirmation, *A Report for Study* (Minneapolis: Augsburg Publishing House. St. Louis: Concordia Publishing House. Philadelphia: Board of Publication, Lutheran Church in America, 1970).
45. The research reports of Arvid Anderson undertaken for the design phase of the present curriculum project (*A Study of Educational Ministry in the Parish*, Task Force for Planning Educational Ministry in the Parish. The American Lutheran Church and the Lutheran Church in America) indicate that most congregations desire alternative routes in at least the youth and adult segments of any new curriculum developed.
46. Specific instances with which this author is familiar include the work of the field staffs of the Boards of Parish Education of both the ALC and the LCA, the Leadership Development Program of the LCA Commission on Youth Ministry, and the new Parish Life Development Project of the LCA which is focusing on the consultative aspects of organizational development.
47. *Individualized Instruction*, p. 159.
48. *Ibid.*, p. 159.
49. Carl R. Rogers, *Freedom to Learn* (Columbus, Ohio: Charles E. Merrill, 1969).
50. Kenneth D. Benne, "Case Methods in the Training of Administrators," in Warren G. Bennis, Kenneth D. Benne, and Robert Chin, eds., *The Planning of Change* (New York: Holt, Rinehart, Winston, Inc., 1964), p. 631.
51. Floyd C. Mann, "Studying and Creating Change," in *The Planning of Change*, pp. 605 ff.
52. *A Report for Study*, pp. 21-22.

A Look At the Future—A Response

J. HARLAN SHORES

In the language of the educator, the educational program of the church means the curriculum—that is those experiences planned and offered under the direct influence of the organized church. Were the word "school" to be substituted for church, the same definition might be used to define the curriculum of public, private and parochial schools as they carry on their programs from nursery school through adult education. The curriculum concept is thus a broad one, but it is also restricted. The many experiences that people have in and through church activities by accident or incidentally *may* be church related but are *not* a part of the curriculum. Nor are the unplanned things that happen *in* churches or *to* churches through community or broader social forces a part of the curriculum. Experiences must be planned and they must be under the direct influence of the church to be a part of the curriculum or educational program.

Whatever competence this author has is in the area of school curriculum development. This chapter then will be an attempt to apply knowledge about the school curriculum to church programs. Trends will be examined as these relate to the curriculum generally and to the church in particular. And, inevitably, there must be some attempt to look into the future. It is recognized, of course, that analysis of trends is likely to be in error, that prediction from trends is dangerous, and that crystal-ball gazing about what things may be like in the year 2000 is even more dangerous. Yet some of all of these must be done if we are to be ready for tomorrow.

One further warning is in order before we begin to consider the church curriculum. Just as the ethnic, economic, political, and other aspects of society are not all of one piece and are not moving in a single conscious and consistent social direction, neither is the curriculum. Current developments and trends in the school curriculum, and surely also in the educational program of the church, are often in basic conflict with one another. Rather than to "ride off in all directions at once" there are choices to be made, and while we would rather

263

call them "educated guesses", they surely show bias on the part of an author or whoever is making these choices.

Realms of Curriculum Choices

No matter how contemporary, futuristic, relevant or innovative a curriculum may be, it must provide answers to five age-old questions. These are what the curriculum is all about, and good answers to these five questions will determine the value of any curriculum or of any church program. Let's consider these five questions, then come back to each in turn as a structure for the body of this chapter.

The first question is, *Who is to be educated?* For which individuals or groups is the program intended? Obviously one would need a different program to serve different people. If the answer is "all the people", its weaknesses in biting off more than can be chewed may show in serving none well. If it is too narrow, and to use another cliché, we put all our eggs in one basket, the program may miss many vital needs. These are hard choices, but they must be made for any church program to be effective.

The second question is, *Educated for what?* What are we really trying to do? What are our objectives, our goals? And, perhaps equally important, what priority do we give to each goal? Where do we put our time, energy and money? Realizing at once that each of these resources is limited, we are again faced with different choices. Where with the first question we may try to serve too many, now we may be trying to offer too much. The result is that none of the dribbles add up to a drop. The opposite error, of course, is to have many goals and to neglect most of them. Clear-cut goals and priorities for each of them are a must.

The third question following directly from the second, is, *Educated with what?* What is the nature of our program? What kind of experiences do we try to provide? How do we go about meeting the goals that have been given high priority? What is the content of our program? We have now raised three questions: Who? For what? With what? It is important that they be answered in this order. Goals cannot be set without people in mind and programs cannot be planned without goals in mind.

Now that we have the scope of a program planned, we must put some order into it. The fourth question is, *When to educate?* The church serves many in many different ways. Which of these experiences should be for the very young? Which for youth, adults, the aged? The good things we have planned must have a sequence. The program must lead to our goals in an orderly and efficient manner.

Now we must get the job done. The fifth question is, *How to educate?* This involves several important questions. Who is to do the job? How is it to be organized for efficient administration? What methods and materials are to be used?

It must be apparent by now that questions about a church program arise in each of these five realms and that answers to any one of them invariably relate to the other four. If a church curriculum were to be built from scratch, the order in which these five big questions have been asked probably is the best order for answering them. But this doesn't happen. Even in a new church at any organizational level, there are ideas about a program even before the church is organized, and these ideas affect the educational program from the outset. In well established churches there are programs in effect that reflect some kinds of answers to all these questions. It is more likely then that we don't approach curriculum development systematically. Instead we work on our most immediate problems—those where the shoe seems to be pinching hardest at the moment. Let's take a brief look then at some of the problems in each of these realms, at some current attempts to solve them, and at what the future might indicate with regard to their solution.

Who Is to Be Educated?

The public school in this democratic society has no choice within its value framework but to answer this question with "all the children of all the people." As a consequence we are constantly aware of shortcomings in our attempts to do a good job of serving so many different individuals and groups. Special attention has been drawn in recent years to the mentally handicapped, the gifted, the educationally disadvantaged, cultural minorities (especially the Blacks, Mexican Americans, and American Indians), and the illiterates among all groups. What seems to be a pendulum-like swing from group to group is not an indication of indecision or vacillation. It is instead a question of priorities. Which segment of the school population is in most dire need now? There are, of course, political considerations as well as moral ones at local, state, and national levels.

One may be sure that the future will see portions of the population singled out for special consideration, and one can be equally sure that different groups will get this increased attention at different times. Another prediction with likely truth is that the side effects from each of these strong pushes will be good for the program of those not immediately involved. Whenever we concentrate on any atypical segment of the people as a whole, we learn much of value to education more generally, and this will continue to be so.

The church must face the same general problem and answer the same general question. Who is to be educated? Who is to be served by the educational program? This question must be answered within the church at all levels, and this author can offer only a few guidelines. One group, to be sure, must be the active members of the church. If they are not served in some manner, they won't long be active. But even this is complicated. Should a Sunday church school be maintained when 60 percent of the students come from families outside the congregation? Does a congregation have responsibilities for youth who use the church's recreational facilities but are not members? Are those who attend services, but do not belong to the church, members? These illustrations could go on and on, and they only point to a few of the problems that must be raised and answered.

Another chapter of this book quotes Ronald Tapp predicting that membership in the institutional church of the future will include few, if any, children, youth, or even young adults. Most churchgoers will be forty-five years old and older. Will we accept this as an inevitable trend and adjust our program to it, or will we attempt to serve children and youth more adequately and make strong efforts to keep these groups within the organized church? As we plan the future, this type of question must be answered.

Just as the school program goes beyond the organized school, the church program goes far beyond its membership. Churches are involved with individuals and groups in the local community, with statewide programs, and, perhaps through the central administration, with national and international service. Few would want to curtail this broad commitment. Many would like to see the church serve segments of the population not now being reached. But again there are practical limits in energy, time and money. Which ones can we serve? How many? How far can we reach? Where will we draw the line?

As these priorities are established, and they must be established now and in the future, we will be looking for those efforts with the largest returns measured in human lives. We will continue to see more needs than can be met, and as our active membership and other social conditions change, so will our commitments. Just as we can be certain of change, we can be certain that there will be people needing our help more than those now served. Never able to do all we would like to do, we might do well to look not only at the largest short and long range returns but also at those efforts yielding the largest side effects. Some direct efforts seem so weak that they are almost futile, but they may have strong side effects on the membership or in showing the way to serve more people or different people in a larger and more effective program.

Educated for What?

Those who don't know the public schools well think that they see a confusion in goal orientation. This is much more imagined than real. In fact a look at city and state curriculum guides and courses of study shows agreement on objectives that is almost frightening in its conformity. The danger, if there is one, is that everyone is trying to do the same thing. One might ask: Where are the new directions? Where are the frontiers?

There is disagreement, and one would hope that there always will be, about how to reach our goals most efficiently, but the contention that exists about objectives is hidden in the priorities that are given to the many goals. It isn't difficult to find almost all worthwhile goals listed, and, as was said, these differ little from school to school, but what is done about them differs much. We have in mind to do everything, but manage to find the time and money to do very little. This same dilemma seems to plague the educational ministry.

No matter what thrust one would like the church to have, he can probably find a firm commitment to it in the program plans at some level. It hasn't been overlooked as an aim, a goal, an objective. It has

267

just been neglected in action. So the real objectives of a school or church are those where we are putting our agencies. We had to set priorities about whom to serve and now we have to set priorities among too many competing goals. We are asking what is most important, and we dare not answer "everything". Even if we manage more time and money, we can't possibly get around to all we would like to do. This is true now and will be true in the year 2000. With a very realistic look at what we have, both the school and the church must trim their objectives to what they can accomplish effectively.

This facing of reality is probably the most difficult task confronting the church in its educational program. There are so many worthwhile goals. Some people have their heart and, perhaps, their active membership in the church in each of them. Everyone can't be pleased with the choices; but, unless the choices are made, we are either deluding ourselves that our program is broader than it really is or we are picking away at so many goals that we reach none of them.

We are helped a bit by our earlier decisions about whom we are serving. Our goals can be for these people. But we are confounded by the problem of testing the relative worth of competing goals. How does one decide what is of most worth? If the answer lies in theology or in the philosophy of religion, this author can't begin to answer. If it lies in practical judgments about what we can do best with what we have at hand, then any Christian or congregation can begin to make these real, difficult, but absolutely necessary choices.

This process, of course, is not something that is done tomorrow for the next decade. It must be done every year and often within the year. The priorities will change with the membership and with the times, but the process must continue as long as does the church.

Educated with What?

It is obvious enough that the program should reflect and be in keeping with the goals. We should have the best program for reaching our objectives. The problem is that no one really knows what is the best program for reaching any goal. We know that some things work and that others don't but it is altogether likely that something not yet tried will work much better than what we know as the best available.

While educators continue the slow process of testing the worth of content (used synonymously here with "experiences" and "programs") for reaching objectives through experimentation, they also consider principles which might be used singly or in combination to judge the worth of content. In the form of questions one might ask the following:

1. Does the content deal with principles that are the most important ones in the subject? In other words, is the content really significant to this organized field of knowledge?

2. Has the content survived? Has it proved to be good over a period of time? Will it continue to do so?

3. Is the content useful? Is it needed?

4. Is the content interesting? This, of course, is related to motivation and the fact that the experiences must be meaningful for those taking part.

5. Is the content related to the maintenance and/or improvement of a democratic society?

6. Is the content relevant? Is it meaningful and important to life as it is lived today? Does it relate to the individual and social needs of today? Does it develop a broader or deeper meaning of Christianity?

When these criteria are used, it is recognized that they are often in conflict with one another. What is basic to a subject may not be useful or interesting. What has survived may be irrelevant, unimportant and no longer useful. And so it goes, priorities must again be established.

A church program might find some of these questions worth asking. For the past two decades, and especially since the advent of Sputnik I in 1957, there has been greatly increased activity in the schools toward the reselection of content for the basic subjects. This began in mathematics, spread quickly to the sciences and foreign languages, and is currently being felt in the English language arts and social science programs. Most of these "new" programs were looking for content more basic, more significant in each organized field. This content, more closely related to the structure of the discipline, was then taught early and in more and more sophisticated forms to more advanced learners.[1] If the church wished to do so, it could use this same principle for the reselection of religious content. Starting with church scholars, fundamental principles of theology might be identified. Looking for those elements most basic to the religion—those with "the most intellectual mileage"—the program from nursery school through adult-

269

hood could be reselected to bring members further and further into understanding of the religion as the church scholars know it.

Dangers of complete commitment to this approach to content selection are at once apparent. Only the first of the six questions cited above has been dealt with. Is learning the religion the only goal? Turning to the principle of survival, what parts of the church program have proved themselves over a period of years? Are these still as effective in today's world?

Even the criteria of usefulness and interest deserve consideration. The program must get to the people being served. It must reach them in this or in whatever society in which they live. And it must be relevant to life as it is being lived. Too often we live in the past, not recognizing that this isn't the society in which we matured. Nor are we the same people who helped bring about these changes. When youth tell us to "get with it", they have a point. We may not want to "get with it" in the way that they want us to, but to try to keep things as they are or as they were is as foolish as it is impossible.

Unclear as we are about who is to be served in the future and about what our goals will be for serving these people, it is impossible to predict what future church programs will be like. It is likely, however, that the six questions listed above will be as pertinent in the year 2000 as they are now. It is also likely that the organized church would profit as much from deliberate attempts to use empirical research to determine the effectiveness of programs as have the schools. If churches have made serious attempts to continuously assess the effectiveness of their programs, these efforts have been poorly publicized.

When to Educate?

Determination of "the teachable moment" will be a perennial problem. We have always tended to teach too early or too late. The two questions of import here are, When *can* a program be effectively carried out? and When *should* a program be offered? The first of these questions lends itself to the kinds of research advocated earlier. Does it work? How well does it work? The second question is not as easily answered. Its answer requires values in the making of judgments. When is the program most needed? What are the side effects if it is offered earlier or later? Just because learnings can be successful earlier is not in itself adequate justification for doing so.

As we determine both the program and its location by age groups, it is important to remember the tremendous advances recently made and those likely to be made in mass communication media. Critical as we may be of radio and television offerings, the fact is that people of all ages have much more knowledge gained in out-of-school and out-of church reading, listening, and viewing than was possible in any past generation. This, of course, is likely to be increasingly true in the future.

Wilbur Schramm, Director of the Stanford Institute for Communications Research points rather dramatically to the influence of television on young children when he reports that children from TV communities come to school with vocabularies about one year more advanced than do children from non-TV communities. He also reports that these children who spend more time viewing TV have significantly larger vocabularies than do those who are infrequent viewers.[2] Considering the fact that Schramm's vocabulary tests didn't include the words directly associated with beer, cigarettes, soaps, cereals, cosmetics and other commercials, it would seem that young children are more ready for any verbal program than they once were. It would also seem that they will be more ready tomorrow than they are today.

How to Educate?

There have been, and are sure to be, so many innovations in this area that it has been difficult to consider it last. Yet this is where it belongs, after considering the who, for what, with what, and when. An early consideration here is: Who is to do the job? Perhaps the schools with a larger variety of specialists have more difficult decisions to make here than do the churches. This is not to deny the many specialties and people to perform these functions within the larger church structure, but is to recognize the fact that the educational ministry, at least at the parish level, will be carried largely by laymen.

With laymen carrying the major burden of implementing the programs at the grass-roots level, the administrative organizations and devices must be those within which these people can operate. It would also mean that, unless the church can afford to employ spe-

271

cialists, continuous in-service training programs are not feasible. Hence the educational ministry must be organized in a relatively straightforward manner, and the materials and techniques employed must be those that can be carried out largely by laymen who move in and out of the leadership positions.

Such conditions would rule out some organizational and methodological choices by churches, just as they rule them out for many smaller schools and school systems. But there are many choices remaining. Unless many churches band together to share costs and the use of facilities, none of the many uses of computers in their present forms is practical. Even now churches could find uses for computers in administrative tasks and in information storage and retrieval. The year 2000 may find them developed in such a way that churches can make these uses of them, but both the expense and the diversity of present administrative organizations effectively rules them out.

Computer use for instruction or for systems analysis is presently ruled out on the same grounds. The programs are too varied and the cost is too high. Looking again into the future it may be that computerized instruction will sometime be so well-branched that it will be more useful to churches than are the relatively straight-line choices now available. Most church concerns offer many more alternatives than does instruction in mathematics, physics, or spelling. For instructional purposes the best of the present computers, expensive as they are, are offering us a Model T when we need the latest model.

Many persons put computers, machine teaching and programming in the same technological basket, but they are different in a number of respects. Some programmed teaching machines are simple and relatively inexpensive. In fact some are being sold for use in homes, and these work reasonably well for lessons that follow an orderly, step-by-step process. None of these is branched in such a way that it can follow many alternate routes to a single conclusion. Nor can any follow different routes to alternative conclusions. Unfortunately, it is the latter that is most needed as we think our way through our religion to its functions in the complexities of living. If the program is carefully developed, as all good programs must be, the present teaching machine can teach facts, simple skills and even values if these are prepared in advance. It cannot involve the learner in solution to his own problems or in solutions to the problems of others. But again, there may come a time when such machines may be built. Looking at the many ways that science and technology have changed our lives, we would be foolish to say that it can't be done.

At the present time programming with the "software" rather than the "hardware" is generally less expensive and more flexible (no pun intended). The same kind of job can be done with facts, skills, and predetermined values. This, of course, means many well-developed programs and lots and lots of paper. It doesn't avoid the great weakness of nearly all programs. The learner responds to the programmer's ideas. His own ideas don't get into the act.

The big push in teaching methodology is now, and will be for many years to come, upon the individualization or personalization of instruction. Programmed instruction has taken beginning steps in this direction by freeing the learner to pursue the program at his own time and at his own rate of progress. When the programs allow the learner many alternatives, including values, and the input of his own ideas, tremendous progress will have been made.

Those producing educational materials, and these now include many of the huge electronic industries, have in recent years turned to a "learning package" concept of production and sales. Instead of buying a textbook, supplementary reading materials, tapes, films, filmstrips and the like separately, the school is offered the entire learning package. Some of the packages may be intended for all the children, some for groups, and some for individuals who are lagging behind or going further than most. This is a difficult kind of programming somewhat akin to the difference between shopping for the separate grocery items for a meal and buying a prepackaged dinner. It's a big dinner and one doesn't have to eat all of it—only the parts that he wants or needs. So again, if the entire package isn't used for all, this is another step toward the individualization of instruction.

It is likely that most churches, as well as most schools, have not taken full advantage of some of the educational hardware that has been around for some time and is constantly becoming more practical and useful. There are times and places where different kinds of projectors, recorders, films, filmstrips, models, mock-ups, and even radio and TV programs or excerpts from these are extremely useful. Perhaps special attention should be drawn to the flexibility and versatility of the small and relatively inexpensive 8 mm projector with its film clips. Some of these are simple enough to be operated by a kindergarten child, but the content could fit any age or developmental level. A very nice feature of this machine is that it can be used effectively for a group as large as twenty-five or thirty or for small groups or individuals. Most of the educational technology, even that designed for mass communication, is being adapted for possible use by individuals and small groups.

Within recent years several administrative devices directed toward more effective utilization of staff efforts and toward attempts to further individualization of instruction have developed as trends. Among these are team teaching, the ungraded school, multileveling of instruction, and ability grouping by classes. As these are tested in practice, some of them seem likely to be refined and used more widely. Others look less promising in the light of both research findings and competing trends.

In its ideal form, team teaching involves cooperative planning, instruction, and evaluation by several staff members who have a special competence in some subject or level of instruction. That part of the rationale for team teaching that contends that several teachers can learn from one another and can pool their special abilities to meet varied student needs is in keeping with the larger trend toward personalized learning. However, that part claiming that certain lessons can be taught better by one member of the team than another which results in teaching a lesson to ninety rather than thirty children surely could make no claim to individualized instruction.

Still many hold that teaching is both more fun and more effective if carried on by a team, and the varied competencies of the many lay members participating in church programs would seem to make this an organizational scheme worth considering for both Sunday church school programs and other educational ministry efforts. With smaller groups than the usual school class size and with many members who would like some but not all of the responsibility, team teaching should be effective. A possible side-effect is coming to know and appreciate the members of the team. There is, of course, the possibility that the team members are incompatible, but this kind of problem may also be a learning experience. As subject matter and various elements of child and adolescent development become more specialized, team teaching probably will continue to grow and develop as an organizational practice. In church programs, it is surely something to experiment with.

The hard and fast lines formerly drawn between school grades have been broken in many schools to better recognize the fact that all teachers must teach at many levels. This is accomplished by multileveling within a subject or even across subjects. Thus the progressive steps in learning to read, for example, might be broken in the kindergarten through grade three sequence into fifteen or twenty levels rather than the four set by rigid grade standards. Any one student can then reach these levels at his own rate and perhaps with different methods and materials. It is obvious that this trend is fully in keeping with personalizing instruction, and it is nearly as apparent that it is possible to ungrade or multilevel instruction in any subject at any or all education levels.

The twin concepts of ungradedness and multileveling would seem to have a long and bright future for education, and would also seem to have strong potential for any kind of sequential educational ministry. If it can be determined what results are desired, what experiences we want, what behavior or actions are the end result, we should be able to move with these from the nursery-school age through to adult church programs. Perhaps the year 2000 is too early to find either school or church programs completely ungraded and multileveled, but this is a goal worth the effort.

In its attempts to reduce the range of individual differences within a class, ability grouping by classes has been practiced by the schools more widely during the past two decades. In this "tracking" system there might be one class of "slow-learning" children, two classes of "average" and one class of "accelerated" children. It would seem reasonable that individual differences in achievement could be cared for more adequately if the very able and very unable students were in separate classes. To put the case simply, it didn't work. Several summaries[3,4,5] of scores of separate research in this field indicate that the range of differences within a class is reduced little if any and that these so-called "homogeneous" groups did not produce improved achievement.

No one really knows why this practice proved to be ineffective in most instances, and there isn't space here to speculate about it. However, the side effects noted in some schools (lowered self-concepts and labeling as "dummies" in the "slow group"; delusions of grandeur or over-expectations in the "high" group; inability to "get along with'" or work with all children or youth; and another version of segregation —all educationally disadvantaged and cultural minorities in the "low" group) should discourage churches from ability grouping by classes.

It has been mentioned often that the overarching, dominating trend, one nearly sure to last beyond the year 2000 will be toward individualizing or personalizing of instruction. If one is to disagree and prescribe the educational needs of people at any age, it will be done individually. Each to his own. Perhaps in a group situation, perhaps toward common goals, but according to his own needs.

Spots of educational research in both the United States[6] and England[7] have found advantages in mixing children from an age and developmental span of two or three years. This is something like the rural school except that only two or three years rather than six or eight are included. The older ones teach the younger, and, perhaps, vice versa. If the gap isn't too large, this plan might deserve trial at all levels of the church program.

Psychologists and professional educators have long deplored the heavy reliance that schools have put on expository methods of teaching. Much of the excitement of learning is lost when too much of it is showing, telling and explaining. A number of pedagogical terms (experience approach, problem-oriented units, discovery methods, learning through inquiry) and adages in education (learning is experience, learning is living) reflect a long-lived desire to move, at least in part, to teaching styles where the learner is a discoverer of knowledge, strategies and skills. Jown Dewey popularized this desire in *Democracy and Education*[8] and this was reflected in the Progressive Education Movement during the 1920s and 1930s. It was called to strong attention more recently in Jerome Bruner's *The Process of Education*[9], and is currently reflected in many new curriculum guides and courses of study.

A learning strategy where basic truths and their applications are arrived at through an inductive approach, a process of inquiry and discovery, may receive increasing acceptance in the schools and may also provide an excellent avenue to some of the church's objectives. Basic beliefs and commitments probably are better internalized when they are thought out rather than given out.

Still another trend quite apparent these days in American and British primary schools (ages 4+ to 11+), and again reflecting some of the ideas of Progressive Education much earlier, is to loosen the curriculum, providing much more student choice and decision making. Learners are helping to determine both what they learn and how they learn it. There are dangers here. Neophytes in any endeavor can and do get lost. They don't have the insights into any of the five big questions raised in this chapter that might be expected of the well-educated adult. Yet there is much the same kind of force in self-determined learning that there is in learning through discovery. A few blind alleys or delayed learnings may be more than worth the price if the learning is more dynamic. And the teacher, of course, is always a member and leader in the group. Perhaps the church program at all levels could profit from a more permissive leadership. Increased involvement might cause the program, and those taking part, to be stronger than would a more direct, highly structured, and seemingly more efficient approach.

This chapter has approached the church's educational program as if it were a curriculum. It has discussed briefly five big problems that must be faced now and in the future when programs are built. Attempts were made to discern trends and to project some of these into the future. It has suggested that the church program might learn something from the mistakes and successes of the public schools. It has not and cannot point a direction for the church. This is the task of the church itself.

NOTES AND REFERENCES

1. Jerome S. Bruner, *The Process of Education* (Cambridge: Harvard University Press, 1961).
2. Wilbur Schramm, J. Lyle, and E. B. Parker, *Television in the Lives of Our Children* (Palo Alto: Stanford University Press, 1961).
3. See the entire April, 1961 issue of *Educational Leadership,* (Washington, D.C.: Association for Supervision and Curriculum Development, National Education Association).
4. J. Harlan Shores, "What Does Research Say About Ability Grouping by Classes?" *Illinois Education* December, 1964, pp. 169-172.
5. Jane Franseth and Rose Koury, *Survey of Research on Grouping as Related to Pupil Learning* (Washington, D.C.: U.S. Department of Health, Education and Welfare, 1966).

6. Joseph J. Adams, "Multi-Age Grouping," in *Research in Elementary School Curriculum* eds. A. Montgomery Johnston and Paul Burns (Boston: Allyn & Bacon, Inc., 1970), pp. 495-501.
7. Vincent R. Rogers, *Teaching in the British Primary School* (London: Collier-Macmillan Ltd., 1970).
8. John Dewey, *Democracy and Education* (New York: The Macmillan Co., 1916).
9. Jerome S. Bruner, *The Process of Education* (Cambridge, Mass.: Harvard University Press, 1961).

Appendix

A Central Objective
for Educational Ministry
in the Parish:
ALC and LCA

THE CHURCH'S EDUCATIONAL MINISTRY

Making a distinction between education and acculturation helps to define the scope and process of education. Acculturation involves the sum total of transactions between a person and the forces his society exerts upon him. The function of acculturation is to establish a viable relationship between the person and his society. Education, as an element of acculturation, shares this function, although it has distinctive and specialized ways of performing it. Education is more systematically planned and implemented than many other elements. It is concerned with analyzing the learning process, selecting objectives, creating teaching-learning environments and opportunities, appraising achievement and sequential progress.

The distinction between acculturation and education applies to the life of the church. A person can, and probably does, learn something from every experience he has in the church. Every experience can have some influence on what he thinks, feels, and does as a Christian. Within the total life of a community of believers there are some activities explicitly labeled as "education." If the life of the congregation does not contain serious self-contradictions, its educational activities share the same broad aims that guide its total life and work. The distinguishing mark of educational activities is that they are not ends in themselves, but are strictly means for enabling persons to participate in God's continuing activity in the human and Christian communities.

In a general sense, the mission of the church is the same for all times and in all places. Yet the church's perception of its mission changes as changes occur in the world. For this reason it is necessary that the church reexamine and reformulate its central educational objective from time to time. The objective presented here is not assumed to be equally valid at all times and in all places. It is intended to point to areas of emphasis especially appropriate for the next ten to fifteen years. It is thought of as a point of reference for the development of educational programs by national units of the church and by congregations.

Educational Objective, Educational Ministry, and Educational Program

The objective indicates the goal toward which educational efforts are directed and suggests key starting points for developing an educational program. The objective does not, in itself, delimit or define the role which education plays in the total life of the church. The distinctive marks of education within the church become visible in program and activities.

The church's educational ministry combines three elements—church, ministry, and education. The concept of educational ministry reflects the biblical description of the church as a fellowship of believers, caring and serving, with each person growing up in every way into Christ. Because the church is not simply a social institution, its educational ministry must be seen as a tripolar process involving God, the church as an educating organization, and the person-in-community. Educational ministry attempts to view the objectives of the church and the goals of persons in light of the redemptive purposes of God.

The concept of the church's educational ministry includes several key elements. Educational ministry is viewed as one aspect of the total work of the church; it should strengthen that work and enhance the life of the church. It is a reciprocal ministry, in which leaders and learners minister to one another. Educational ministry is concerned with the growth of persons in Christian faith and life. Organizationally, no one unit of the church has responsibility for the total educational ministry of the church. Rather, several units have responsibility for various aspects of it.

Persons should be central in the church's educational ministry. The total life involvement of the person provides the context for educational ministry. The primary aim is to assist persons to respond to God's continuing revelation and to participate in God's ongoing activity both in the human community and in the community of believers. The church's educational ministry will attempt to help persons to recognize that God is active in the world and to respond to him in their day-to-day lives.

282

Concerns of the church's educational ministry take tangible form in programs, services, and materials. Educational ministry should consist of a cluster of resources and activities designed to support and supplement one another in an effort to help persons respond to God's revelation. A prerequisite for coherent educational ministry is that units designing educational activities for the congregation do so on the basis of a central objective.

A Concept of the Chuch

The New Testament pictures the church as the redeemed community. Within this community God communicates his love and care for his children and through Jesus Christ offers the gift of the forgiveness of sins. In this gathering all human divisions such as station in life, race, or gender are not to be means of separation. Each person stands as an equal within the community. God imparts righteousness and holiness to the community and to the individual. The church is a community of hope, a hope that throughout all ages God will continue to love and redeem as he has in the past. This hope is wrapped in the life, death, and resurrection of Jesus. The community believes Jesus is the Messiah, the chosen revelation of God, and that baptism, the forgiveness of sins, and the gift of the Holy Spirit are important aspects of the faith (Acts 2:38). In response to God's love, the church is the gathering together of the faithful in worship, communion, and as means of sharing love and forgiveness with one another.

Institutions such as The American Lutheran Church and the Lutheran Church in America may be regarded as empirical, historical manifestations of theological concepts of the church. While institutions such as denominations and congregations are not to be equated with the theological concepts, they can be regarded as concrete, though incomplete and imperfect, expressions of such concepts as "the communion of saints." Since this is what the institutions, as institutions, claim to be, they attempt to use theological concepts of the church as norms for their life and work.

It is possible to speak of the church's nature, of its message, and of its mission. In earlier centuries much energy was expended in efforts to clarify the nature of the church—"one, holy, catholic, and apostolic." In more recent times emphasis was placed on the message of the church—the gospel, the life, death, and resurrection of Jesus. At present, discussions of the church tend to center on its mission—its function in relation to the world.

Three ideas underlie current concepts of the church's mission. First, the world is acknowledged as the setting of God's activity and the object of his love. The world is God's creation from the beginning. It antedates the church. On it God lavished his creative powers and love. He continues to create and to sustain it. It is his will that all men should know that they are the object of his love. The world is the place in which men find and fulfill his purposes for all.

Second, the church is seen as a community of faith and love, a self-conscious vehicle of God constantly called into being by the Spirit to confront men with the Word and to minister to human need. This is not to say that God has left himself with no other witness in this world. However, God has made himself most clearly known in Christ. Through him God gathers men in order to bless them so that they may in turn be a blessing to others.

Third, God's activity in the past and present is seen as moving toward a future fulfillment. This view regards the present as temporary and tentative. It is open to the surprises of God even while attempting to discern where his present activity is leading. It affirms a belief in the ultimate realization of God's intention for man, the world, and the universe. It is a theology of hope.

Although the church does not presume to be the only vehicle which God uses to perform his work in this world, it does see itself as that vehicle in which the presence of God ought to be most clearly visible. In this role it will continually seek to articulate and interpret to contemporary man God's self-revelation as it proclaims the gospel and witnesses to God's action in Christ. At the same time the church will provide the opportunities for worship, for the study of Scripture, and for members to prepare themselves through a deepened understanding of Christian faith for carrying out personal ministries in daily life, at work and leisure, in family and neighborhood, as responsible citizens. In such a way will the church hold before its people an image of a style of Christian life which is open to the future and to the exercise of responsible personhood.

Centers of Responsibility

There are several centers of responsibility for planning the educational program of the church. One is the congregation, which is responsible for conducting an educational program and for providing a climate which supports the objectives it seeks through education.

A second center of responsibility is the national church body, which provides resources (materials and services, both traditional and innovative) for educational programs conducted by congregations. Such resources must take into account the array of differences among congregations and the variety of abilities, interests, and needs found among members of a congregation.

Additional centers of responsibility are located in synods, regions, districts, conferences, and local groups of congregations. Congregations grouped together in these ways can establish procedures and draw upon resources for improving their educational programs.

The Role of the Congregation in Educational Ministry

Essential to any structure, either traditional or innovative, is some sort of community of believers, a group of persons who are in enough continuing relationship with each other to develop a sense of group identity. This community of believers, regardless of locale or form, is the setting within which the education of Christians takes place. It is the responsibility of that community, the congregation, to develop both its educational ministry and its life together.

The Christian community is a community with a history and a hope. The history is important since it is a medium through which God continually reveals himself. The hope is to be realized in the coming of God's kingdom. Members of the community can assimilate and use those elements of its heritage which are most valued and relevant only if they have the opportunity to perceive these elements of the heritage. This may imply teachers, classes, curricula, time schedules, although increasing variety in congregational structures may raise questions about the continuing viability of some of the traditional agencies for Christian education.

Educational ministry in a congregation has a responsibility to equip the members of the Christian community for their task of mission in the world. This involves not only transmitting the Christian heritage, but also interpreting its relevance for life today. It entails an understanding and acceptance of self as a person and a child of God, the development of meaningful relationships with others, the continuing acquisition of new knowledge and new skills, insights into the vital issues and needs of our time, empathy with people in need. Members of the Christian community must be helped to accept responsibility for becoming change agents in the world.

By its whole spirit and life together the congregation teaches the nature and implications of Christian faith and life. Parish organization is in itself a strong influence, for the ways in which persons are related to each other and enabled to share in the mission of the congregation have a profound influence on their understanding of the Christian gospel and their growth in Christian living. The structures and processes of the community can be so planned that learning will occur as persons participate in the total life of the community.

Convictions and values affirmed by Christians need to be communicated through affiliation as well as through instruction and assent. An individual's convictions and values are powerfully influenced by the convictions and values of persons and groups that are important to him. When membership in a congregation has significant personal meaning for an individual and when strong interpersonal ties exist, there will be more effective communication of convictions and values affirmed by his fellow Christians. An increased emphasis on and provision for varieties of planned learning opportunities will multiply the possibilities for the formation of strong interpersonal ties within the congregation and ultimately lead to a stronger total congregational life. They will also serve to equip ". . . the saints for the work of ministry, for building up the body of Christ, . . ." (Ephesians 4:12). If the climate of the congregation is to be effective in teaching and reinforcing Christian beliefs and values, more and better planned learning opportunities must be provided at all levels.

Every aspect of this total approach to congregational life and program demands greatly increased emphasis on leadership development as well as participant training. A more flexible and comprehensive program of instruction demands teachers who have the background, knowledge, skills, and confidence to use flexible approaches and resources. Development of congregational life demands that congregational leaders have a basic understanding of the mission of the church, the skills of organizational development, as well as a knowledge and appreciation of people. A strengthened educational ministry, especially at the youth and adult levels, will create a membership better prepared for the participation, leadership, and teaching tasks necessary to a vital congregational life and expanded program.

The congregation must look analytically at its total program, life together, and the mission of its members, in order to make the kinds of decisions about both formal program and congregational life which will foster Christian growth. This involves serious and sustained attention to articulation of objectives, analysis of the existing situation in the light of these goals, setting priorities, making decisions, and taking steps which will move the total life of the congregation in the direction of the objectives. This process must be based on responsible and widespread participation by members of the congregation.

The Role of the National Church in Educational Ministry

The role of the national church in educational ministry is to support, stimulate, serve, and provide resources for congregations. Such resources include those for instructional programs and for development of congregational life.

The changing nature and increasing variety of congregational life demands that educational resources be adaptable for use in many different settings. Congregations must be assisted to explore opportunities for educational ministry in new settings beyond the traditional agencies which have served as the vehicles in the past. The resources must also take into account the social setting and the varying abilities, interests, and needs, found among members of a single congregation. The assumption that one curriculum can meet the needs of all situations and individual differences must be reexamined.

If learning takes place in all aspects of life in the Christian community, there must be a vital interrelationship between the educational program of the congregation and its total life. The program and resources required should not be developed unilaterally by any one existing unit of the national church, but through a shared responsibility of those agencies concerned with varying aspects of educational ministry in congregational life.

Congregations look to the national church for assistance in the process of organizational analysis, decision making, and innovation. These processes, which have a strong influence on educational climate, are new for many congregations and involve specific skills which can be taught. Resources needed to implement these processes should be made available to congregations by the national church.

GOD'S CONTINUING ACTIVITY AND REVELATION

The uniquely Christian emphasis of the central objective for educational ministry is articulated in the words "God's continuing activity and revelation, particularly in Jesus Christ." To speak of God's continuing activity is first of all to bear witness to his being. It is to say in as direct a way as possible that God is a personal reality and can be known in human experience.

To speak of God's existence is to indicate something about his nature or character. He is the God who acts. He enters into a dynamic and continuous relationship with his creation in such a way that man can say, "He is not far from each one of us, for 'in him we live and move and have our being'" (Acts 17:27)). To speak of God's continuing activity is to say that God is continually, dynamically involved in the universe. He is active as a Father in his continuing work of creation, as Son in carrying out his redemptive promises, and as Holy Spirit in his ongoing presence in the lives of men.

God's activity cannot be restricted to any specific time, or place, or type of action. He is present and active in what takes place in and through religious groups, agencies, or institutions consciously dedicated to the carrying out of his redemptive purposes. He is present and active in the world of political, social, and economic events and activities as well. He is active both in holy history and in all of history. To speak of "assisting persons to perceive, respond to, and participate in God's continuing activity" is to say that ministry will help people identify and live in relationship to God in all of life.

God's relationship with his creation provides man with the continuing possibility of knowing him. However, man does not and cannot know God except as God takes the initiative. It is only as God reveals himself that he can be known. Revelation is always God's act. It is an event unlike other events in that its apprehension is a matter of faith. Revelation may take place at any time in any situation.

To speak of God's continuing revelation is to view revelation from the divine side, to see God always and everywhere at work revealing himself. From the human side God's revelation appears episodic, occurring only at certain specific times and places, only in certain events and circumstances. To man, God is both hidden and revealed. An important part of the task of educational ministry is to assist persons to develop an awareness of God's continuing revelation and to help them develop insights and skills for discerning the content of the revelation. Educational ministry should provide situations, opportunities, information, and experiences that will enable persons to struggle with the question as to what God may be saying at any time and to provide the community of believers with appropriate resources.

In addition to the strong emphasis on the contemporary character of God's revelation, renewed emphasis is to be placed on the continuing importance of the revelation of God recorded in the Bible and in the heritage and witness of the people of God. One of the problems associated with any emphasis on God's continuing revelation is how to discern what God is saying in the midst of the clamor that engulfs us at any point in history. How does one know whether he is perceiving and responding to God's revelation? Precisely at this point the Bible and Christian heritage and witness become important. In the Bible and in the heritage and witness of the Christian church, we find testimony to the ways God revealed himself in certain specific events. These provide clues and criteria for identifying God's activity and revelation in the contemporary world.

The Bible will have a central place in the church's educational ministry. The major thrust will be to know what God has said in time past that may open us to what he is saying and doing in the world today. The hermeneutical process may offer the most viable way for persons to respond to God's continuing activity. The interpretation of the Bible will be a continuing task in educational ministry and will involve the entire community of believers in interpretation. Those who prepare educational resources will have to be open to a variety of approaches and emphases in both Old and New Testament studies.

In the Christian community the continuing activity and revelation of God in the world is interpreted in light of the person and work of Jesus Christ. The Christ event is therefore the clue to the meaning of all other events.

The words "particularly in Jesus Christ" intend to refer to all that is related to the Christ event in the life of God's people: Scripture, history, writings, confessions. It is the basis for a Christian interpretation of the meaning of evil, suffering, death, resurrection. It also leads to a view of the purpose of history and to a hope for the future. Everything that is done in educational ministry is to center in the redemptive purposes of God revealed in Jesus Christ.

Perceive, Respond, and Participate

The ultimate goal of educational ministry is to assist persons to become personally involved in the continuing activity and revelation of God both in the human and Christian communities. This is the thrust of the words "perceive, respond to, and participate in." While these words are related to the cognitive, affective, and executive domains of personality, their sense cannot be adequately understood from the phychological point of view alone. They must also be considered in a theological context.

The order in which the words "perceive, respond, and participate" appear in the central objective is not intended to imply that the action indicated always takes place in that sequential order. It is just as likely for perception to take place through participation as it is for perception to lead to participation. The ordering of the three verbs does not in any way indicate a hierarchy of educational goals proceeding from perception to participation. Perception and response are inherently related to the nature and quality of participation.

To perceive means to become aware of something through some kind of sensory experience. It includes the element of discovery and implies a measure of understanding.

Educational ministry must help persons see that God is involved in all of life everywhere. If educational ministry is to focus on God speaking and acting in the midst of contemporary events and experiences, then educational ministry must deal directly and specifically with these events and experiences. Educational ministry will have to make a realistic assessment of the Christian's relationship to such social institutions as schools, social agencies, political parties, occupational and professional organizations, family life. This may mean that the church will have to consider an educational ministry that is able to work through nonchurch structures of society, in which people are already deeply involved.

Educational ministry is to assist persons to respond to God's continuing activity and revelation. The objective of educational ministry has not been reached when men simply perceive that God is speaking and acting in the affairs of the world. The response should include concern for the welfare of all people as well as activities of worship and praise.

Response involves a wide range of human behavior. Some responses are internal, some external; some have both aspects. Responses may be unconscious, almost instinctive; they also may be clearly recognized and reasoned. Some responses are primarily cognitive, some are primarily in the realm of emotion, and some are manifest in a person's actions. The broadest sense of the term refers to responses which possess all three characteristics. In this broad meaning of the term, educational ministry is to assist persons to respond to God's continuing activity and revelation. This allows for emphasis, as various points in educational ministry, on one or another type of response.

One meaning of the word "respond" carries the implication of decision making. The term "respond" implies the necessity of an educational atmosphere in which people are free to make decisions about the nature and meaning of God's activity and revelation, free to disagree, free to choose not to participate in it in any way. Educational ministry should provide materials, information, and experience in such a way that people may obtain the information, community acceptance and support that will enable and permit them to make a personal response.

To participate in God's continuing activity includes involvement not only in those activities conducted by the church, but also in activities in the world through which God's concerns for the welfare of all people can be expressed. Educational ministry should be directed to the equipping of the saints for the work of ministry, by providing knowledge to discern what God is saying or doing as well as training in the skills necessary to serve God in the world.

It may be helpful to identify three forms of participation. First, persons may at any time or any place participate unknowingly in what God is saying or doing. Anyone or anything may be used as an instrument of God for the accomplishment of his purposes. If God is, through his action, continually revealing himself, any person may knowingly or unknowingly be a participant in that revelation. In the Old Testament, pagan nations were used as instruments or tools to chastise wayward Israel and thus became participants in the activity and revelation of God. The ecclesiastical and political powers and structures of Judaism and Rome participated in the life, death, and resurrection of Jesus Christ, unknowingly and unwillingly, but nevertheless effectively.

291

Secondly, persons may participate as self-conscious agents for God in carrying out his purpose for the world. This kind of participation takes many forms, including identification with the Christian community and its ongoing life of worship and service. God uses the community of believers as bearers of the means of grace in Word and Sacrament. Through identification with it, members of the Christian community participate consciously in the continuing activity and revelation of God.

A third form of participation in God's continuing activity and revelation is that of witness. Witness to what God is saying and doing takes the form of action through involvement as well as verbal forms of witness by those who knowingly participate in God's work in the world.

Human Community and Christian Community

"Human community" is the world of persons, social institutions, and forces. Life together in love in the human community is an eschatological hope for Christians. The more immediate goal is the achievement of a human community (locally, nationally, internationally) in which there is freedom and justice for all. It is clear that the goal is far from being realized. Christians have a responsibility under God to participate fully in human community. This involves voluntary sharing of suffering and positive action to achieve social justice and human fulfillment.

"Human community" may also be interpreted more broadly to refer to all aspects of creation—the physical world and the universe—since this is the environment in which persons live. In this broad meaning, human community is the object of God's love and the context of his activity. It is his creation. He continues to sustain it. His will is that all men know that they are the object of his love and the human community is the arena in which they are to express and fulfill his purposes. He guides men to discern his workings in human community and his will for it; for those who have eyes to see, he reveals himself in and through human community.

The term "Christian community" or "community of believers") is used to refer to congregations or other groups of Christians. Theologically the congregation (or other group of Christians) is viewed as an embodiment of the church as the Body of Christ and the people of

God, a community of faith and love rooted in Jesus Christ and characterized by shared life, mutual concern, responsibility and participation. There are many members of a single body. Empirically, quite different characteristics exist in many or most congregations. The specific mission of congregations at various times and places may differ. One of the goals of educational ministry is to assist persons to participate fully in the life of the community of believers in whatever form its ministry to those within and without it may take.

God speaks to man in and through the church, the community of believers. He intends it to be the salt or yeast which, through the efforts of its members, will work with him toward the fulfillment of his purposes for the human community. The church is included within the human community. Persons who belong to the Christian community belong just as fully to the human community. The church believes that in Christ God has revealed himself and thereby enables his followers to know within creaturely limits his purpose and intention for his creation. It views the Scriptures as a record of God's redemptive act in Christ, through which he continues to speak. The church regards itself as a means God uses to make his will known to mankind. Its mission is to witness to God's self-revelation and to participate responsively in the human community.

CONTINUAL LIFE INVOLVEMENTS IN CHRISTIAN PERSPECTIVE

Finding ways to communicate Christian faith so that it becomes meaningful to modern man is one of the serious problems of the contemporary church. It is a problem for the entire life and work of the church, including the church's educational ministry. Unless persons perceive the gospel as meaningful and pertinent, Christian faith is not being communicated.

The problem of communication occurs in virtually all educational endeavors, inside and outside the church. Designers of educational programs are constantly struggling to find organizing principles and teaching styles which will deal with content in a way that is meaningful to persons.

The concept of continual life involvements incorporated in the central objective is suggested as an approach to educational ministry that will facilitate communication of Christian faith, that will enable persons to perceive the gospel as meaningful for their lives. The concept suggests that the process of perceiving, responding to, and participating in God's activity is a continuing process. It is not an isolated event that occurs only at a single point in time. The person brings his own history to each moment. Decisions and actions taken at a moment in time have implications and consequences for the future. The central element in the process is the person's own life. By virtue of being a human being living in society, the person is involved in various sets of relationships. Even though the person cannot avoid the fundamental involvements of being a person, relating to persons and groups, and living in society, culture, and the physical universe, nevertheless he may decide on the nature of these involvements.

Each person grows and learns in his own way according to his circumstances, dispositions, and capacities. The church's educational ministry must place high value on individual uniqueness. It must help the person to be himself and to develop his unique potentials in every aspect of his life. Education is not simply preparation for the future, nor is it achievement of a specified level of development.

This view of education requires a central objective and an organizing principle relevant to persons at all stages of life and experience. In order to do this, it must identify broad areas of experience which are common to human beings. It must indicate a direction for continuing growth and development rather than attempting to describe the complete Christian as an end-product of the educational process.

Any educational program must face the question of whether each person is so unique that he bears no resemblance to other persons. If this is the case, an individual educational program must be prepared for each person. However, many significant aspects of a person's life stem from experiences which he has in common with others by virtue of being a human being living in society. Each person becomes involved in many situations, faces many demands, responsibilities, and opportunities which are essentially the same as those faced by others. These are the person's continual life involvements—areas of experience and relationships which persist throughout life with changing shapes and significance.

In order to help a person understand, interpret, and implement his life involvements in the light of his religious commitments, the church's educational program must deal with the relationship between the witness and heritage of the church and the person's own experiences. The heritage includes biblical, doctrinal, and historical aspects as well as the contemporary life of the church. The continual life involvements concept is an attempt to find an effective and realistic way that will enable the person to discover the relevance of the Christian heritage to his own experiences and to find out how his total life is bound up with his relationship to God.

Using continual life involvements as an organizing principle for the church's educational ministry provides a way of bringing Christian witness to bear on the concerns which people face, whether or not they are aware of facing them. It is consistent with current and emerging theological viewpoints about the relationship between God, world, and church and about the nature of Christian faith and life. It provides a way of relating Christian convictions and values to all of life rather than treating them as a distinct and separate segment of life. The gospel, the Scriptures, the heritage and living testimony of the church become meaningful and significant for persons by virtue of the fact that they are related to continual life involvements. They are basic resources for helping persons in their Christian faith and life.

Continual life involvements include three basic dimensions of: (1) being a person, (2) relating to persons and groups, and (3) living in society, culture and physical universe. Recognition must be given to the interrelationships of these three dimensions as they occur in the actual life experience of persons. This can be done by thinking of them as three dimensions of a cube.

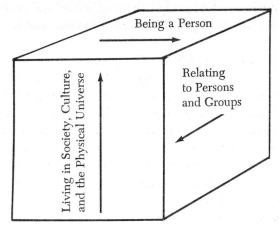

The three dimensions pervade one another. All three probably are present to some degree in every human experience, but in many experiences one or another of the three dimensions is central.

Using these three dimensions, it is possible to examine the range of human experience and to identify areas of experience which are virtually inescapable for any member of North American society. Even though specific content of the experiences varies from one person to another, the areas of experience are common to all.

Elements of a Christian Perspective for Our Time

Continual life involvements provide a description of where man lives. They point to the psychological, behavioral, and social aspects of the person's life. They represent an ecology, describing situations which all people face. Similarly the basic elements of the Christian faith, central in any generation, could be stated. These would be based on the Scriptures, confessional statements, worship traditions, and the witness of the community of believers.

What is needed for the development and planning of educational ministry is a way of relating life involvements and the core of the Christian faith. The result might be called a Christian perspective on the continual life involvements in our time.

A Christian perspective enables man to find meaning in his life involvements. It is a view a person has as he finds the involvements having meaning, in relationship to God as he is known in Jesus Christ. It helps Christians develop ways of thinking, acting and feeling. It is a stance of grace and faith. It is a process of thinking and living theologically.

A Christian perspective helps to interpret life itself. It assists the person in meaningful perception, response to, and participation in life itself and thereby helps the person to establish meaning for his involvement in God's continuing activity. It leads to a style of life that inquires, interprets, and calls for meaning. This hermeneutical living is the nature of the Christian community, and its way to live out its mission. This style of life employs the resources of the Christian community as the person lives and becomes involved in every kind of situation throughout all of life.

The fast changing nature of society today and the individual's involvement in it makes it difficult to state with certainty a Christian perspective for every life involvement. Nevertheless, the nature of the gospel, God's love for his world, and his involvement in the world, compels us to try to relate the meaning of the gospel to every life involvement in planning the church's educational ministry.

The task is to identify what might be the most crucial continual life involvements and to describe what would seem to be the most relevant Christian perspective on them. For example, "change and uncertainty" is a universal life involvement, but the particular nature of the future may call for a form of Christian perspective characterized by urgency and hope, rather than by quiet trust and confidence as in a former era.

This approach to educational planning seeks to bring together present day human experience and Christian heritage and hope in a dynamic way. There is the danger that we may misread the signs which point toward the decade ahead. However, we live in challenging times and overcautiousness has the opposite danger of being out of touch with contemporary human experience and what the gospel has to say about it.

The task of arriving at a Christian perspective on continual life involvements can be approached from two directions. One is to ask some crucial questions; the other is to make some descriptive statements. Both of these directions have been followed.

A Christian perspective on continual life involvements is based on the following premises.

It views all person as created by God,
and as redeemable.
It is an interpretation of life by Christians together
and individually.
It views all interpersonal situations as potentially
open to God's redemptive purposes.
It views the universe as God's universe.
It assumes that God is involved with man and his society.
It views the situation from the historic as well as
the eschatological perspective with God's revelation
in Christ central to both.

Questions such as the following are helpful in a Christian perspective on continual life involvements.

What do Christian heritage, freedom, and hope say about this life involvement?

What aspects of the life involvement are of greatest
  concern to Christian people?
What does the gospel, particularly as proclaimed in the
  Scriptures, have to say about the personal and
  corporate meaning of the life involvement?
What kinds of educational goals are most relevant for
  the Christian in this life involvement?

Being a Person

Being a person in the fullest sense means having a sense of personal
identity, with personal goals and purposes, in the midst of society and
in the face of conflicting demands which threatens one's identity. It
involves dealing with the events and circumstances of life, relating to
other persons and to what a person considers to be life's ultimates.

Being a person is a basic human experience: a Christian perspective
comes from the *interpretation* and *meaning* which one gives to this experience. The source of Christian meaning for the person is in the witness of the Christian community of which he is a part. However, the
person has to discover and interpret that meaning for himself as he
seeks to be a person in the fullest sense.

The witness of the Christian community, particularly as proclaimed
in the Bible includes several essential elements in relation to being a
person. One of the basic elements is that of relationship. Creation means
there is a Creator and a creature. Redemption means there is One
who redeems, and one who is redeemed. This provides a perspective
which helps a person to find the center of life in his relationship with
God, who creates and redeems, and is present and active as Spirit.

Such a perspective has important implications for what it means to
be a person, implications which are deeply imbedded in the Christian
heritage. Man's self-image and worth is enhanced by God's love as
shown in his creation and redemption of man. Personal rebellion and
social evils are signs of a broken relationship and loss of direction
which must be restored and healed by the Redeemer. The new life
which comes through redemption and man's response of faith provides
new purpose and meaning for the person.

In Christian perspective, one finds personal fulfillment in wholeness,
freedom, being for others, affirmation of life. True individuality occurs

when the individual lives in encounter with God and with fellow human beings. In every age there are forces and events which are in conflict with Christian perspective. As the person lives in the midst of these conflicting forces, his efforts to be a person are often thwarted. In our own time, there are strong forces which the individual must face in his efforts to find and maintain a sense of personal Christian identity.

Relating to Persons and Groups

It is necessary to view all the dimensions of man, all of his life involvements, and to educate him as a whole person. Human relationships as experienced with other persons, other groups, large and small, and in families are an integral part of human life. This interpersonal nature of living is also an essential concern of the Christian community and of the gospel. The people of God are a nomadic people, open and flexible to the present and to the future. They encircle, incorporate, and call people into fellowship in the body of Christ. Man finds completeness as he relates to the people of God.

Interpersonal relationships are one of the continual life involvements of man. A Christian perspective implies that a man should know what others are asking, saying, and doing and should relate to them in lives of mutual service. People of all places and ages and walks of life are involved directly or indirectly. Community is an essential human and Christian concept.

A Christian perspective implies that a person will acknowledge and respect the integrity and worth of other person as created by God. It implies that he will value their well being as much as he values his own. It implies that his participation in family and other groups will be guided by these convictions.

Living in Society, Culture, and the Physical Universe

In a Christian perspective persons are of supreme worth. Persons are always located within a contextual situation which has social, cultural, and physical aspects. Within this context, the Christian seeks to identify, call into question, and interpret important forces and systems.

Persons with a Christian perspective are concerned with active involvement in society, culture, and the physical universe in ways that call attention to the truth that God's creation and redemption extend beyond the world of persons to the whole of reality. Christian persons interpret scientific discoveries as evidences of the mystery and complexity of God's creation. Increasing knowledge of social systems and processes provides possibilities for further actualizing human potential. Therefore, the Christian person speaks clearly for man, for human community, for Christian community, and for the continuing relationship of each with the other.

Persons with a Christian perspective regard the nation and its communities as the arena in which God's justice and love are to be carried out. It is especially difficult for persons to see God moving in a society which is itself in the process of developing and in which individual persons are also in the process of change. A Christian perspective, however, sees Christ precisely in the center of the tensions and forces of society. The Christian congregation is called to increase its involvements in both the immediate and wider communities. It is called to be a faithful witness to the person and work of Christ, and to minister to the needs of persons who are neglected and oppressed.

Persons with a Christian perspective will operate in the political arena through a sense of personal and social responsibility for the decisions and direction of government, especially where government is the primary agency of change. Problems of church and state relationships also make it necessary for the Christian person to clarify and articulate the nature of his commitment. In the area of international politics, the Christian person will press for understanding, peace, and justice, among all nations, especially taking into account the needs of developing and disadvantaged nations.

Persons with a Christian perspective are on guard against the false values and self-concern which may develop in a consumer economy that is becoming increasingly impersonal and complex. Persons with a Christian perspective become sensitive to the mood of the times and find indications of the shape of the future in literature and art forms. A Christian's means of expression and communication will be those that have the greatest relevance for the day. No single type of expression or communication will be meaningful in the same way for all. This requires increasing involvement in dialogue and creative kinds of service.

Persons with a Christian perspective see reality in a transcendent dimension. They see God active not only in the past and the present but in the future as well. They see the future with the eye of hope based on God's faithful fulfilling of the promises given in Jesus Christ.

CENTRAL OBJECTIVE FOR EDUCATIONAL MINISTRY IN THE PARISH

The central objective for educational ministry in The American Lutheran Church and the Lutheran Church in America shall be
to assist persons,
to perceive, respond to, and participate in
God's continuing activity and revelation,
particularly in Jesus Christ,
in the human and Christian communities
as they deal with their continual life involvements of
being a person,
relating to persons and groups, and
living in society, culture, and the physical universe.

OUTLINE OF CONTINUAL LIFE INVOLVEMENTS*

I. Being a Person

A. Developing a Sense of Personal Identity, which involves
   1. self-image
   2. purpose and meaning, goals, commitments, self-evaluation
   3. personal abilities, self-expression
B. Dealing with the Givenness and Inevitables of Life, which involves
   1. success and failure, health and illness, life and death, change and uncertainty
   2. personal potentials and limitations
   3. events and circumstances
   4. forces and effects of contemporary society
   5. personal feelings and reactions

---

* This outline does not intend to suggest any priority or chronological sequence for the three major dimensions. Nor does it intend to suggest that any life involvement can occur in isolation from other life involvements.

301

C. Dealing with Ultimates, which involves
   1. recognition
   2. interpretation
   3. response

II. Relating to Persons and Groups

A. Relating to Other Individuals as Persons, which involves
   1. recognition of one's relatedness to other persons
   2. recognition of their needs, interests, and values
   3. awareness of social forces which influence personal relationships
   4. levels of affective relationships
   5. cooperation, competition, and conflict
   6. communication with others
   7. role differentiation
B. Relating to One's Family, which involves
   1. role differentiation
   2. levels of affective relationships
   3. empathy and compassion, tension and conflict
C. Relating to Small Groups, whic hinvolves
   1. membership in various small groups
   2. participation
   3. conflicting group claims and personal priorities
D. Relating to Larger Groups, which involves
   1. membership and selection
   2. level of participation
   3. personal role and function
   4. conflicting claims and personal priorities
   5. relationship to groups with which one is not identified

III. Living in Society, Culture, and the Physical Universe

A. Understanding and Responding to the Physical Universe, which involves
   1. awareness of being in and a part of the universe
   2. human existence in and use of the natural world
   3. the contributions of the natural sciences
   4. feelings about the world and the universe

B. Understanding and Responding to One's Society, which involves
1. the values, institutions, and activities which shape contemporary society
2. mutual responsibilities of the individual and society
3. individual freedom and social conformity
4. relationships between one's own society and other societies

C. Understanding and Responding to One's Culture, which involves
1. cultural expressions and communications such as art, music, poetry, literature, cinema, television, mass media
2. the intellectual and cultural heritage
3. educational patterns and influences
4. the individual's contributions to the culture
5. relationships to other cultures

D. Understanding and Participating in Political Processes, which involves
1. political forces and processes
2. political systems and structures
3. political conflicts and tensions
4. personal political roles that are domestic and international

E. Understanding and Participating in Economic Processes, which involves
1. economic forces and processes
2. economic systems and structures
3. economic conflicts and tensions
4. personal economic roles—occupations, leisure time, use of money, goods, and services

F. Understanding and Responding to Religious and Philosophical Processes, which involves
1. religious and philosophical forces and movements
2. religious and philosophical systems and structures
3. religious and philosophical conflicts and tensions
4. personal religious and philosophical involvements

OUTLINE OF CONTINUAL LIFE INVOLVEMENTS IN CHRISTIAN PERSPECTIVE

A WAY OF STATING OBJECTIVES FOR EDUCATIONAL MINISTRY

One way of arriving at objectives for educational ministry is to look at continual life involvements in Christian perspective. The educational objectives stated in this section grow out of the central objective, which emphasizes assisting persons to deal with continual life involvements as the context for perceiving, responding to, and participation in God's continuing activity and revelation.

Each of the general objectives on the succeeding pages is to be a point of reference for the development of more specific objectives for persons of various age groups living in different situations. Each continual life involvement ought to be probed for basic meaning and implications. Questions which need to be asked include:

(1) What are the behavioral dimensions most appropriate for each age group and situation, in terms of the specific objectives which grow out of the basic objectives?

(2) What are the theological, or Christian perspective, dimensions in the basic objective which are most meaningful for the persons in a particular situation and age level?

I. *Being a Person*

A. Developing a Sense of Personal Identity in the light of having been created in God's image, which involves

1. regarding oneself as a child of God

2. developing purpose and meaning, goals, commitments, and self-evaluation as ways for expressing and fulfilling God's intention for one's life

3. employing personal abilities and self-expression as ways of carrying out God's goals and purposes

B. Dealing with the Givenness and Inevitables of Life as the context for personal Christian growth related to life's meaning, potentials, and limitations, which involves

1. regarding success and failure, health and illness, life and death, and change and uncertainty as experiences in which Christian faith and commitment find meaning
2. regarding personal potentials and limitations as clues to one's place in the Christian and human communities
3. participating in events and circumstances as activities in which self-identity as a Christian is created and maintained
4. viewing forces and effects of contemporary society in terms of their potential for personal growth, for good or evil
5. feeling and reacting in ways that make one free and whole

C. Dealing with Ultimates through the ultimate of God's continuing activity and revelation, particularly in Jesus Christ, which involves
   1. knowing God through his people and the Scriptures
   2. developing an interpretation which sees God in Christ at the center of life
   3. responding to God in ethical decisions, in worship and in service, in light of an understanding of God's purposes

II. Relating to Persons and Groups

A. Relating to Other Individuals as Persons and viewing these relationships as a way in which God gives meaning to life, which involves
   1. regarding other persons as also being loved by God
   2. respecting the uniqueness of other persons
   3. recognizing the social forces which influence personal relationships and responding to them on the basis of the value God places on each person
   4. responding with concern for individuals within all levels of affective relationships
   5. seeking the well being of other individuals in the midst of cooperation, competition, and conflict
   6. communicating with other individuals in ways which foster respect and reconciliation

7. viewing personal roles as ways in which the creative work of God is expressed

B. Relating to One's Family as a way in which God gives meaning to life, which involves
   1. viewing roles within the family as ways for mutual service and support
   2. improving affective relationships within the family and finding appropriate ways of expressing them
   3. responding with empathy and compission to tensions and conflicts in family relationships

C. Relating to Small Groups as a way in which God gives meaning to one's life, which involves
   1. accepting membership in various small groups as a way of furthering God's purposes
   2. participating in small groups as a way of discovering the meaning of life together
   3. recognizing that conflicting group claims and personal priorities provide the stimulus for decisions and needed changes

D. Relating to Larger Groups as a way in which God gives meaning to their life, which involves
   1. accepting membership in various larger groups as a way of furthering God's purposes in the human and Christian communities
   2. deciding upon the degree of participation in larger groups on the basis of purposes of the groups and personal convictions
   3. accepting responsibilities on the basis of one's own abilities and the needs of the group.
   4. recognizing that conflicting group claims and personal priorities provide the stimulus for decisions and needed changes
   5. recognizing the need to evaluate groups with which one is not identified on the basis of God's purposes for human community

III. *Living in Society, Culture, and the Physical Universe*

A. Understanding and Responding to the Physical Universe as created and sustained by God, which involves

1. perceiving the interrelatedness of everything in God's universe
2. using the natural world as the setting for finding resources for meaningful existence
3. viewing the contributions of natural science as affirming God's power
4. expressing feelings about the universe which reflect the mystery and complexity of God's creation

B. Understanding and Responding to One's Society as a meeting place in which God confronts man, which involves

1. examining the values, institutions, and activities which shape contemporary society on the basis of their contribution to and effect on human community
2. recognizing the mutual responsibilities of the individual and society
3. evaluating the place of individual freedom and social conformity in light of God's purpose for human community
4. acknowledging the validity of different ways of organizing society and seeking to establish meaningful relationships among societies in the world community

C. Understanding and Responding to One's Culture as a meeting place in which God confronts man, which involves

1. appreciating and interpreting cultural expressions and communications such as art, music, poetry, literature, cinema, television, mass media
2. interpreting the heritage of one's culture in the light of insights of the Christian community
3. recognizing that educational patterns and influences should be functional communication channels in the human and Christian communities
4. participating and contributing to one's culture according to one's own ability and sense of purpose
5. appreciating the values in other cultures as a means of expressing and experiencing the wholeness of mankind

D. Understanding and Participating in Political Processes as avenues through which the continuing activity of God can take place, which involves
   1. viewing and interpreting political forces and processes on the basis of their effect on individuals and society
   2. evaluating all political systems and institutions on the basis of their effect upon human beings
   3. responding to political conflicts and tensions in light of their potential for creating or destroying community
   4. participating in political processes on the basis of one's own ability and sense of purpose, so as to contribute to the well being of persons and society

E. Understanding and Participating in Economic Processes as being a meeting place in which God confronts man, which involves
   1. viewing economic forces and processes as means through which Christian stewardship, choice, and initiative can be expressed
   2. using economic systems and structures as means for establishing equitable distribution of material goods as an expression of God's justice and love
   3. responding to economic conflicts and tensions in light of their potential for creating or destroying community
   4. participating in meeting economic needs through personal roles related to one's abilities, resources, and sense of purpose

F. Understanding and Responding to Religious and Philosophical Processes as meeting places in which God confronts man, which involves
   1. viewing all religious and philosophical forces and movements in light of the gospel
   2. evaluating all religious and philosophical systems and structures in light of the Christian heritage and witness
   3. using religious and philosophical conflicts and tensions as opportunities for examining the meaning of life
   4. participating in person religious and philosophical roles as means of Christian witness and for enhancing human community and Christian community